An Age of Equipoise?

An Age of Equipoise?

Reassessing Mid-Victorian Britain

Edited by

MARTIN HEWITT

Ashgate

Aldershot • Burlington USA • Singapore • Sydney

Published by
Ashgate Publishing Limited
Gower House
Croft Road
Aldershot
Hants GU11 3HR
England

Ashgate Publishing Company
131 Main Street
Burlington
Vermont 05401–5600
USA

Ashgate website: http://www.ashgate.com

British Library Cataloguing in Publication Data

An Age of Equipoise? Reassessing Mid-Victorian Britain.
  1. Great Britain—Social life and customs—19th century.
  2. Great Britain—Social conditions—19th century. 3. Great Britain—Intellectual life—19th century.
  I. Hewitt, Martin.
  941'.081

Library of Congress Cataloging-in-Publication Data

An age of equipoise? Reassessing mid-Victorian Britain/edited by Martin Hewitt.
  p. cm.
  Includes bibliographical references and index.
  ISBN 0-7546-0257-5 (alk. paper)
  1. Great Britain—History—Victoria, 1837–1901. 2. Great Britain—Civilization—19th century. 3. Burn, William Laurence. Age of Equipoise.
  I. Hewitt, Martin.
  DA550.A35 2000
  941.081—dc21   00-57605

ISBN 0 7546 0257 5

This book is printed on acid free paper

Typeset in Sabon by Manton Typesetters, Louth, Lincolnshire and printed in Great Britain by Antony Rowe Ltd, Chippenham, Wiltshire

Contents

List of figures and tables

Figures

Tables

Notes on contributors

Brenda Assael is a lecturer in Modern Britain in the History Department of the University of Wales, Swansea. Her forthcoming book, *The Circus and Victorian Society*, will be published by the University Press of Virginia. She has also written numerous entries for the *New Dictionary of National Biography* on Victorian performers and her essay on 'Theatre History' appears in the *Encyclopedia of Historians and Historical Writing*, edited by Kelly Boyd.

Tim Barringer is Assistant Professor in the Department of History of Art at Yale University. He has written widely on nineteenth-century visual culture. He is co-editor of *Colonialism and the Object* (with Tom Flynn, 1998) and *Frederic Leighton: Antiquity, Renaissance, Modernity* (with Elizabeth Prettejohn, 1999) and is author of *Reading the Pre-Raphaelites* (1999).

David Brown is a field co-ordinator for History at City College, Norwich. With the help of a British Academy award, he is completing research on the subject of 'New men of wealth and the purchase of land in the United Kingdom 1780–1879'.

Matthew Cragoe is a senior lecturer in History at the University of Hertfordshire. He is the author of *An Anglican Aristocracy: the Moral Economy of the Landed Estate in Carmarthenshire 1832–95* (OUP, 1996) and has published widely on the history of Victorian Wales. He is currently writing a political history of the principality during the nineteenth century.

Ross G. Forman is a research fellow in English at Kingston University (UK). His work focuses on nineteenth-century British imperialism in Latin America and China. He is currently completing a book manuscript on Victorian and Edwardian images of China.

Martin Hewitt is Director of the Leeds Centre for Victorian Studies and editor of the *Journal of Victorian Culture*. Along with Robert Poole he has recently produced an edition of *The Diaries of Samuel Bamford, 1858–61* (Sutton, 2000).

Peter H. Hoffenberg (PhD, University of California, Berkeley) is Associate Professor of History at the University of Hawaii, Manoa. He is the author of *An Empire on Display: English, Indian and Australian Exhibitions from the Crystal Palace to the Great War*, forthcoming from the

University of California Press. His work also includes the study of nineteenth- and twentieth-century Australian political culture and the life and times of John Lockwood Kipling, artist and art-school administrator.

Stephen L. Keck is currently working on projects which involve both Ruskin and Helps. Having taught at the College of Charleston (USA), he is currently Assistant Professor of History at the National University of Singapore.

Roland Quinault teaches modern British history at the University of North London. He has published extensively on Victorian political and social history and is currently writing a book on prime ministers and democracy. He was formerly Honorary Secretary of the Royal Historical Society.

Sheila Sullivan received her PhD in English from the University of Chicago in 1995 and teaches at St Mary's College of Maryland. She has written articles on late Victorian masculinity (Sherlock Holmes), Newgate fiction, illustrated journalism, Victorian scandal (the Road Murder and *The Woman in White*) and Madeleine Smith. She is completing a book tentatively titled *Authorizing Gestures: Gender, Criminality and the Creation of Professional Authority in the 1860s*. She is also working with a collaborator on a book of essays: *The Function of the Courtroom at the Present Time: Rereading the English Trial (1840–1920)*.

Martin J. Wiener, Mary Gibbs Jones Professor of History at Rice University, is the author of *Between Two Worlds: The Political Thought of Graham Wallas* (1971), *English Culture and the Decline of the Industrial Spirit, 1850–1980* (1981) and *Reconstructing the Criminal: Culture, Law and Policy in England 1830–1914* (1990). He has recently published in the *Journal of British Studies*, the *Journal of Modern History*, *Social History* and *Law and History Review*. The essay here is part of a book project on the role of law in 'reconstructing' manliness in nineteenth-century Britain.

Prologue:
reassessing *The Age of Equipoise*

Martin Hewitt

... a fair appraisal of the Victorian commonwealth demands a
knowledge of historiography as well as of history
Asa Briggs, *Age of Improvement* (1959)

W.L. Burn's *The Age of Equipoise* is one of those books that have
attained classic status. Few serious students of mid-nineteenth-century
Britain can be unaware of the book and its characterization of the
period. In print at least until the later 1970s, it was for the twenty or
twenty-five years after its publication in 1964 a virtually ubiquitous
presence on the bibliographies and lists of recommended reading for the
period. Of course, G.M. Young's *Victorian England: Portrait of an Age*
(1936) remained – and in many respects remains – unassailable as the
fundamental interpretation of the Victorian era; but Burn's book was
usually the *proxime accessit*, showered with praise by subsequent scholars as 'indispensable for an understanding of the cross-currents and
anomalies of mid-Victorian society', and 'perhaps the best general study
of mid-Victorian life in every aspect'.[1]

Admittedly, it is a text that has fallen out of favour in recent years.
In the 1970s Geoffrey Best commented that by the 1990s 'hard-pressed
historians who have no time to read the book will still be using the
concept'.[2] And so it has proved. *The Age of Equipoise* has suffered the
fate of most classics, increasingly passing out of the purview of scholarship, becoming a book more cited than read.[3] Recent studies of the
mid-Victorian period have ceased to feel the need to give it even token
acknowledgement as part of the literature which defines current interpretations of the period.[4] At the turn of the twenty-first century,
attempts to generate a discussion of the book among Victorianists are
likely to be met by nostalgic, but time-dimmed, encomiums from the
generation which read it with pleasure in the 1960s and 1970s, and
vague acknowledgements of an indirect knowledge of the book from
younger scholars.[5] At the Brotherton Library, University of Leeds,
even the hardback first edition has been transferred from the main
academic collection to the student collection. Here, alongside its bat-
tered paperback successor, it is apparently reduced to supplying regular
service to undergraduates in search of an interpretative text for the

period.[6] It is clearly not thought to have an enduring use for the faculty.

Nevertheless, for a good part of the nearly forty years since its first appearance, *The Age of Equipoise* was unquestionably a central text in the canon of interpretations of the Victorians. At the time of its publication, reviewers were quick and fulsome in their praise. There was a general sense that this was an important and impressive book, in the tradition of the 'overall impressionistic survey' established by Young.[7] For the 'popular' reviewers in particular, the association with Young was too easy to resist, and *The Age of Equipoise* was widely welcomed as a masterly, impressionistic and personal analysis of an age in the grand tradition of the *Portrait*.[8] In *Punch*, R.G.G. Price remarked that though Burn was certainly 'less bubblingly allusive than G.M. Young', he had 'the same kind of learning and the same gift for showing the unfamiliarity of a familiar landscape'.[9] In the scholarly journals too there were generous tributes: a 'vivid recreation of a vanished society [which] cuts through the deadening layers of over-simplified generalisations, labels, categories and catchwords to reveal a rich diversity of life and thought buried beneath them', remarked one reviewer;[10] 'profound and lively', suggested another.[11]

The Age of Equipoise quickly became a staple of Victorian reading lists and annotated bibliographies as a general interpretative essay. Recommendation was often preceded by comment on the extent to which it might be 'too specialized for the novice', or at least likely to 'give greatest pleasure to those who already have some acquaintance with the period'.[12] But it still featured prominently in the general reading cited by standard texts for both British and American students. Hence R.K. Webb, in his widely used *Modern Britain*, recommended it as close to Young in 'learning, provocativeness and idiosyncrasy'; John Roach deemed it 'magisterial', Norman McCord pronounced it *'inter alia* a subtle and perceptive analysis of relations between government and society, and currents among the legislative innovations of these years', while Joseph Altholz described it in 1976 as quite simply an 'essential study of the mid-Victorian period'.[13] Even those who remained sceptical about its overall arguments showed little hesitance in recommending it. Hence D.G. Wright, who spoke of the 'so-called "age of equipoise"', still recommended it as 'a scholarly and subtle analysis of the balance of interests in mid-Victorian society'.[14]

Burn's book also rapidly achieved a central place in the scholarship of the period. In the later 1960s H.J. Dyos, driving force in the development of urban history in Britain, and also co-editor of the influential volumes of essays on *The Victorian City* (1973), treated *The Age of*

Equipoise, along with Young's *Portrait* and Kitson Clark's *The Making of Victorian England* (1962), with what one reminiscence has described as 'affection bordering on awe'.[15] It was quickly installed in the small (and variably defined) canon of key interpretative texts on the Victorian period, alongside Young, Kitson Clark, Walter Houghton's *The Victorian Frame of Mind* (1957), Asa Briggs's *Victorian People* (1954) and *The Age of Improvement* (1959), and Jerome Buckley's *The Victorian Temper* (1951).[16] Above all, the idea of mid-Victorian Britain as 'the age of equipoise' has sunk deeply into the scholarly consciousness. So much so that authors no longer feel obliged to link their usage of the concept back to Burn's book, almost as if, like the 'railway age' or the 'age of Palmerston', the notion is felt to have some natural connection with the period.[17]

Of course, the book is now nearly forty years old, and it is perhaps unsurprising that its key idea has passed into a currency sufficiently general to obviate the need for repeated genuflection to the initial text. Indeed, the drifting of the text beyond the horizon of most current scholars might be entirely unproblematic were it not for the fact that *The Age of Equipoise* remained until very recently unsuperseded as the standard scholarly interpretation of the mid-Victorian period. It is true that G.F. Best's *Mid-Victorian Britain* (1971) provided a later and more encyclopaedic view of the mid-century, but the years between 1964 and 1998 saw no systematic attempt at reinterpretation. Perhaps the publication in 1998 of Theodore K. Hoppen's *The Mid-Victorian Generation* might have marked the final eclipse of Burn's text; but while this is a magisterial volume, drawing together the state of scholarship at the end of the twentieth century, and will undoubtedly be the bedrock of further examination of this period over the coming decades, it quite explicitly eschews the establishment of a major new interpretative frame for understanding the period. One of the ironies of its appearance is that its implicit claims to establish a new historiographical standard have prompted reviewers to cast back to Burn's book as the orthodox standard against which it is to be judged.[18]

So, *The Age of Equipoise* is back on the agenda. Its position as an important text in current understandings of the mid-Victorian period has been partially reaffirmed, even if with a certain scholarly embarrassment, and this has in turn brought into play more general questions about the development, or lack of it, of the historiography of the Victorian period. And yet, the closer one considers the impact of Burn's book, the more difficult it becomes to sustain the impression of its influence. Indeed, it is possible to argue that the wide divergence between the apparent importance of the text and its actual scholarly impact (as well as the lack of an obvious replacement) is symptomatic of the difficulties of Victorian Studies as an interdisciplinary field – of the extent to which the notional key texts of the field have failed to constitute it as a coherent arena of scholarly activity. For these reasons amongst others a reappraisal of the author, his text and its relationship with the broader scholarship of the mid-Victorian period itself would seem timely.

A reluctant Victorianist?

The position that W.L. Burn occupied for so long, and indeed continues by default to occupy in part, would probably have surprised him, for it might be said that he was a reluctant Victorianist. At the very least he came late to the Victorians, and he was never preoccupied by them to the extent that many of the other scholars with whom he came to be bracketed were. His early work concentrated on eighteenth-century government and society, especially in Scotland, but also with an interest in the history of British North America which he retained to the end of his life. His first (and only other) major scholarly work was a study of *Emancipation and Apprenticeship in the British West Indies* (1937). Even in the post-1945 period, when his attention turned increasingly to the Victorians, he retained broad historical interests, from Gibbon to the Chamberlains, from early British imperialism to American foreign policy in the twentieth century. Much of his writing in this period appeared not in specialized academic journals, but in the pages of the intellectual monthlies, the *Quarterly Review*, the *Listener, Parliamentary Affairs*, and above all *The Nineteenth Century and After*. In these journals Burn's writing revealed as much interest in the contemporary world and the ability of the nineteenth century to speak to it as it did a passion for the period itself.

Burn's engagement with the Victorians was that of an outsider. G.M. Young had written as a Victorian seeking to stem the tide of Bloomsbury group anti-Victorianism, convinced that the age, and especially the mid-Victorian years, were the period out of all British history when a wise man would choose, if he could, to be young.[19] His was the view of the mandarin and the metropolitan, secure in its classical education, its gentility and its persistent preference for style over substance, emotionally rooted in the nineteenth century and steeped in the values of that century's liberalism. Burn, in contrast, was a post-Victorian, dryly sceptical of the Victorian revival which was gathering pace around him, and this, along with the changed intellectual climate in which he wrote, produced a quite different emotional engagement with what he called the 'nostalgic dream' of mid-Victorian England (p. 25). In writings throughout the 1950s he warned against the dangers of, as he put it in one review in 1960,

> making the mid-Victorian scene the object of an uncritical and disingenuous admiration. We are apt to select what pleases us and to ignore the rest. We are careful to see the merits of the closely-knit family life, but less careful to see that it depended in the last resort on a system of family law which few of us would wish to have re-enacted.

Under the sanction of commentators such as Bagehot, he cautioned, there was a tendency to overlook the 'rigid Sabbatarians, the rabid teetotallers, the readers of the *Record*, the men who courted bribes at elections ... '.[20]

Like many of his contemporary Victorianists, Burn was philosophically conservative, abidingly unsympathetic to Liberal idealism, and with strong Leavisite concerns about the decay of British culture in the second half of the twentieth century. His antipathy to post-war Britain under Labour, a society in which 'too many people want too many things too urgently',[21] would have struck a chord widely. But Burn was not just culturally conservative, he was politically Conservative. He was quite happy needling colleagues of more liberal inclinations by preaching to them the virtues of what he described as 'the essential Toryism'.[22] Partly out of a natural desire to rein in some of the more uncritical exuberance he saw around him, and partly out of his real philosophical antipathy to some key aspects of the period, Burn presented a much more jaundiced view of the mid-Victorians than was common during the post-war revival. It was, as he noted in one of his essays from the later 1940s and early 1950s, 'not an attractive [period] in its public aspects',[23] chilled by the 'damp fog of liberalism', an era in which expediency dominated over principle, in which politics was 'drab utilitarianism behind an aristocratic façade'.[24]

His was not a view from the centre of the academic universe, like Houghton's or Kitson Clark's. Although an undergraduate at Oxford in the early 1920s, and a civil servant during the Second World War, he was as essentially provincial as they were not.[25] His roots were firmly in County Durham, and his only extensive period of time spent away from the North-East was his period in the 1920s and 1930s at the University of St Andrews. His work as a barrister was focused on the north-eastern circuit, and in the post-war period in which *The Age of Equipoise* took shape, he was a country landowner and JP, as well as Professor of History at Newcastle, dividing his time between the university and fishing, shooting and looking after his farms in his native Weardale.[26] Like Asa Briggs, Burn homed in on the 1850s and 1860s as the essence of 'Victorian' civilization; with Briggs he shared the provincial's suspicion of the cultural and political élites; but while Briggs's Victorianism was rooted in the emerging cities and the urban middle classes who dominated them, Burn was more at home in the gentler and more longstanding traditions of the county towns and country districts which were in the process of being pushed aside by the forces of 'progress'. As he wrote at the outset of *The Age of Equipoise*,

> My England ... is rural rather than urban, professional rather than industrial or proletarian; the England of the rectory and the modest mansion-house and the farmhouse, of the courts and the clubs and the 'public offices', rather than that of the manse and the factories and the co-operative stores and the Positivist congregations'. (p. 7)

He shared with many of the founding fathers of Victorian Studies an immense knowledge of the by-ways of the period. Yet his view of Victorian culture was in many respects an external one. His use of the conceit of an imaginary photograph of the Victorian rector's family for his famous exploration of selective Victorianism was suggestive in this regard, for his was the photographer's view: worldly, perceptive, brought to bear from many angles, but detached. While Buckley and Houghton and other scholars of Victorian literature and intellectual history were beginning to explore for the first time the complex emotional and intellectual make-up of the Victorian mind, Burn was more comfortable discussing the outward forms, the social practices, the legal forms, and the institutions which both embodied and sought to assuage the contending forces of optimism and pessimism. The breadth of his knowledge enabled him to produce rich and densely packed canvases which were a triumph of analytical illustration; but his engagement with the Victorians was not such that he either attempted, or was capable of, the encapsulation of the whole culture in the way that Young had managed, and to which others aspired.

Characterizing *The Age of Equipoise*

Just as Burn can be seen as a Victorianist of unusual stamp, so *The Age of Equipoise*, on closer analysis, is much less of a comprehensive portrait, in the manner of Young, than has often been assumed. That it was able to attain and retain the status of a central interpretative text of the high Victorian period for as long as it did indicates the difficulties Victorian

Studies as an interdisciplinary field has had in producing interpretative paradigms. Despite the way in which it has been conventional to bracket it with Young's *Portrait* – to present them as two of a kind, allusive, personal, idiosyncratic, and above all patrician cultural history – on closer inspection, Burn's book is of a different kind altogether.

This difference is shown at the outset by the much-praised first chapter, 'The Distorting Mirror', in which Burn took considerable pains to construct a warning of the perils of 'selective Victorianism', especially of the type which took mid-Victorian self-satisfaction at face value. The task of the historian, Burn commented, was to navigate a middle way between emphasis on 'individual idiosyncrasies' and 'wide generalisation about classes, types and occupations' (p. 23). Reading an imaginary photograph of a comfortable clerical family on a sun-drenched lawn, he uncovered piece by piece the potential disruptions of the idyll which lay behind the image, the intellectual indifference of the cleric, the genteel poverty which wears down his wife, the doubt which assails his son, the sexual exploitation of at least one of the servants. The mid-Victorian period, Burn was at pains to demonstrate, shared many of the problems of the 1960s; but it was also separated from that time by a historical gulf which ought not to be underestimated. 'Over and over again', he reminds us, 'in examining mid-Victorian England, one comes across modes of thought and action so bizarre, so little credible, that the men and women who practised them appear as inhabitants, not just of another century, but of another world' (p. 38).

In deference to these insights, Burn did not attempt a comprehensive survey of the Victorians, concentrating instead on a slice of less than two decades. It is true that the years chosen are those most usually identified as the heart of the high Victorian period, the quintessentially Victorian decades of the 1850s and 1860s, which had themselves engrossed more than their fair share of Young's attention, and tended to be over-represented in other contemporary attempts at encompassing things 'Victorian'. But his explicit concern with 'mid-Victorianism' and his desire to consider the nature and timing of the moves into and out of this era mean that Burn was much more concerned with issues of periodicity than Buckley, Houghton or Young.

Hence two of the book's six chapters, 'The Day After the Feast' and 'The End of an Epoch', consider the nature of the transition into and out of the age of equipoise. Of these the first was the more searching and successful. In it Burn was careful not to present the mid-Victorian years as the product either of some sudden political demobilization or material amelioration effected in the 1840s, but rather to tease out shifts in the culture drawn from broader and more diffuse sources. His central assertion was that far from being an age of repression, the early Victorian years were best seen as decades of Romanticism, emotionally charged, intellectually heated, febrile and passionate, principled and gripped by agitations of many sorts, shot through with the fear of revolution. In part the years after 1851 represented a closing down of some of the vitality of these years: 'doors which had been open too long and wide, with great gusts of wind and rain sweeping through them, were being closed' (p. 71), and a move towards more mundane ambitions, as 'speculative theology gave way to speculation in railway shares' (p. 72); but they also represented the achievement of new vistas, a pausing for breath and to appreciate the view, after a long climb up a steep hill. His concluding chapter, 'The End of an Epoch', was less sharply sketched, not least because Burn spent much of it considering the longevity of landed power, and the persistence of patterns of rural landownership, governance and social relations well into the later century. Nevertheless, he suggested that the degree of contrast between the 1870s and 1860s, exemplified by the more open agnosticism, the revivified republicanism, the perceptible shift from statutory permission to statutory compulsion, and the expansion of the bureaucratic apparatus, all indicated that '[a] dam, of some sort, had burst' (p. 329). If England in the 1850s and early 1860s had been surfeited after the feast, by the mid-1860s 'appetites were sharpening again', and as the impetus for reform gathered pace on various fronts, so the comfortable – and only partly illusory – mid-Victorian freedom derived from the 'preservation of an inner sphere, exempt from state power' (p. 330) was rapidly eroded.

Notwithstanding that in the first of these two chapters Burn provided enough of a sense of the early Victorians to permit the illusion that his text aimed at a general interpretation, the compression of his study of the end of the age of equipoise should alert us to the book's partial coverage of the Victorian era. At the same time, The Age of Equipoise is also explicitly partial in its thematic coverage, omitting, in particular, any substantial reference to politics (Burn explained that he had drafted two chapters on the subject, but had eventually decided – on what grounds it is not entirely clear – to omit them). It is also – as the subtitle announces – 'a study of the mid-Victorian generation', and this generation most often turns out to be the children of the 1790s rather than the 1820s, not those who were in the first flush of adulthood as the 1850s broke, but rather those comfortably ensconced in middle age. Its list of dramatis personae is dominated by those – like Joseph Parkes (1796–1865), a Birmingham radical who talked of revolution in 1832, but who from the late 1840s settled for service as a functionary of the

Chancery court, Matthew Davenport Hill (1792–1872), defender of advanced radicalism in the 1820s and 1830s, but advocate of extreme caution in the 1850s, and John Fife (1795–1871), radical surgeon turned lieutenant-colonel in the rifle corps – for whom early radicalism had mellowed with age into a more comfortable and – the word is almost inevitable in dealing with the period – complacent acceptance of the prospect of gentle and moderate 'progress'.

Above all, however, what marks Burn's book off from Young's is the extent to which it is not so much a general interpretative survey in the grand manner as an analysis which addresses specific – if broad – questions. Burn's enquiry starts from the paradox of a society in the throes of substantial social, economic, political and intellectual trans-formation managing to maintain its cohesiveness and avoid any conflicts sufficiently powerful and fundamental to threaten violent upheaval, while at the same time boasting of its almost complete individualism and absence of forces and institutions of control. His concern is to dispel the notion of mid-Victorian Britain as an age of *laissez-faire* and the unfettered freedom of the individual. The mid-Victorians might have believed that they lived in this kind of world, but this was merely the kind of 'comfortable illusion' to which every age is entitled (p. 7). Instead they inhabited a society marked by various types of discipline. These were not merged into a single force, and as such it was possible, especially for the rich, to evade most of them for most of the time. Nevertheless, commented Burn, 'England, as I see it, was more notable in this period for discipline than for freedom from discipline' (p. 7). To this end, the three central chapters of the book sought to examine the balances of freedom and constraint which characterized the period.

The first of these (the third chapter of the book), entitled 'Getting and Spending', while providing evidence of the fragile and circumscribed nature of mid-Victorian prosperity, used it to consider the play of *laissez-faire* and interventionism in contemporary attitudes to wealth and poverty. The emphasis on the insecurity of success and the ever-present spectre of poverty needs to be underlined, in the light of the way in which Burn has at times been invoked as a conjuror of comfortable prosperity. To the contrary, Burn was quite explicit that 'the abyss' was all too real for most mid-Victorians, and that the rising wealth of many groups only intensified the apprehension of want. At the same time he pointed out that the threat of poverty was enshrined in mid-Victorian social thought; indeed it was central to that thought that the threat of poverty and the stimulus to exertion it provided was a vital social discipline. Remove it, especially (but not only) from the poor, and the result would be idleness, improvidence and ultimately immorality. State intervention needs must be heavily circumscribed for this reason, but also because as much scope as possible had to be left to private charity 'because it constituted for those who practised it a moral and social discipline' (p. 115). It was easy, as Burn conceded, for such attitudes to be deployed in the self-interested defence of wealth from the burdens of increased taxation; but for the majority, he argues, a genuine belief in the double disciplines of philanthropy underpinned the restricted role of the mid-Victorian state, and the extended discipline of mid-Victorian earnestness.

The second central chapter examined 'Legal Disciplines', illustrated by five case studies, of legislation on the police, prisons, the endowed schools, the medical profession, and the 1866 cattle plague. After an especially active period of legislation around 1850, Burn noted that these years were marked, if not by a lull, then at least by a confusion in which it is difficult to trace clear lines of policy. Without doubt the action of the state was constrained by the transitional position of parliamentary politics, the disinclination of the state to formulate long-term plans and policies, the passion for public economy, defects in the administrative structure (with respect both to the formulation of policy and its implementation by the central administration and by local bureaucracies). In some respects it might be argued that individual liberty was extended, but in others it was curtailed; and if, more significantly, there was a shift in the balance of discipline from the localities to the centre, this shift was made uneven by the greater tolerance which had to be shown to local government than to other corporations, and unpredictable by the permissive cast of much legislation, and the reliance on delegated authority (to inspectors, the Privy Council) for a good deal of the rest. Nevertheless, wherever the absence of legislative intervention gave rise to palpable evils or obvious abuses, or wherever it was in the interests of powerful social groups that the regulatory authority of the state be extended, the mid-Victorians proved themselves quite capable of extending legal disciplines. Hence not just the extension of sanitary legislation, but the Vaccination Act of 1853, Police Act of 1856, the Prisons Act of 1865, the (albeit belated) Cattle Plague Act of 1866. There remained the steady accumulation of knowledge for which, before 1867, the will to act did not exist; but mid-Victorian citizens still lived in an increasingly disciplined environment, even if the discipline had 'come to be so quietly and decorously applied that they could almost ignore its existence' (p. 136).

In any case, wide-ranging as legal disciplines might be, the reach of the mid-Victorian state was limited, and there were what might at best be described as 'awkward gaps in the administrative chain' (p. 291), and here, where the state could not or would not provide, argues Burn, a range of non-statutory bodies and non-legal codes of behaviour stepped in – the 'social disciplines' which formed the basis of his fifth chapter. In practice it was difficult to draw a hard and fast line between the legal and the social, and to an extent, this was a residual category, encompassing all that was not legal, and some at least of the forces Burn identified, including the 'discipline of dependence' and of the family, were perhaps more economic than social. Nevertheless, Burn suggests, it might be that the latter were ultimately more important than the former. Certainly, mid-Victorian culture contained a range of practices which themselves placed considerable constraints on individual freedom of action, such as the obligations and expectations enshrined in codes of gentility, the hierarchical subordinations of the family, the moral codes which prevailed even as religious doctrines and beliefs fell increasingly into doubt, and the over-arching constraints of the press and publicity by which discovery and disgrace threatened those who transgressed. The authority of the newspaper editor, the factory paternalist, the domestic patriarch, the country gentleman, the dissenting minister, even the professional association, might be subject to a constant process of piecemeal challenge, but viewed in the round constituted a society more 'strongly authoritarian' (p. 286) than conventional invocations of *laissez-faire* individualism could possibly encompass.

The result is a book whose commitment to a specific focus should not be underestimated. While his range of example was imposing, Burn never strayed long from the tensions which were at the root of his enquiry, individualism versus collectivism, the centralizing state *versus* local autonomy, freedom versus discipline, licence versus authority, and his discussions of such central topics as religion, gentility, even sport, were refracted through this strong diagnostic impulse.

The influence of *The Age of Equipoise*

It is no easy matter to assess the significance of a single book, to attempt to isolate the impact of one text among the myriad influences and juxtapositions that comprise the texture against which all scholarship is written. It is doubly difficult for a book which ranged as broadly as *The Age of Equipoise*, and which, conventionally at least, became one of the standard treatments of its period. It is likely that much of the impact of the book was felt obliquely and indirectly, more in the habit of mind with which historians approached the Victorians, and in the place allotted to the mid-Victorian period in general interpretations of the reign, than in specific and acknowledged debts. Hence even Asa Briggs, whose seminal reinterpretations of the Victorians in the 1950s and early 1960s were much influenced by Burn's early thoughts on mid-Victorian equipoise, makes no formal acknowledgement of the fact in his various studies of Victorianism.[27]

Indeed, it is difficult to know precisely what might be expected to be the impact of the book. It is noticeable for example that among the welter of praise which Burn received on the book's publication in 1964, the reviewers collectively displayed considerable uncertainty about the contribution it might be said to make. Beyond the general tributes, they clearly found it difficult to pin down the significance of Burn's arguments. 'Enormously rewarding and stimulating', concluded David Owen, the doyen of American historians of the Victorian period.[28] But his difficulty, and that of all the reviewers, came in pinning down the exact nature of this reward and stimulation. Some reviewers gave particular praise to Burn's dissection of 'selective Victorianism', 'a classic of witty precautionary reading'.[29] Others chose to highlight the extent to which Burn disposed of the notion of the period as one of individualism and individual liberty, or at least established that 'Laissez-faire itself was enforced by a great structure of coercion'.[30] But others sought refuge in suggestions of relatively narrow significances, as in John Roach's judgement that it was 'primarily a study of power and authority in Victorian society, rather too much dominated by the debates of administrative historians',[31] or the idea that the book operated more successfully as a series of essays than as a general interpretation of a period, that 'it open[ed] up many more lines of enquiry than the author can fully deal with'.[32] And lurking behind the comments of many reviewers was the impression that in much of the book there was little that was particularly new or original, that, as Asa Briggs put it, 'much of what Professor Burn says on these general themes has become commonplace in recent years'.[33]

Part of the problem lay in the prolonged genesis of the book, for many of its key ideas had been floated by Burn during the late 1940s and early 1950s in a series of papers, lectures and articles, most importantly 'The Age of Equipoise: England, 1848–1868', first delivered to the Conference of Anglo-American Historians in July 1949, and subsequently published in *The Nineteenth Century and After*.[34] Through the 1950s and early 1960s Burn's ideas, often taken and developed by Briggs, Kitson Clark and others, seeped slowly into the consciousness of Victorianists. So much so that in 1963 one literary critic could describe the mid-Victorian decades as that era 'which historians increasingly have called "the age of compromise" or the "age of equipoise"'.[35]

At the time Burn was commencing his rethinking, interpretations of mid-Victorian Britain were overwhelmingly dominated by perceptions of a fundamental watershed around the time of the Great Exhibition in which the country passed from the troubled 1840s to the unthreatened 1850s. In his *Portrait* Young had remarked that 'fear abated, hatred subsided, pride remained',[36] and in his 1951 article 'Mid-Victorianism' he conjures up halcyon years of compromise between *laissez-faire* and state intervention, perfect confidence in Parliament, unchallenged belief in individual improvement, 'wonderful receptiveness, tireless energy', 'an unchallenged success' in material things, and (quoting *The Times*) '"a degree of general contentment to which neither we nor any other nation we know of ever attained before"'.[37] Contemporary historical treatments, such as the chapter on mid-Victorianism in David Thomson's *England in the Nineteenth Century* (1950) and literary treatments, including Graham Hough's *The Last Romantics* (1949), concurred in presenting an essentially untroubled era never far from Trevelyan's 'complacency and cocksureness',[38] shaped by values of industriousness, tolerance, self-reliance and self-help, secure in its belief in the benevolence of progress, a society whose prophets were themselves a sign of the assuredness and confidence which made such self-criticism possible. It was still all too easy for analysis to drift into Stracheyite characterizations of smug, self-satisfied hypocrites.[39] It is important that hindsight should not lead us to underestimate the persistence of these frames. The second edition of Llewellyn Woodward's volume in the Oxford History of Britain, *The Age of Reform*, published in 1961, retained its uncomplicated Whiggish picture of the mid-Victorian period characterized by a single vector of improvement.[40] As Burn himself remarked in 1964,

> It is difficult for any of us, and especially for the older of us, to rid our minds of the picture of a country where Cotton was King, where industrialization had made agriculture obsolescent, and where Bright and Cobden, backed by what are vaguely but respectfully called the middle-classes, were the dominating figures.[41]

Burn's achievement was to play an important part in the dismantling of such unitary and Whiggish visions. Although *The Age of Equipoise* contained much that was absent or only slightly alluded to in his earlier essays, the dozen or more articles he published between the end of the Second World War and the early 1950s did go a long way towards outlining his ideas on the nature of Victorian, and especially mid-Victorian, Britain. They established his sense of the 'depth and intensity' of the period which underpinned his later attack on 'selective Victorianism': 'the mid-Victorian scene', he argued, 'was too complex, too heterogenous [sic] in its structure, for description by any one simplifying adjective'.[42] They clearly expressed the extent to which the much-vaunted material success of the mid-Victorians was a creation of nostalgia: the working classes were only an accident away from misery, the middle classes were under constant pressure to keep up appearances, while 'the preoccupation of the mid-Victorian parliaments with bankruptcy law tells its own tales'.[43] They enunciated the degree to which the watershed of the 1840s, although bringing a real change in temper, had to be kept in perspective: the reforms of the 1830s and 1840s could not be said to have effected any wholesale shifting of social or political power: the middle-classes were rebuffed, despite the lessons sometimes drawn from the repeal of the Corn Laws, and 'the aristocracy was able to retain possession of the controls'.[44] Although Leeds and Sheffield were integral to any discussion of mid-Victorian England, notwithstanding them,

> mid-Victorian England was *not* the frontier society it might so easily have been. The state was still weak, and politics confused, but the frontier areas were humanised and disciplined and civilised by the adaptation of old institutions and the development of new.[45]

By the time of the appearance of *The Age of Equipoise* in early 1964, such arguments had obtained quite wide currency. The book was preceded by the publication of many of the classics of the emerging Victorian Studies canon, Houghton's *Victorian Frame of Mind*, Briggs's *Victorian People* and *The Age of Improvement*, and George Kitson Clark's *The Making of Victorian England*. But if the readers of the book in the mid-1960s found the ideas encapsulated in the label the 'age of equipoise' unsurprising, they needed to remember, as indeed Briggs reminded them in his own review, that they were 'far less taken for granted when he first coined the phrase to describe the period'.[46] Burn's article had clearly been one of the central influences on Briggs as he was writing the key essays of *Victorian People* (especially 'Samuel Smiles and Self-Help', and 'Trollope, Bagehot and the English Constitution'), and this is apparent also in his extraordinarily prescient and influential *Age of Improvement*.[47] For Briggs, Trollope and Bagehot 'expressed more clearly than any other writers the equipoise of mid-Victorian England'. If Kitson Clark's *Making* eventually adopted different modulations from Burn's, his influence was acknowledged at the outset, and implicit in the recognition of the new task of revisionism with which the book began.[48] For an article in a relatively unfashionable general-interest review, Burn's essay appears to have been widely read, and cited more frequently than might have been expected, both before and after the publication of *The Age of Equipoise*: for example, by Houghton in *The Victorian Frame of Mind*, Olive Anderson in her *A Liberal State at*

War (1967), F.B. Smith in *Disraelian Conservatism and Social Reform* (1967) and by Michael Thompson in his *English Landed Society in the Nineteenth Century* (1963).[49]

It may be the extent to which *The Age of Equipoise* was thus in many respects rounding off a historiographical revolution rather than opening up new lines of enquiry that helps explain how surprisingly difficult it is to find explicit traces of Burn's impact on subsequent scholarship. Whatever the reason, it must be said that the recognizable impact of the book on the scholarship of the Victorian period after 1964 has been extraordinarily limited. This is not to say that it has not been much cited. Indeed, it has been mined mercilessly. A systematic survey would almost certainly reveal that it has been less often invoked than not only Young, but also Briggs's *Age of Improvement*, and his *Victorian People* and *Victorian Cities* volumes; but the range of contexts in which reference to *The Age of Equipoise* pops up is still impressive. Quite often it seems to have served as a useful repository of contemporary comment and incident.[50] But in other instances a more telling influence is apparent in a reliance on Burn's perceptive observations and judgements. This use was particularly common amongst literary scholars, and for a while *The Age of Equipoise* was relatively widely used in literary circles as an important 'background' text.[51] As late as the mid-1980s it was extensively quarried in Joseph Kestner's *Protest and Reform* (1985). But it was also frequently worked by historians: hence David Cannadine's appeal both in his *Lords and Landlords* and in his *The Decline and Fall of the British Aristocracy* to Burn's observation that 'the Duke of Omnium and the small squire were half a world apart',[52] or Frank Prochaska's summons of Burn's comment that the dependent daughter was 'that fundamental prop of the Victorian home'.[53] The vein is far from exhausted: Theodore K. Hoppen's recent volume in the new Oxford History of Britain, *The Mid-Victorian Generation. Britain 1846–86* (1998), as well as borrowing Burn's subtitle ('A study of the mid-Victorian generation'), cites Burn's specific observations and judgements on numerous occasions.[54]

It is possible to discern some influence on general surveys of the period. There is little doubt that Burn played a part in the reconceptualization of Victorian periodicity from the binary split between 'early' and 'late' which had been the dominant mode of the interwar years, to the tripartite division of early, mid- and late which became orthodox from the 1960s onwards (although this division was clearly articulated by Thomson in 1950).[55] He contributed to the extent to which it became commonplace to reject *laissez-faire* labels, and to present the period as one of 'quiet consolidation' legislatively. In comments such as Derek Beales's suggestion in his 1969 text that in the mid-Victorian period 'Spontaneity and heedlessness have gone. So Victorian Britain disciplined herself', we have unmistakable echoes of Burn.[56] The idea of 'equilibrium' was widely deployed. Citation of Burn was, at least for a while, apparently *de rigeur* for texts surveying the Victorian period.

Yet, on closer inspection, much of the complexity of Burn's position had failed to register. The mid-Victorian period was still characterized by many historians as anti-reforming, increasingly prosperous, moderate, consensual. It was still possible to invoke Burn, but also to argue, as Hamish Fraser did in 1974, that

> It is hard not to see the third quarter of the nineteenth century as, in so many ways, a lacuna in British history. The very confidence in itself which permeates society gives the period a uniqueness. The middle classes, above all, had reason to feel confident that at last they were coming into their own, though all levels of society were touched by it. It was a confidence built on stability ... Gone was the trepidation of the 1840s. Yet to come was the self-doubt of the 1880s. For three decades one can see 'Victorianism' at its high noon.[57]

Literary scholars were rarely so uncircumspect, but for many of them, too, 'the age of equipoise' became a formulation which validated a view of an essentially untroubled and settled period, a period, as Patrick Brantlinger portrayed it, 'of relative social stability and security' characterized by the cult of progress, a 'surge of industrial expansion and relative prosperity', and hostility to reform, or as Roger Henckle put it, 'good times – of peace, prosperity, stability and assurance, that the social historian W.L. Burn characterises as the Age of Equipoise'.[58]

At the level of specialist studies, such fragility of influence is even more apparent. In some cases this may be understandable, though not necessarily justifiable. From the outset, perhaps prompted too easily by his omission of the planned chapters on politics, although also reflecting their preference for presenting cut flowers rather than rooted plants, historians of politics, both national and local, appear to have rejected the book as even a framing device for their analyses.[59] Unsurprisingly, historians of foreign policy, even of imperial expansion, continued to write internalist accounts of diplomatic manœuvrings which made little effort to position themselves in any broader interpretative frame.

In other cases, however, the extent to which *The Age of Equipoise* is excised from the debate is less easily explained. Social and cultural studies of aspects of the mid-Victorian period which were published in the later 1960s and early 1970s, when one might expect its influence to be at its apogee, almost universally ignored the text. In his *The Origins of Modern English Society*, Harold Perkin felt able to proceed without direct reference to Burn, even though the heart of his thesis was the creation in mid-Victorian Britain of a 'viable class society' in which the entrepreneurial ideal dominated. The renewed attention to the dynamics of post-Chartist stability, in many respects pioneered by Tygryve Tholfsen's 'The Intellectual Origins of Mid-Victorian Stability' (1971), proceeded happily with barely a reference to Burn's sustained attempt to comprehend the cohesive forces of mid-Victorian society.[60] Even studies which drew on forces which had been a central element of Burn's analysis preferred to position themselves against other texts.[61] It would be foolish to posit reference to *The Age of Equipoise* as some test of adequacy for studies of the period: there is no suggestion here that every study *ought* to have referenced Burn. But the number and range of books which excluded him is remarkable. To give just a few selected examples, *The Age of Equipoise* is omitted even from the bibliography of R.A. Church, *The Great Victorian Boom* (1975), though he does list both Young and Kitson Clark, and of Alastair Reid, *Social Classes and Social Relations in Britain, 1850–1914* (1992), even though he too is interested in the transition from what he sees as the traditions of Halevy, Young and Kitson Clark to those of post-1960s social history. Others which ignore.Burn while citing other classics include Christopher Kent, *Brains and Numbers* (1978), T.R. Wright, *The Religion of Humanity* (1980), T.W. Heyck, *The Transformation of Intellectual Life in Victorian England* (1982). Even within literary studies it is much easier to find works which, despite their attention in period and problem to matters which Burn had confronted, chose to ignore the book. Many continued to use Briggs as their guide.[62] By the mid-1980s, in works such as Catherine Gallagher's *The Industrial Reformation of English Fiction, 1832–67* (1985) and Rosemary Bodenheimer's *The Story of Politics in Victorian Social Fiction* (1988), there was no place for Burn.[63] Ironically Burn's most direct influence in literary studies was not via *The Age of Equipoise*, but through his earlier study of Trollope.[64]

The same is true for specialized sub-disciplines within History. Take the case of 'administrative history'. Admittedly something of a backwater today, during the 1950s and early 1960s the debate on the nature of the development of the Victorian state and its legislative and bureaucratic presence was a vigorous one, and our sense of the developments of the mid-Victorian period is still vital for an understanding of the nature and dynamics of the emergence of the modern state.[65] As has been suggested, it was undoubtedly one of the key influences on Burn while writing *The Age of Equipoise*, and a substantial part of the book is taken up with observations intended to intervene in the debate, his discussions of the nature of the legislative process (more patchy and unpredictable than perhaps the MacDonagh model suggested), and his argument that the traditional individualism versus collectivism dichotomy was less useful than a localism versus centralism one. This line quickly established itself as the conventional picture.[66] Yet the debate on the 'Victorian revolution in government' continued to rumble into the 1970s with merely the sketchiest of references to Burn. Neither MacDonagh in his summative *Early Victorian Government*, nor Harold Perkin, in his 'Individualism versus Collectivism in Nineteenth Century Britain: A False Antithesis', give any direct notice to Burn.[67] In the same way, examination of the burgeoning literature on nineteenth-century social policy in these years again reveals at best scattered reference to *The Age of Equipoise*.[68]

Little changes if we cast the net somewhat more broadly to consider Burn's suggestions about mid-Victorian Britain as an era of increased authority and disciplinary forces. The writings of Thornton, Roberts, Moore and others explored the disciplinary roles of deference and paternalism without reference to Burn's broader framework.[69] The history of crime and of policing also showed little willingness to build on Burn's situation of the development of the police in its broader legislative and social contexts, despite its broad interest in the agencies of order.[70] When, in the later 1970s and 1980s, 'discipline' became a central trope of Cultural Studies, the lineage was back to Michel Foucault, and his hugely influential *Discipline and Punish*,[71] not to Burn, despite the useful complementarity of Burn's ideas to Foucault's much more theoretically fertile work.[72] Hence more recently the work of Gatrell and others on the emergence of the 'disciplinary state' makes no attempt to position their narrower and more coercive notions of discipline against Burn's more open-ended usage.[73] With rare exceptions such as Martin Wiener, whose essay in this volume (Chapter 6) continues a long-standing engagement with Burn's ideas,[74] legal historians failed to explore the opportunities of interpreting the law in the broad ideological and cultural context which Burn had sketched out, and on the few occasions when they did move in this direction, proved themselves happier at denying Burn any *locus standi* as a historian of the law.[75] And perhaps most poignantly of all, despite his self-confessed concentration on the England of county town and village rectory, Burn is quickly lost to historians of Victorian rural society.

Why should this be? A good deal of this invisibility perhaps derived from the rather marginal position Burn occupied in the British academic world in the 1950s and 1960s, because of his position at Newcastle rather than at Oxford or Cambridge, and because his scholarly activities had to share space with his wider interests, as landowner, magistrate and essayist.[76] His sudden death in 1966 meant that Burn himself was unable to exercise any influence over the ways in which his text was interpreted and adopted. Hence, in contrast to Kitson Clark, ensconced in Cambridge with his coteries of students, or Briggs with his central role in the institutional development of the historiography of nineteenth-century Britain in the 1960s, Burn was not an active presence in the new scholarship of the later 1960s and 1970s.

This might not have been a decisive handicap, had it not been for Burn's conservatism, which distanced him from the emerging generation of social, labour and cultural historians who would seem to have identified him as a representative of the kind of patrician social history they sought to supersede.[77] Although Burn could (and was) easily claimable as either social or cultural historian, these two fields, as they emerged in Britain especially, were dominated by quite different traditions. In Cultural Studies the defining approaches were those of Raymond Williams, above all in his *Culture and Society*, and of the Birmingham Centre for Contemporary Cultural Studies. Meanwhile British Social History tended to derive its historiographical coherence from a leftist if not *marxisante* tradition established by the Webbs, G.D.H. Cole, and figures such as E.P. Thompson and Eric Hobsbawm.[78] Although these fields emerged almost contemporaneously with Burn's book, they adopted what Stefan Collini has recently described as 'the hermeneutics of suspicion',[79] and in doing so took a very different approach from Burn's to the question of social order and cultural discipline. For many on the Left, Burn represented the kind of élitist, lettered, social-history-from-the-top-down which they were determined to repudiate.[80] And repudiate him they did: as Alastair Reid has remarked, the scholarship of the younger social historians of the 1960s 'usually depended on a rather deterministic elimination of precisely that intimate acquaintance with the detail of Victorian life which had characterised the work of the previous generation'.[81] Hence from the 1960s to the 1980s historiographical debate on the mid-Victorian period was constituted in terms of accounting for the demise of the working-class challenge and the causes and nature of mid-Victorian 'stability', centred on issues such as the labour aristocracy thesis, the 'liberalization' of the state in the 1840s, ideological co-option or 'embourgeoisiement'. All of these, not least because of the degree to which they were rooted in class-based social analysis, scarcely drew at all on Burn's analysis of the era's social and cultural cohesiveness.[82]

The abuses of equipoise

What all this suggests is that the enduring significance of Burn's work, if there is any, rests not in the substance of his text, but with the idea he enshrined in its title, that mid-Victorian cohesion derived from a field of forces which achieved (if this is the right word) a relatively short moment of 'equipoise'. 'Equipoise' quickly became a conventional label for the mid-Victorian decades. By the 1970s it was invoked at will in studies of the period, both by those who accepted it as a useful description, and those who felt the need to signal some form of unease with it. Yet in many respects it was the concept of equipoise which created the greatest degree of unease among the reviewers of the book when it first appeared. Llewellyn Woodward dismissed it as unconvincing, especially as a way of encompassing many of the key political facets of the period. J.F.C. Harrison rather disingenuously remarked that it was not a concept which could with any utility be applied to the Victorian period as a whole. And Derek Beales, while giving the clearest discussion of Burn's use of the term of any of the contemporary reviews, thereafter quickly proceeded to argue that 'some of the most telling passages, though, are those which bring out, not the balance between opposed forces but consensus and cohesion'.[83]

It is thus perhaps not so surprising that the number of studies which have sought to apply equipoise as an analytical tool is remarkably small. Geoffrey Best's *Mid-Victorian Britain* (1971) was written in the shadow of Burn, and although, as a whole, it is a much broader and in many respects more conventional social history text, its concluding chapter, 'The Social Order of Mid-Victorian Britain', covered much of Burn's ground, in very much the same terms. Dennis Smith's *Conflict and Compromise* (1982) and Richard Price's *Labour in British Society* (1986) both gave considerable weight to ideas of a contested, fractured, but nevertheless significant mid-Victorian period of equipoise.[84] Likewise, François Bedarida's *A Social History of England, 1851–1975* (1979), where the characterization of the mid-Victorian period as being in 'a state of equilibrium. Not an equilibrium resulting from stagnation and archaic routines ... but an equilibrium achieved in the face of the rapid movements of a country in full growth', was a straightforward restatement of Burn's position.[85] Nevertheless, such self-conscious and substantial deployment by historians was rare. In Literary Studies, the only sustained application of the notion of 'equipoise' which I have located is that of Geoffrey Harvey in his *The Romantic Tradition in Modern Poetry. Rhetoric and Experience* (1986). But here the concept of equipoise, as applied to the 'poetry of equipoise', is a formal and internalist one, characteristic of a 'quintessentially English tradition' stretching from Wordsworth to Betjeman. There is a passing attempt to make an explicit linkage between Burn's characterization and mid-Victorian literature in Robin Gilmour's *The Novel in the Victorian Age. A Modern Introduction* (1986), but it is in no sense a sustained analysis; otherwise it seems that all that is to be found is the kind of fleeting reference made in John Lucas's 1964 essay 'Dickens and *Dombey and Son*'.[86]

There are numerous other instances where it appears that equipoise is being deployed as a central analytical concept, but where closer examination reveals a usage that is perfunctory, if not sloppy. The difficulties are hinted at by Bedarida's choice of 'equilibrium', and his concurrent usage of other formulations, balance and so on, even if, in his hands, the shift is achieved without injury to Burn's intentions. In less careful hands, the transition often means the loss of the instability, imprecision and flux which were central to Burn's analysis.[87] And indeed, rather than invoking 'equipoise' as a specific analysis of mid-Victorian England, the tendency has been to deploy it fairly indiscriminately as one of a number of alternative ways of describing the period. Hence, for example, the way in which Peter Mandler's *Aristocratic Government in the Age of Reform* (1990) feels at liberty to shift without preamble between an initial presentation of the period as underpinned by the 'Victorian compromise' (even if 'bumpy, circuitous, and built on a bed of political conflict, high as well as low') to a designation of the era as one of equipoise.[88]

The casualness of many such invocations is a reflection of the way in which, as the notion of equipoise has become progressively detached from *The Age of Equipoise* itself, it has been emptied of most of its analytical substance. Increasingly equipoise has come to stand for stability without any of the dissensions, perturbations, disagreements and centrifugal forces that were inherent in Burn's usage.[89] There has been a remarkable readiness to hitch the concept to innumerable distinct and less useful paradigms for understanding the mid-century: perhaps as indicating '[t]he economic stability ... and the appearance of social consensus'.[90] In the last decade or so 'equipoise' has been most often invoked only to establish a crude Aunt Sally of the very kind Burn had been attempting to dispel: of a reductionist account of the period which hides the disparities and contradictions of a complex culture;[91] or even worse, of smug, self-satisfied, complacent mid-Victorianism, grown fat on the British economic miracle and unwilling to confront the social inequalities, moral compromises and intellectual uncertainties which from the 1870s refused to be bottled up. Hence the 1988 presentation of 'the age of equipoise' as a 'simplistic characterisation [of] ... British prosperity and social stability'.[92] One might even venture to say that over the last ten or fifteen years there has been a tendency to reduce 'the age of equipoise' to merely a phrase.[93]

The interpretative problems of mid-Victorian Britain

This decay of 'equipoise' highlights the interpretative uncertainties that continue to dominate the study of mid-Victorian Britain. Few would now subscribe to the interpretations against which Burn was reacting in 1964. Although there is general agreement that mid-Victorian Britain saw a significant shift in atmosphere from the more troubled 1830s and 1840s, it is recognized that this transition was less abrupt, less decisive and less fundamental than had once been thought. There is little dispute over the economic transformation in which the frequent cyclical depressions of the early Victorian decades made way for the greater prosperity and stability of the 1850s and 1860s, even if the 'mid-Victorian boom' or the 'golden age' must both now be treated with scepticism. The break-up of Conservatism in the wake of Peel's decision to repeal the Corn Laws in 1846 clearly helped usher in a period of political incoherence which did much to give the mid-Victorian period its sense of transitional stasis. Likewise, the defeat of Chartism in 1848 was not a watershed in nineteenth-century labour history, in which class confrontation was abandoned in favour of strategies of conciliation and co-option, but merely a stage in the fluctuations of a radical tradition that resurfaced within Gladstonian Liberalism. It has long been clear that the 1830s and 1840s did not see the triumph of a new middle class, and that it was not until much later that urban–industrial society achieved even parity with older agrarian forms. The debate on the nature of the Victorian state and the philosophies which dominated it has settled down into a comfortable acceptance that while before the 1870s or 1880s the first inclination of the policy-makers and their social allies was to leave the field free for the operation of individual effort and voluntary action, this inclination never acquired the status of dogma, and did not preclude the substantial extension of state interference, legal and administrative, central and local, from the 1840s to the 1860s. Beyond this, however, confusion reigns, and the precise nature of the mid-Victorian culture which emerged, and the interpretation of its causes, remain riddled with analytical confusions.

In part, the dissonances are disciplinary. Within literary scholarship the period seems increasingly to be perceived in terms of pessimism, doubt and anxiety, not just in the growing challenge to biblical literalism and hence Christian doctrines, of which *The Origin of Species* was in many respects the final great blow rather than the first, but also heightened concerns about the very nature of Victorian civilization, its philistinism, preoccupation with wealth at the expense of beauty, the intensifying pressures of everyday living. The literature of the period, not least the emerging sensation fiction, is deployed to uncover a welter of neuroses: the threat to privacy posed by the new police, the dangers of insanity, the uncertainties of a world in which personal connection is being superseded by the impersonality of the city. Mid-Victorian Britain is presented in pathological terms, its sages and novelists 'empowered to diagnose the moral and social ills of society'.[94] The period is perceived as experiencing, in Norman Vance's words, 'a general sense of religious and social crisis'.[95] In contrast, historians, although they are at last becoming more willing to accept not only that the mid-Victorians faced unprecedented challenges, but also failed to find the certitude and solidity which they craved,[96] are still wedded to a view of the period which stresses above all its economic success, its political stability, and the almost unchallenged dominance of liberal optimism, faith in progress, in the assuredness of British superiority, and still prepared to assign the world of Victorian doubts and troubles to a later, more complex late Victorian period.[97] At times, such interpretations can produce characterizations which achieve almost Stracheyite hues, with overtones of complacency, self-satisfaction and smug superiority.[98]

These dramatic differences of tone indicate the further difficulties, the analytical ones of explaining how this society, under the various economic, social and psychic strains which affected it, achieved the degree of stability and self-satisfaction which it did. On this question there is no agreement. Instead the period has come to be hitched to a variety of distinct (although often interchangeably employed) metaphorical frames: balance/equilibrium, compromise, consensus, control and discipline.

At first glance the notion of equilibrium or balance would seem to be close to, if not synonymous with, 'equipoise', and indeed the conflation has been widely practised, both explicitly and implicitly. In the 1950s Briggs presented mid-Victorian Britain as characterized by 'a balance of interests'[99] and he has been widely imitated (so much so that D.G. Wright went so far as to suggest that the primary focus of *The Age of Equipoise* was an analysis of the 'balance of interests' in mid-Victorian society).[100] Used carefully, the idea can illuminate aspects of the mid-Victorian period. But as a concept it does have drawbacks. It is one-dimensional, and tends to encourage the privileging of one vector or axis over others (hence it is often deployed to suggest that the

defining interaction of the period was between rural and urban societies). It overplays stability, conjuring a sense of stasis and weightlessness.
It implies a mechanical relationship in which fixed quantities cancel
each other out, and thus denies figurative space for the interaction and
modification of the two sides.

Perhaps in part for these reasons, balance has tended to be used as a
useful alternative descriptor, rather than an over-arching interpretative
frame. Two more flexible approaches have more consistently been
adopted: compromise and consensus. The idea of compromise, with its
associated notions of 'negotiation' and 'accommodation', has a long
pedigree. Indeed, it was central to the first attempt to produce a comprehensive analysis of Victorian literature (if not the entire culture),
G.K. Chesterton's *The Victorian Age in Literature*. Although Chesterton
is rarely invoked nowadays, his work was widely taken up by writers
before Burn, including Young, who had spoken of 'the Victorian compromise between laissez-faire and state intervention',[101] and more recent
scholars have on occasion followed suit.[102] One of the attractions of the
idea of compromise is that it can encompass a range of social processes,
including industrial relations, popular and parliamentary politics, and
religion. It does nevertheless have drawbacks, in particular the extent to
which it requires the identification of collective social actors who can be
seen to effect the compromise. As current scholarship calls into question
the stable class identities on which, in particular, such approaches had
been founded, so it becomes difficult to sustain general, rather than
specific, models of negotiation or accommodation.

Indeed, as a result in large part of the 'linguistic turn', the prevalent
interpretation of the mid-Victorian period is one of consensus. There is
again a long-standing tradition of tracing the roots of mid-Victorianism
back to the establishment of shared ideas and value systems. Scholars in
the 1970s concentrated on theories of embourgeoisiement, or of hegemony, in both cases arguing that the years after the collapse of the
Chartist movement saw the successful promulgation, by a range of
social institutions and practices, of middle-class ideas and values. This
was the central thesis of Perkin's *Origins of Modern English Society*,
and was largely taken up by subsequent writers such as Geoff Crossick
and Robbie Gray.[103] The most complete expression of this interpretation can be found in the works of Tholfsen, both his 1971 article and
his subsequent *Working Class Radicalism in Mid-Victorian England*
(1976). During the 1980s and 1990s the idea of a mid-Victorian consensus has very nearly acquired the status of orthodoxy.[104] While studies
written within the older tradition of cultural materialism continue to
see the creation of consensus as contributing to a disempowerment of

the working classes, much of this recent work has seen the mid-Victorian consensus as marking the reunification of long-standing shared political traditions temporarily fragmented in the early decades of the century.

Yet it has to be said that, as a central explanatory axis for comprehending the cohesiveness of mid-Victorian Britain, consensus is far from wholly satisfactory. At the very least it tends to underplay the persistence of conflict in the period – over values, economic, social and political theories. It also privileges ideas and the cultures and practices which can be said to embody or reproduce these ideas over broader economic, social and institutional practices. In their different arenas the work of figures such as Peter Bailey, Neville Kirk and F.M.L. Thompson have demonstrated how difficult it is in many instances to see an effective, and more particularly a stable, consensus at work.[105]

Equipoise as analysis

In this context, perhaps it is time to look again at 'equipoise' as an analytical frame. If it can be rescued from the kind of casual deployment which has marked the last fifteen or twenty years, it might provide important opportunities for overcoming some of the interdisciplinary contradictions which have grown up in the characterization of the period and for moving towards a more inclusive and multidimensional account of the mid-Victorian decades. This is not necessarily to urge a rehabilitation of *The Age of Equipoise* itself. The text is nearly forty years old, and its basic framework over fifty. It was, as has already been acknowledged, very much a book of its time, and its key preoccupations can say relatively little to our current concerns. Questions of the nature of mid-Victorian administration, and the philosophical positions which underpinned it, are no longer live. It suffers from a tendency (notwithstanding Burn's discussions of selective Victorianism) to analyse the Victorians largely through concepts of their own making, while at the same time relegating some of the most important critics and observers, including Arnold and Ruskin, to the peripheries. But above all, it does not in the end provide an especially effective or fully developed discussion of 'equipoise' as an organizing concept.

Burn, of course, had borrowed the nomenclature from G.M. Young, for whom the word had been little more than a throwaway, his 'moment of equipoise' merely one facet of the gem he was cutting. In 1949, when Burn extended the moment into an age, and used 'equipoise' as the thematic glue for his interpretation of the entire mid-Victorian period, it was utilized really as an equivalent to 'balance', between the different classes and between the individual and the state. But by 1964, even though Burn still hinted occasionally at unease with the term,[106] the usage was much more studied and self-conscious. '[W]hat I sought', Burn explained, 'was a generation in which the old and the new, the elements of growth, survival and decay, achieved a balance' (p. 17). This equipoise 'was not deliberately planned or contrived. It was the outcome of a temporary balance of forces; but of forces struggling, pushing, shoving to better their positions' (p. 82; see also pp. 326–7). There was nothing complacent here. 'The "good" mid-Victorians did not for a moment assume that the nation was safe on a plateau of goodliness; their insistence on the need for honesty, chastity, temperance and thrift was dictated by the threats of dishonesty, sensuality, drunkenness and improvidence' (p. 41). Hence it was a period of considerable strife, of ongoing struggles; there was 'a large number of contests in which, for the moment, neither side could claim anything like complete victory' (p. 328). Hence

> The 'age of equipoise' did not aim at equipoise; it was querulous and excited and impatient as often as it was calm and lethargic. But it accepted most aspects of the present with a satisfaction which sometimes verged on the myopic and faced the future with less apprehension than the contemplation of any future can reasonably provoke. (p. 331)

Fragmentary and unstudied as these comments were, there can be little doubt that 'equipoise' was being offered as a distinct pattern for mid-Victorian England, and that Burn was explicitly rejecting the other dominant tropes used to analyse mid-Victorian society. In particular, Burn saw little of the stability and explicit accommodation between opposing forces, and even less of the deliberate concession on both sides, which were central to the idea.

At times, it is true, his discussion of the working out of equipoise brought him to suggest areas in which a certain (temporary) consensus had emerged; hence, for example, his comment that

> Mid-Victorian simplicity ... did something to bridge the gap between the rich and well-educated and the semi-literate poor. The same poems, the same hymns, the same pictures were capable of appealing to both; and this (with the widespread acceptance of certain religious beliefs) gave coherence and stability ... (p. 50)

But he was always careful to hedge such generalizations about with powerful exceptions: thus the proponents of the gospel

> preached assiduously on an adequate basis of belief and met with enough success to convince them that their creed was substantially

valid. Yet the balance of success over failure was not so great or so
sure as to encourage complacency. It was recognized that there were
many among the working-classes who had never been 'converted' at
all and others whose 'conversion' was only skin-deep. (p. 112)

It is this emphasis on the fragile, fractured and fragmentary nature of
the bonds of coherence that differentiates the notion of 'equipoise' from
the potentially very similar idea of 'balance'; the difference is apparent
in the contrast between Briggs's analysis, in which mid-century balance
was contrasted with the late-century tension, and Burn's, in which
tension is fundamental to equipoise. Whatever else it was, we can now
have little doubt that the mid-Victorian period was a period of considerable imbalances, but imbalances tied together by a complex series of
centripetal forces. Far from being 'a lull, a centre of indifference',[107] as
Kitson Clark put it in 1962, it was a period of conflict and contestation
on an almost unprecedented scale. Ideals such as respectability and
gentility did function to establish superficial consensus around certain
values, and considerable political and cultural effort was invested in
nurturing these nodes of agreement. Their ability to contain significant
divergences of opinion was sustained by the willingness Burn noted in
the mid-Victorians to rest satisfied with expedients and rough-hewn
distinctions, to avoid hardening areas of potential disagreement. The
number of axes of contestation and the extent to which the centres of
conflict were dispersed also helped to prevent the gathering of forces
around single issues or symbols, which had been the defining feature of
the 1830s and 1840s. For this reason, too, equipoise would seem a
more useful notion than balance, encompassing as it does the sense of
the multivalences of the culture.

Preview

Although they engage in different ways and in differing degrees with the
notion of equipoise, the essays in this collection are all driven in part by
this sense that the idea of equipoise can help illuminate the mid-Victorian
period in ways that alternative formulations cannot. Some develop
arguments which were embedded in Burn's own study. Martin Wiener,
long a champion of Burn's pioneering ideas on the role of legal disciplines in mid-Victorian Britain, demonstrates how the law engaged with
a social discipline, the idea of 'domesticity', to produce new forms of
regulation of the activities of men. David Brown's study of landownership addresses Burn's discussion in the final chapter of the longevity of
aristocratic wealth and influence in this period, and also the realities

underlying the ideology of 'removable inequalities'. While suggesting that Burn might have overestimated the barriers to entry into the landed élite in this period, and as a result paid insufficient attention to a significant process of social absorption, Brown also demonstrates the extent to which the myth of an open élite was sufficiently grounded in social realities to sustain itself, and hints at the importance of changes in landownership, however marginal, in sustaining this myth. Matthew Cragoe takes up another question raised by Burn – the response to the cattle plague in the mid-1860s. He explores the ways in which geographical and religious loyalties both reinforced and cut across each other. In the decline of belief in a providential God, and the alienation of the rural interest from the urban populace evinced by reactions to calls for a day of humiliation in 1866, we can see the cross-cutting alignments which inhibited the consolidation of lines of conflict.

Several of the chapters address the nature and extent of the supposed mid-Victorian consensus. Peter Hoffenberg contributes to the renewed debate in recent years on the meaning and impact of the 1851 Great Exhibition, and its successor, the 1862 London International Exhibition. He explores the ways in which the exhibitions represented 'systems of order', manifesting authority, but also making it vulnerable to criticism and dissent. Tim Barringer explores similar tensions in his study of the institutional history of the Victoria and Albert Museum, which was one consequence of the Great Exhibition. Even questions of taste, he demonstrates, could not be extricated from the broader processes of social exchange which marked the design movement in the 1850s and 1860s. Roland Quinault demonstrates not only the extremely undemocratic nature of the mid-Victorian political system, but also the complete absence of agreement on the issue of the right to vote, an absence which made the period 'surprisingly disturbed' and 'marked by a prolonged, if rather intermittent, popular agitation', and a debate in which the 'equipoise' of the constitution itself became an important locus of argument. Stephen Keck's chapter takes up one of the many challenges inherent in The Age of Equipoise – how to respond to Burn's explicit exclusion of Ruskin, as 'perhaps too exotic a figure', and his willingness to embrace the largely forgotten writings of Sir Arthur Helps as more representative of the mid-Victorian temper. By taking parallel elements of their writings on war, Keck is able to show not only the degree to which equipoise might be constituted in the cross-fertilization of their ideas, but also the way in which even the forward-looking Ruskin was deeply implicated in the bonds of equipoise.

Other essays take up issues which were largely absent from The Age of Equipoise. As Brenda Assael notes, children were neither seen nor heard in Burn's book, except where matters of education were raised. Nevertheless, as has long been recognized, the position of children was one issue over which the contradictory pressures of regulation and *laissez-faire* in Victorian Britain were especially exposed, and her chapter explores the ambiguities and equivocations centred on discussions about the protection or regulation of circus children in mid-Victorian Britain. Ross Forman's essay takes up questions of Britain's interactions with the wider world at mid-century, a question which was largely confined in *The Age of Equipoise* to discussions of episodes such as the Governor Eyre affair. By considering mid-Victorian Britain through Brazilian responses in Portuguese to an episode of mid-Victorian imperialism, Forman is able to demonstrate the broad and unstable range of meanings attached to the British imperial presence in these years. Sheila Sullivan, while trenching on several issues significant to Burn's original argument, not least the 'discipline of publicity', explores one dimension of the 'cultural trauma' which seems to have maintained a strangely symbiotic relationship with the easy confidence which marked so much of mid-Victorian culture – the emerging threats to a stable masculine identity.

Taken together, these essays achieve, I believe two modest but important tasks. They demonstrate the intricacy and turbulence of the forces for cohesion in mid-Victorian Britain, along with the remarkable success of the culture in achieving a working, if constantly shifting, *modus vivendi*. And they substantiate the suggestion that, notwithstanding the ambiguous status of *The Age of Equipoise* as an interpretative text, and notwithstanding the widespread abuse its central concept has suffered at the hands of subsequent scholarship, 'equipoise' deserves rehabilitation as a powerful conceptual frame for making sense of the mid-Victorian period.

Notes

1. Richard Altick, *Victorian People and Ideas* (London: Dent, 1974), pp. 320–21; Arthur Pollard, *The Victorians* (London: Barrie and Jenkins, 1970), p. 40.
2. G.F. Best, 'W.L. Burn: a recollection', *Durham University Journal* (1974), p. 1; this recollection is accompanied by Lionel Madden's 'A [selective] Checklist of Books, Articles and Reviews by William Laurence Burn', pp. 4–12.
3. Hence the brief citation of Burn in Jeffrey Auerbach, *The Great Exhibition of 1851. A Nation on Display* (New Haven, CT: Yale University Press, 1999), which cites the Exhibition as the 'high point' of Burn's 'age

of equipoise' (p. 1), even though Burn explicitly excluded it, commencing his age, with some deliberation, in 1852.

4. Margot Finn, *After Chartism: class and nation in English radical politics, 1848–1874* (Cambridge: Cambridge University Press, 1993), Miles Taylor, *The decline of British radicalism, 1847–1860* (Oxford: Oxford University Press, 1995), my own *The Emergence of Stability in the Industrial City. Manchester, 1832–67* (Aldershot: Scolar Press, 1996). Symptomatic perhaps is the way in which Burn takes his place easily among the standard interpretations of the period in Richard Price, 'Does the Notion of Victorian England Make Sense?', in D. Fraser, ed., *Cities, Class and Communication. Essays in Honour of Asa Briggs* (London: Harvester Wheatsheaf, 1990), pp. 153 and 164–5, but has slipped quietly out of view by the time of Richard Price, 'Historiography, Narrative and the Nineteenth Century', *Journal of British Studies*, 35 (April 1996), pp. 220–56.

5. See for example the scattered references to Burn in the files of the VICTORIA discussion list.

6. Taken together, the two loan copies have been issued 70 times between 1993 and 1999; and this does not take into account usage of the copy in the reference section, for which figures are of course unavailable. Ironically, of course, in reading lists prepared with students in mind, the classic surveys have been squeezed out by the proliferating modern textbooks; for one example see C. Cook, *The Longman Companion to Britain in the Nineteenth Century, 1815–1914* (London: Longman, 1999).

7. Derek Beales, review of *The Age of Equipoise*, in *Historical Journal*, 8 (1965), p. 417; see A.J.P. Taylor, 'After the Feast', *New Statesman*, 24 January 1964, p. 129.

8. See the comments which adorn the paperback edition; also, *The Economist*, 29 February 1964, pp. 806–7.

9. R.G.G. Price, review of *The Age of Equipoise*, in *Punch*, 22 January 1964, p. 144.

10. J. Tumelty, review of *The Age of Equipoise*, in *Durham University Journal*, LVIII (1965–66), p. 100.

11. Beales, review, p. 417.

12. Altick, *Victorian People and Ideas*, p. 320; D. Nicholls, *Critical Bibliographies in Modern History: Nineteenth Century Britain, 1815–1914* (Folkestone: Dawson, 1978), p. 21.

13. R.K. Webb, *Modern England. From the Eighteenth Century to the Present* (London: Allen and Unwin, 1980; 1985 edn), p. 331; N. McCord, *British History, 1815–1906* (Oxford: Oxford University Press, 1991); John Roach, *Social Reform in England* (London: Batsford, 1978), p. 250; J. Altholz, *The Mind and Art of Victorian England* (Minneapolis, MN: University of Minnesota Press, 1976), p. 195.

14. D.G. Wright, *Democracy and Reform, 1815–1885* (London: Longmans, 1970), pp. 55 and 151.

15. Patrick Scott, on the VICTORIA list, 15 April 1996, archived at http://listserv.indiana.edu/archives/victoria.html.

16. For a good example of this, see the comment of R.K. Webb that it was one of 'four marvellous syntheses which still dominate our historical awareness', *Modern England*; see also, for example, R.B. Henkle,

Comedy and Culture. England, 1820–1900 (Princeton: Princeton University Press, 1980), p. 182, and Patrick Brantlinger, *The Spirit of Reform. British Literature and Politics, 1832–67* (Cambridge, MA: Harvard University Press, 1977), p. 2.

17. For examples of this kind of usage see Lawrence Goldman, 'The Social Science Association, 1857–1866: a context for mid-Victorian Liberalism', *English Historical Review* (1986), p. 108 (though Burn is later brought explicitly into the analysis, pp. 126–7); Tony Taylor, 'Commemoration, Memorialisation and Political Memory in Post-Chartist Radicalism: the 1885 Halifax Chartist Reunion in Context', in Owen Ashton et al., eds, *The Chartist Legacy* (London: Merlin Press, 1999), p. 257.

18. See Miles Taylor, 'Review of K. Theodore Hoppen, *The Mid-Victorian Generation, 1846–1886*', Reviews in History. Institute of Historical Research, at http://www.ihrinfo.ac.uk/ihr/reviews/hoppen.html; Rohan McWilliam, review in *Journal of Victorian Culture*, 5.1 (Spring 2000).

19. Young, unlike Burn, has attracted a good deal of attention from subsequent scholars. See W.D. Handcock, 'Introduction' to his edition of Young's *Victorian Essays* (London: Oxford University Press, 1962); John Gross, 'G.M. Young and his England', *Encounter*, 20 (1963), pp. 79–84, Sheldon Rothblatt, 'G.M. Young. England's Historian of Culture', *Victorian Studies* (Summer 1979), pp. 413–29, G. Kitson Clark, 'Introduction' to his annotated edition of the *Victorian England* (London: Oxford University Press, 1973), and Asa Briggs, 'G.M. Young: The Age of a Portrait', in his *Collected Essays. Volume II* (Brighton: Harvester, 1984), pp. 253–71.

20. Burn, review of Norman St John Stevas, *Walter Bagehot* (London: Eyre and Spottiswoode, 1959), *History*, 45 (1960), p. 168.

21. Burn, 'The last of the Lynskey Report', *The Nineteenth Century and After* (hereafter *TNC*) (1949), p. 223.

22. Best, 'Recollection', p. 2.

23. Burn, 'English Conservatism', *TNC* (Jan./Feb. 1949).

24. Burn, 'Anthony Trollope's Politics', *TNC* (March 1948), p. 161. For further evidence of this lack of enthusiasm, see his reviews of MacDonagh, *A Pattern of Government Growth* in *Historical Journal*, 6 (1963), p. 140 and of St John Stevas, *Walter Bagehot* in *History*, 45 (1960), p. 158.

25. See his welcoming of Briggs as a 'fellow provincial', review of *The Age of Improvement, Victorian Studies* (1959–60), p. 208.

26. See brief tribute of R.A. Humphreys, *The Times*, 19 July 1966.

27. See Briggs's chapter 'Victorianism' in *The Age of Improvement* (London: Longmans Green and Co., 1959), and in *The Social History of England* (London: Weidenfeld and Nicolson, 1983), esp. pp. 269–71. See Martin Wiener's chapter 'The origins of Victorianism: impulse and moralisation' from his *Reconstructing the Criminal: Culture, Law and Policy in England, 1830–1914* (Cambridge: Cambridge University Press, 1990) (even though *Equipoise* is cited approvingly later).

28. David Owen, review of *The Age of Equipoise, American Historical Review*, 70 (1964–5), pp. 438–9.

29. *Times Literary Supplement*, 30 January 1964, p. 129. This is an element of the work which did subsequently leave its mark; see, for example, Frank Turner, *Contesting Cultural Authority. Essays in Victorian Intel-*

lectual Life (Cambridge: Cambridge University Press, 1993), p. 8, though the tendency to note but then ignore is also apparent on occasion, as in M.J. Salevouris, *'Riflemen Form!'. The War Scare of 1859–60 in England* (New York: Garland Publications, 1982), pp. 197–8.

30. Taylor, 'After the Feast', p. 129.
31. See Jennifer Hart, 'Nineteenth Century Social Reform: A Tory Interpretation of History', *Past & Present*, 31 (1965); Owen, review of *The Age of Equipoise*, pp. 438–9.
32. J.B. Conacher, review of *The Age of Equipoise*, in the *Canadian Historical Review*, 47 (1966), p. 79.
33. See reviews of Conacher and Beales, which both minimize the importance of the first three chapters and the final one; there is a similar tone in Taylor, 'After the Feast', Asa Briggs, review of *The Age of Equipoise*, in *English Historical Review* (January 1966), pp. 192–3.
34. W.L. Burn, 'The Age of Equipoise: England, 1848–1868', TNC, CXLVI (October 1949), pp. 207–24; see a series of other essays and reviews, including 'Anthony Trollope's Politics', *TNC*, CXLIII (March 1948), pp. 161–71, 'Victorian Political Martyr', *The Listener*, 6 July 1950, pp. 23–5.
35. M.A. Goldberg, 'Trollope's *The Warden*: a commentary on the "Age of Equipoise"', *Nineteenth Century Fiction* (March 1963), p. 382.
36. Young, *Portrait*, p. 13.
37. G.M. Young, 'Mid-Victorianism', *History Today* (1951), pp. 11–17.
38. G.M. Trevelyan, *English Social History* (London: Longmans and Co., 1944), pp. 561–2.
39. See, for example, T.M. Parrott and R.B. Martin, *A Companion to Victorian Literature* (New York: Scribner, 1955), pp. 45 and *passim*.
40. E.L. Woodward, *The Age of Reform* (Oxford: Clarendon Press, 1938; 1961).
41. Burn, review of F.M.L. Thompson's *English Landed Society*, *History*, 49 (1964), p. 343.
42. Burn, 'The Age of Equipoise', p. 208.
43. Ibid., p. 209.
44. Ibid., p. 218.
45. Ibid., p. 215.
46. Briggs, review of *The Age of Equipoise*, pp. 192–3.
47. Burn's influence is not readily apparent in the volumes of *Victorian People* itself, which dispensed with footnotes, although the attentive reader will see numerous echoes of Burn's ideas in Briggs's essays, but is made clear in some of the original essays which formed the basis of the volume, which were initially published with notes; see the version of 'Trollope, Bagehot and the English Constitution' published in *Cambridge Journal* (1952), reprinted in Robert O. Preyer, *Victorian Literature. Selected Essays* (New York: Harper & Row, 1967). Similarly, in *The Age of Improvement*, Briggs tends to cite Burn's essay for matters of detail (e.g. p. 415, n. 2, p. 426, n. 1), rather than in support of his general interpretations, but the influence of Burn, perhaps mediated through the earlier volume, is still clear; to take one example, in his observation that in mid-Victorian Britain, 'expediency was the "only principle to which allegiance is paid"', p. 416.

48. Although by no means as widely acknowledged as an influence in the published scholarship of the 1950s as Kitson Clark, who influenced much of the key work of this period, Burn's influence is also visible in the acknowledgements of other scholars, for example, Oliver MacDonagh, *A Pattern of Government Growth, 1800–1860*. *The Passenger Acts and Their Enforcement* (London: MacGibbon and Kee, 1961), p. 9; Norman McCord, *The Anti-Corn Law League, 1838–1846* (London: George Allen and Unwin, 1958), p. 10; John Roach, 'Liberalism and the Victorian Intelligentsia', *Cambridge Historical Journal*, XIII (1957), p. 58, n. 1.

49. Thompson indeed recommends it as a key text for 'further reading', p. 351.

50. G.H.L. Le May, *The Victorian Constitution* (London: Duckworth, 1979), p. 13. Interesting in this regard are the comments of Patrick Leary that 'Whenever I do look at it again, though, I'm struck by how thickly strewn it is with memorable quotations and anecdotes, many of which stayed with me long after I'd forgotten where I first encountered them', VICTORIA, 4 December 1999.

51. For a rare explicit positioning see R.D. Whitlock, 'Charles Dickens and George Eliot: Moral Art in the "Age of Equipoise"', unpublished PhD thesis, University of Washington, 1974; Laurence Poston, 'Philip van Artevelde: the politics and poetry of equipoise', *Victorian Poetry*, 18 (1990), pp. 383–91.

52. David Cannadine, *Lords and Landlords. The Aristocracy and the Towns, 1774–1967* (Leicester: Leicester University Press, 1980), p. 37; see *The Decline and Fall of the British Aristocracy* (New Haven, CT: Yale University Press, 1996), p. 22.

53. F.K. Prochaska, 'Female Philanthropy and Domestic Service in Victorian England', *Bulletin of the Institute of Historical Resarch*, LIV (1981), pp. 79–85.

54. K. Theodore Hoppen, *The Mid-Victorian Generation. 1846–1886* (Oxford: Clarendon Press, 1998), pp. 55, 154–61, 171, 175, 211, 328, 357, 483.

55. The binary divide was of course central to Young's *Portrait*, which sprang from the two volumes on *Early Victorian England* which he edited, and to Trevelyan's *Social History*, as well as literary criticism such as David Cecil's *Early Victorian Novelists* (London: Constable and Co., 1934).

56. Derek Beales, *From Castlereagh to Canning* (London: Nelson, 1969), p. 195.

57. W.H. Fraser, *Trade Unions and Society. The Struggle for Acceptance, 1850–1880* (London: Allen and Unwin, 1974), p. 11.

58. Brantlinger, *Spirit of Reform*, pp. 2–7, Henkle, *Comedy and Culture*, p. 186; or the picture presented in Richard Faber, *Proper Stations. Class in Victorian Fiction* (London: Faber and Faber, 1971), that 'the old social system continued and flourished ... react[ing] to change by developing a greater self-consciousness and rigidity ... stable and intricate ... a combintion of complexity and stability, of vigour and strict form that seems to confer on mid-Victorian society its classic quality ...', pp. 20–21.

59. See J.B. Conacher, *The Aberdeen Coalition 1852–1855. A Study in mid-*

nineteenth century party politics (Cambridge: Cambridge University Press, 1968), Angus Hawkins, *Parliament, party and the art of politics in Britain, 1855–59* (London: Macmillan, 1987), John Garrard, *Leadership and Power in the mid-Victorian Town* (Manchester: Manchester University Press, 1983).

60. T. Tholfsen, 'The Intellectual Origins of mid-Victorian Stability', *Political Quarterly*, LXXXVII (1971).

61. Hence J.M. Compton in his examination of mid-Victorian gentility and its implications for the Indian civil service preferred to go back to Briggs's *Victorian People*; see 'Open Competition and the Indian Civil Service, 1854–1876', *English Historical Review* (1968), pp. 265–84; Olive Anderson, 'The growth of Christian militarism in mid-Victorian Britain', *English Historical Review* (1971), pp. 46–72.

62. See, for example, Françoise Basch, *Relative Creatures. Victorian Women in Society and the Novel, 1837–67* (London: Allen Lane, 1974).

63. Bodenheimer is an interesting case in that she draws on most of the other central texts, including several of Briggs, Cole, Hammond, Stedman Jones, Patrick Joyce, Edward and Dorothy Thompson, Patrick Brantlinger, Catherine Gallagher, Kathleen Tillotson, Norman Vance, etc.

64. See J. Halperin, *Trollope and Politics* (London: Macmillan, 1977), citing 'Anthony Trollope's Politics', *TNC*, March 1948.

65. From the later 1950s this centred on the ideas of Oliver MacDonagh, most fully expressed in 'The Nineteenth Century Revolution in Government: a Reappraisal', *Historical Journal*, 1 (1958). For a good summary of the debate see Hart, 'Nineteenth Century Social Reform'. Subsequently, listings of the historiography of this debate, even A.J. Taylor's *Laissez-faire and State Intervention in Nineteenth Century Britain* (London: Macmillan, 1972), give no space to Burn; see for a good example G. Finlayson, *Citizen, State and Social Welfare in Britain, 1830–1990* (Oxford: Clarendon Press, 1994), pp. 2–3, n. 6. Given that, as Henry Pelling observed, many of the key figures in this debate had studied under Kitson Clark at Cambridge, this might in part reflect Burn's marginal institutional position in the field.

66. See the summary in Pat Thane, 'Government and Society in England and Wales, 1950–1914', in F.M.L. Thompson, ed., *Cambridge Social History of Britain, 1750–1950. III. Social Agencies and Institutions* (Cambridge; Cambridge University Press, 1990); and the various bibliographic summaries of the debate, such as Gash in *Aristocracy and People* (London: Edward Arnold, 1979), p. 362, J.T. Ward, 'Introduction' to *Popular Movements, c.1830–50* (London: Macmillan, 1970), p. 30, n. 36.

67. For Perkin's essay see *Journal of British Studies* (1977), reprinted in his *The Structured Crowd: Essays in English Social History* (Brighton: Harvester, 1981), pp. 57–69.

68. The exception is Roach, *Social Reform in England*, where Burn provides the frame for the chapter on mid-Victorian society, and is frequently cited; but elsewhere Burn is briefly quoted in D. Fraser, *The Evolution of the British Welfare State* (Basingstoke: Macmillan, 1984 [1973]), pp. 105 and 112, and belatedly in Finlayson, *Citizen, State and Social Welfare*, pp. 104–5; but not cited at all in U. Henriques, *Before the Welfare State* (London: Longman, 1969), Anne Digby, *Brit-*

ish Welfare Policy: Workhouse to Workfare (London: Faber, 1989), or K. Jones, *The Making of Social Policy in Britain, 1830–1990* (London; Athlone, 1991).

69. See A.P. Thornton, *The Habit of Authority. Paternalism in British History* (London; George Allen and Unwin, 1966), David Roberts, *Paternalism in Early Victorian England* (London: Croom Helm, 1979).

70. John Stevenson and Roland Quinault, *Popular Protest and Public Order. Six Studies in British History, 1790–1920* (London: George Allen and Unwin, 1975). For example in C. Steedman, *Policing the Victorian Community: The Formation of English Provincial Police Forces, 1856–80* (London: Routledge and Kegan Paul, 1984), despite her complaint at the 'silence' of commentators (and implicitly at least, historians) on provincial policing in the mid-Victorian period; and others, including D. Jones, *Crime, Protest, Community and Police in Nineteenth Century Britain* (London: Routledge, 1982), Donald C. Richter, *Riotous Victorians* (Athens, OH: Ohio University Press, 1981).

71. M. Foucault, *Discipline and Punish: The Birth of the Prison* (London: Allen Lane, 1977); cf. his earlier *Madness and Civilisation* (New York: Vintage Books, 1971) and *The Birth of the Clinic* (London: Tavistock Publications, 1973).

72. See Mary Poovey, *Making a Social Body. British Cultural Formation, 1830–64* (Chicago: University of Chicago Press, 1995), esp. 'Thomas Chalmers, Edwin Chadwick and the sublime revolution in Nineteenth Century Government'; P.A. Dale, 'Realism Revisited: Darwin and Foucault among the Victorians', *Review*, 12 (1990), pp. 303–21.

73. See V.A.C. Gatrell, 'Crime, Authority and the Policeman State', in Thompson, ed., *Cambridge Social History of Britain. III*, pp. 243–310.

74. Cf. his observation in *Reconstructing the Criminal* (1990), that 'In a path-breaking [study] in the 1960s, W.L. Burn rescued the criminal legislation of the 1860s from obscurity and linked it with other neglected legal disciplines of the time', p. 152, and his development of ideas of the coerciveness of the mid-Victorian liberal state.

75. Hence the interesting positioning of Burn in G.R. Rubin and David Sugarman's *Law, Economy and Society, 1750–1914; Essays in the History of English Law* (Abingdon: Professional Books, 1984), as one of a group of 'economic historians' (including W.J. Ashley, R.M. Hartwell, R.S. Neale and Thorold Rogers (!)), who 'have attempted to connect legal and economic history from a variety of different perspectives', p. 110. For a good example of the failure to invoke Burn, even in a study explicitly considering issues of moral regulation versus moral libertarianism, see M.J.D. Roberts, 'Morals, Art and the Law: the passing of the Obscene Publications Act, 1857', *Victorian Studies* (Summer 1985), pp. 609–29.

76. An interesting picture of the emerging circles of British Victorian Studies, at least in its historical wing, which would lead one to such a conclusion, can be found in Brian Harrison, 'Introduction' to *Drink and the Victorians. The Temperance Question in England, 1815–1872* (2nd edn, Keele: Keele University Press, 1994), pp. 11–19.

77. See comments of J.F.C. Harrison, even in his review of John Roach, *Social Reform in England*, *Victorian Studies* (Spring 1980), p. 400. Even

sympathetic commentators tend to place Burn in stark opposition to the new theoretical trends; hence Patrick Scott's linking of Young, Burn, Humphrey House and Kitson Clark as the 'characteristically anti-theoretical almost Podsnappian anti-continental rich-thick-allusive-descriptive school' of early Victorian cultural history, VICTORIA archive, 21 August 1995.

78. The nature of this influence is clearly seen in a range of reviews and position papers in the 1970s and 1980s; for example, E. Hobsbawm, 'From Social History to the History of Society' in *Daedalus* 100.1 (1971), pp. 20–45, R.S. Neale, *Class in English History, 1680–1850* (Oxford: Basil Blackwell, 1981).

79. S. Collini, *English Pasts* (Oxford: Oxford University Press, 1999), p. 253.

80. This, as much as anything else, would seem to lie behind the studied silence of what we might call the Nuffield coterie; Gareth Stedman Jones (in his *Outcast London* (Oxford: Clarendon Press, 1971)), Brian Harrison in *Drink and the Victorians* (1994), Patricia Hollis, *Pressure from Without in Victorian England* (London: Edward Arnold, 1974), Robert Currie, *Methodism Divided: A Study of Sociology of Ecumenicalism* (London: Faber, 1968).

81. Reid, *Social Classes and Social Relations in Britain, 1850–1914* (Basingstoke: Macmillan, 1992), p. 10. This exclusion is most apparent in the extraordinary omission of any mention of Burn in Harold Perkin's 'Social History in Britain', first published in the *Journal of Social History*, X (Winter 1977), pp. 129–45, and reprinted in his *The Structured Crowd*, pp. 212–30.

82. See David Kynaston, *King Labour* (London: Allen and Unwin, 1976), Neville Kirk, *The Growth of Working Class Reformism in mid-Victorian Britain* (London: Croom Helm, 1985), E.H. Hunt, *British Labour History, 1815–1914* (London: Weidenfeld and Nicolson, 1981), R.Q. Gray, *The Aristocracy of Labour in Nineteenth Century Britain, 1850–1900* (London: Macmillan, 1981). A partial exception is Keith Burgess, *The Challenge of Labour. Shaping British Society, 1850–1930* (London: Croom Helm, 1980), pp. 25 and 30.

83. Beales, review of *The Age of Equipoise*, p. 418.

84. Dennis Smith, *Conflict and Compromise. Class Formation in English Society, 1830–1914* (London: Routledge and Kegan Paul, 1982), pp. 79–103; Richard Price, *Labour in British Society*, (London: Croom Helm, 1986), whose post-mid-Victorian chapter is entitled 'The Disruption of Equipoise'.

85. F. Bedarida, *A Social History of England, 1851–1975* (London: Methuen, 1979), p. 73 and *passim*.

86. For Gilmour's use, see *The Novel in the Victorian Age* (London: Edward Arnold, 1986), p. 145; Lucas's essay is in David Howard, John Lucas and John Goode, eds, *Tradition and tolerance in nineteenth-century fiction: critical essays on some English and American novels* (London: Routledge and Kegan Paul, 1966), p. 102.

87. For use of equilibrium in this way see Janet Roebuck, *The making of modern English society from 1850* (London: Routledge and Kegan Paul, 1974), pp.1, 7 and 15–37.

88. Peter Mandler, *Aristocratic Government in the Age of Reform* (Oxford: Clarendon Press, 1990), p. 4, see also pp. 6, 276, 281. For another

example, see John Belchem, *Popular Radicalism in Nineteenth Century Britain* (Basingstoke: Macmillan, 1996), p. 103.

89. See for example Laurence Goldman's description of 'the "Age of Equipoise" Britain enjoyed in the mid-Victorian decades ... the social stability, liberal political consensus and balance that Britain came to achieve ... a society that had come through class division to re-establish national unity and, above all, deference to traditional social and intellectual leadership', in his 'Exceptionalism and Internationalism: The Origins of American Social Science reconsidered', *Journal of Historical Sociology*, 11.1 (1998), p. 21 (the views of the period are not Goldman's but those of American sociologists, but the idea that this is a classic version of ideas of 'equipoise' appears to be the author's). Compare with the suggestion that the 'thesis' of Burn's book was of 'a period of economic and social stability' which ended in the mid-1860s, Jonathan Loesberg, 'The Ideology of Narrative Form in Sensation Fiction', *Representations*, 13 (Winter 1986), p. 123.

90. Simon Cordery, 'Friendly Societies and the Discourse of Respectability in Britain, 1825–75', *Journal of British Studies*, 34 (1995), p. 46.

91. See James Epstein, 'Victorian Subjects: Introduction', *Journal of British Studies*, 34 (1995), p. 296.

92. W.E. Van Vugt, 'Prosperity and Industrial Emigration From Britain during the early 1850s', *Journal of Social History*, 22 (1988–89), p. 339. See case of M. Scott Baumann, ed., *Years of Expansion. Britain 1815–1914* (London: Hodder and Stoughton, 1995), where not only is it suggested that the concept of the 'age of equipoise' is 'questioned' by Tholfsen's description of the mid-Victorian period as 'a stable culture in a state of inner tension', but Burn is also renamed Burns, p. 232.

93. Significantly it is described as such in both Gilmour, *The Novel in the Victorian Age*, p. 108, and H.G.C. Matthew, *Gladstone, 1809–74* (Oxford: Oxford University Press, 1988), p. 104; compare with the remark that 'the age of equipoise' is 'the title of a book', J. Breuilly, *Labour and Liberalism in Nineteenth Century Europe* (Manchester: Manchester University Press, 1992), pp. 35 and 70.

94. See Sally Shuttleworth, *Charlotte Brontë and Victorian Pyschology* (Cambridge: Cambridge University Press, 1996), p. 14. Similarly Poovey, *Making a Social Body*.

95. Norman Vance, *Sinews of the Spirit* (Cambridge: Cambridge University Press, 1985), p. 3; compare with David Carroll's argument for what he terms 'the Victorian crisis of interpretation', *George Eliot and the Conflict of Interpretations. A Reading of the Novels* (Cambridge: Cambridge University Press, 1992), p. 4, and Alexander Welsh, *George Eliot and Blackmail* (Cambridge, MA: Harvard University Press, 1985). For other, at times more extreme, interpretations along the same lines see Nicholas Rance, *The historical novel and popular politics in nineteenth-century England* (London: Vision Press, 1975).

96. Clearly in evidence in Hoppen, *The Mid-Victorian Generation*. For good recent examples of such acknowledgements, see G.R. Searle, *Morality and the Market in Victorian Britain* (Oxford: Clarendon Press, 1998), esp. pp. vii–x.

97. True even of Searle, *Morality and the Market*.

98. Hence the comment about the 'complacent bellicose national pride characteristic of mid-century Victorians' made in Wendy C. Hinde, *Richard Cobden. A Victorian Outsider* (New Haven, CT: Yale University Press, 1987), p. 213.

99. This notion is a recurring theme in his *Victorian People*; see pp. 10, 31, 99, 105, and in the title of his mid-Victorian chapter in *The Age of Improvement*.

100. Wright, *Democracy and Reform*, p. 151.

101. Young, *Portrait*, p. 14.

102. See, for example, Finn, *After Chartism*.

103. G. Crossick, *An Artisan Élite in Victorian Society, Kentish London, 1840–1880* (London: Croom Helm, 1978), R.Q. Gray, *The Labour Aristocracy in Victorian Edinburgh* (Oxford: Clarendon Press, 1976). See also the important early expression of this approach; Brian Harrison and Patricia Hollis, 'Chartism, Liberalism and the Life of Robert Lowery', *English Historical Review*, 82 (1967).

104. See, for example, Stuart Angus Weaver's *John Fielden and the politics of popular radicalism* (Oxford: Clarendon Press, 1987), Theodore Koditschek's *Class formation and urban–industrial society Bradford, 1750–1850* (Cambridge: Cambridge University Press, 1990), Karl Ittmann's *Work, Gender and Family in Victorian England* (Basingstoke: Macmillan, 1995), as well as a range of studies written more explicitly within the new history of popular politics pioneered by Patrick Joyce and Gareth Stedman Jones, including Eugenio Biagini's *Liberty, retrenchment and reform: popular liberalism in the age of Gladstone, 1860–1880* (Cambridge: Cambridge University Press, 1992), and James Vernon's *Politics and the People* (Cambridge: Cambridge University Press, 1993).

105. Peter Bailey, *Popular Culture and Performance in the Victorian City* (Cambridge: Cambridge University Press, 1998), Neville Kirk, *Change, Continuity and Class: labour in British society, 1850–1920* (Manchester; Manchester University Press, 1998), F.M.L. Thompson, *The Rise of Respectable Society. The Social History of Victorian Britain* (London: Fontana, 1988).

106. As when, for example, he commented that 'There is a temptation here to revert to the term "equipoise"' (p. 270).

107. Kitson Clark, *Making of Victorian England*, p. 43.

CHAPTER ONE

Equipoise and its discontents: voices of dissent during the international exhibitions

Peter H. Hoffenberg

Introduction: equipoise, exhibitions and the Victorian public

'All London is astir ... and some part of all the world', noted John Ruskin in his diary for the first day of May in 1851.[1] Although the metropolis was in a frenzy over the official opening of the Great Exhibition at Hyde Park's unprecedented Crystal Palace, the famous art critic remained at home, ignoring the public birth of the international exhibition movement. 'Sitting in my quiet room, hearing the birds sing', he began the second volume of his *Stones of Venice*, while the city's streets overflowed with goods and people. Among those striding to and fro or in carriages were men and women from overseas nations and kingdoms, Britain's own colonies, provincial regions and London itself. Metropolitan dandies, merchants and workers mingled with Indian princes, Australian politicians and French businessmen.

Overcoming his initial scepticism about the event, Thomas Babington Macaulay wrote enthusiastically about those crowds on the same day. 'I should think that there must have been near three hundred thousand people in Hyde Park at once. The sight among the green boughs was delightful ... the boats; the flags; the music; the guns; everything was exhilarating.'[2] Macaulay's celebratory letter reflected the general sense that this was a moment of triumph for England, free trade and, perhaps, Victorian equipoise. Like all celebrations, though, this one also included its discontents.

The Great Exhibition and its most immediate English successor, the 1862 London International Exhibition, provided moments for various critics to attack what W.L. Burn called 'the mid-Victorian equipoise', most particularly the representation of some of its fundamental building blocks, such as political economy, the state, the cultural élite and the working class.[3] Voices of dissent included those of Victorian public moralists, among whom was Thomas Carlyle, who called upon a

tradition of cultural criticism of the market society, and of those occupying a very different position along the nineteenth-century spectrum,
frustrated scientists and advocates of political economy, including Charles
Babbage. The working-class, socialist and radical press also participated in the public debate about the mid-Victorian exhibitions. They
interpreted the events through class-coloured lenses, at times critiquing
organizers and displays with the passion of their anti-aristocratic and
anti-capitalist visions of 'Englishness'.

Burn's *The Age of Equipoise* emphasizes a series of disciplines and
network of authorities which preserved the sense of order within England between 1852 and 1867. Burn explored the contours of authority
and power at that time by asking about the ways in which society was
held together with all of its apparent contradictions and complications.
Here are the 'elements of stability' empowering Victorian confidence;
the various structures wove together a seemingly bearable and workable
philosophy, which, as we know, was filled with paradoxes and anxieties. What lay beneath the deceptively peaceful surface of the 1850s and
1860s? How did this complex society work if it were neither strictly
mechanical nor simplistically functional?[4]

The 'great' exhibitions of the mid-Victorian era help us better understand the ways in which Burn's society functioned. They represented the
systems of order which intrigued him. In doing so, the popular shows
also revealed to critics the tensions and ironies inherent in that equipoise. Representations of the economy and society were embraced
mystifications for some, but also, for others, demystifications of those
same ideas and practices. For such critics, the exhibitions were not
revelations of Heaven on Earth, but of Hell, most particularly concerning issues such as national identity, the market society and labour. The
shows confirmed the power of a cultural élite and the state at the same
time that they made those vulnerable to attack. Here were national
celebrations which often excluded a significant public role for the largest social group within the nation, the working class. And, in a final
irony, the grand spectacles celebrated a view of work which iconized
machinery and obscured human labour, the largest source of work
during the mid-Victorian era.[5]

Exhibitions are not discussed at length in Burn's work. He briefly
stopped amid discussion of 'The Day After the Feast' to suggest that the
Great Exhibition was both a symbol of 'the utilitarian, commercial,
middle-class age' and 'the culmination of the romantic age'.[6] His lack of
interest in exhibitions is understandable, since, at one level, his work
commenced with England in 1852, one year after the Great Exhibition;
but at a deeper level, he was more concerned with enduring institutions

and ideas, rather than temporary forms of entertainment, or 'feasts'. Legal and social disciplines, not the cultural world of music halls, museums or their complements, filled his pages. Yet the exhibitions in 1851 at the Crystal Palace and at South Kensington in 1862 were integral parts of the sense of equipoise. The Great Exhibition prefigured that equipoise; the London International revealed many of its tensions.

Was there a celebration of 'equipoise' at the 1851 and 1862 exhibitions? Yes, although not necessarily as an explicit objective of the events, as if commissioners and the general public intended the Great Exhibition as a celebration of equipoise itself, rather than of its causes and signs, such as free trade and relative political stability. But it was a self-conscious celebration of the ways in which official commissioners, as representatives of the state and a new cultural élite, linked together the material world and organized not just objects, but also the visitors themselves: not only Victorian things, but also the Victorians. Burn's sinews of authority and power provided the girders of these ideological structures, just as new building materials provided the superstructure for the Crystal Palace and the later South Kensington halls.

This is not to suggest that exhibitions elided the ideas and spaces of civil society and the public sphere, but that experiencing them helped mediate between the private sphere, those very public ones, and the mid-Victorian state.[7] Participation in the exhibitions helped create the sense of a Victorian public, particularly if we conceptualize the public as a process, or as Mary Poovey has argued, as a social body being formed and made, rather than the public as a thing or a condition of stasis.[8] This was the case in large part because visitors participated in the shows by purchasing commodities, consuming food and beverages on the premises, and turning the cranks of working machines. Perhaps even observing and being observed were forms of participation. This was a seductive invitation to help build the mid-Victorian equipoise rather than a unilaterally imposed official ideology. Exhibitions suggested one nexus of a fluid civil society: policed participation, contest within limits and articulated dissent.

Exhibition commissioners expressed a symmetry between the shows and the public. John Forbes Watson, commissioner for British India at a series of exhibitions in England and France, including the London International, argued that the popularity and success of the shows depended on exhibitors and visitors, 'the real actors in the Exhibitions'.[9] In a series of letters to *The Times*, later published as a single volume, Watson addressed characteristics of exhibitions twenty years after the Crystal Palace.[10] He concluded that '[e]verything is done in reference to the public in general', echoing the Victorians' obsession with public opinion, and recognizing that that public was increasingly complex and sophisticated. Exhibitions mirrored and shaped the dynamism of an increasingly multifaceted public, while commissioners addressed the relationships between those exhibitions and that 'public'.

Watson's public included 'well defined special classes' in society and at the exhibitions, such as producers, traders and consumers, but also 'in a wider sense', the public included the private community and the state itself. The commissioner suggested that there was a mirroring between society and the exhibitions, that the latter helped create and shape the former as the 'public'. Watson argued that the interests of the various sections of the public (economic, special, private and the state) were different and conflicting, but that exhibitions could appeal to and reconcile these special classes. In a formulation which hints at Burn's 'equipoise', the commissioner added that '[t]he promotion of every one of these interests may, and should, be made the subject of specially devised measures, while preserving harmony' in the working of the exhibitions and society. The link was Watson's definition of the public, both inside and outside the exhibition experience and space. The public, or civil society, was formed and represented by participation at the shows.

The exhibitions represented the momentary and often unstable equilibrium of mid-Victorian society, what Burn called the 'unruffled calm ... the outcome of a temporary balance of forces struggling ... to better their positions'.[11] At the same time, the shows suggested the potential for a more permanent realization of balance, or equilibrium. They represented the apparent counterpoise of various forces and institutions, such as the middle and working classes, the colonies and England. The exhibitions were not only signs of equipoise, but also the living and material experience of such equipoise; not just the idea, but also the social fact of placing and holding society in equipoise. The processes of organizing and visiting the shows revealed the sources of stability which interested Burn; those very processes, or practices, were themselves targets of contemporary criticism, and, to such critics, sources of instability.

Not surprisingly, Thomas Carlyle was among those critics, and, in contrast to Macaulay, he wrote about the Great Exhibition in a far less benign manner, concluding that '[s]uch a sanhedrin of windy fools from all countries of the Globe were surely never gathered in one city before'.[12] The critic longed for some 'silence' in place of 'the Wind-dustry involving everything in one inane tornado'. From the other side of the political playing fields, The Friend of the People asked 'What have exhibitions done for the people?'[13] The answer for the republican-socialists?

Not much, at least for the people, or labourers of England, but plenty for its aristocrats and swindlers.

Conservatives and socialists contested the political economy celebrated by the shows. Exhibition commissioners and executive committees were attacked as part of the governing élite, a 'Science and Art Clique' at the heart of the state, or in the words of one MP, as 'the Kensington Party', misusing public funds and their own authority at the centre of political power.[14] *The Bee-Hive*'s banner headline declared the 1862 International Exhibition a 'FAILURE', in good part because of the commissioners' 'jobbery and robbery', which lined their élite pockets at the expense of the nation.[15] Those were sustained and systematic voices of dissent during the exhibitions, rather than momentary bursts of public outcry about ephemeral fears, such as the possible visitation of the Plague in 1851.[16] Little if any was heard about those concerns once the Great Exhibition was officially opened.

Exhibitions and markets: the equipoise of political economy?

Representations of the market as an idea and process were at the heart of the exhibitions, reminding contemporaries of the market's power, promises and failures. Commissioners and merchants hoped that improvements in trade and production would result from touring the commercial collections and studying both the discrete national exhibits and the over-arching worldly treasure chest. Charles Babbage wrote that the Great Exhibition was 'calculated to promote and increase the free interchange of raw materials and manufactured goods between all the nations' and, in doing so, would 'instruct the consumer in the art of judging the character of the commodity'.[17] Shows in 1851 and 1862 offered idealized markets: seemingly limitless in wealth and variety, and, at the same time, founded upon a direct relationship between producers and consumers. One contemporary read the colonial displays at the 1862 London International Exhibition as a sign of a working free-trade empire, the commercial ties foreshadowing future viable political federation.[18]

Sir Henry Cole, Keeper of the South Kensington Museum and Executive Commissioner in 1851 and 1862, noted how such shows allowed producers and consumers to compare the economic strengths of participating countries. In a neo-Ricardian turn on comparative advantages, this strong advocate of the exhibitions argued that they provided opportunities to develop and experience each nation's 'natural tendencies'.[19] Cole concluded: 'Every nation has something peculiar to itself which is useful to another, and it is the increased ease of interchange which international exhibitions chiefly promote.' France could exhibit 'wines, silks, and all kinds of articles connected with the luxuries of civilized life', while English exhibitors displayed 'iron and coal'. Direct and open connections between commercial parties at the exhibitions replaced the 'mysteries' of hidden, or private, production and consumption, such as that practised by older guilds. The shows were political economy in practice, examples of how its advocates, such as Cole and Babbage, thought the market might instruct, civilize and promote equipoise.

Recently, Thomas Richards has suggestively argued that the Great Exhibition offered the spectacle of commodities and the emergence of a new capitalist form of representation.[20] Here were consumers and consumerism, or, in his words, 'a functioning microcosm of mid-Victorian capitalism', centred by the distinctive ways in which the commodity was represented. Commissioners undertook that representational project at the exhibitions for economic, cultural and political reasons. The development of industrial capitalism as a particular form of social relations paralleled the ideas of nation-building and colonial federation, such as those being tossed about in Canada and Australia at the time. Consumers were, after all, citizens and subjects, and consumerism was both an ideology for and mode of participation in the nation and empire. If the Crystal Palace made the commodity the focal point, as Richards argues, it and its successors also offered the visitors' relationship to commodities as a metaphor for political and social relations.[21] This association was fluid and mutable, adjusting to ideas about the market's benefits and deficiencies.

Economic displays in 1851 and 1862 created pictures of national and imperial commercial equipoise. Differing and often conflicting groups participated as producers and consumers. The market offered a reconciliation of distinctions and similarities, a redefinition of racial and social communities. In doing so, it provided an idealized representation, almost a metaphor, of the nation and the normative relationship among its various 'interests'.[22] The market and its functioning were both the practice and the image of equipoise at the exhibitions; the market symbolized a cluster of ideas and processes to explain and describe social relations and the English nation. Exhibitions provided comparison, competition, demonstration and evaluation of economic goods by jurors and visitors.

Babbage believed that the staging of exhibitions linked the ideal types of the nation and the market; citizens participated as producers and consumers, most strongly if the principle of 'competition' were guaranteed by including prices for the exhibits. He was outraged when the commissioners did not provide such prices in 1851.[23] That competitive moral found little favour with alternative nationalists who promoted cooperation, rather than competition, or with public moralists wary of the market as a source of authority, taste and order. They criticized the exhibitions as representations of modern political economy.[24] Those critics had no doubts that this was a brave new world with an equipoise vastly different in style and scope from previous ones.

Carlyle was among those drawing upon and contributing to this tradition of cultural criticism. Readers can perceive in his response to the Great Exhibition his general disdain for political economy and its child, the modern, urban society seemingly filled with social chaos and disintegration. The new, more democratic age of the market could not be restrained by the glass and iron of Paxton's Crystal Palace: it was the permanent future, not an ephemeral moment. Carlyle's correspondence at the time to family and friends reveals in no uncertain terms his strong reactions of disdain and antipathy for the event and its participants. Whereas Ruskin and Macaulay had appreciated to some degree the noise and crowds, Carlyle concluded just before the show closed that 'Palaver, noise, nonsense and confusion, in all its forms, have been the order of the day.'[25] This is not to say that Babbage as an advocate of political economy would not have heard 'noise' at the Crystal Palace, but his would have been the sounds of a creative marketplace, the sensible echoes of dynamic mid-Victorian capitalism, rather than its 'nonsense'.

Carlyle wrote to Ralph Waldo Emerson that the Great Exhibition had depressed local and national trade, although its organizers had promised just the opposite results, and that the spectacle had put him in a 'pathetic grandfatherly feeling'.[26] The exhibition was a 'universal Children's Ball, which the British Nation in these extraordinary circumstances is giving itself!' Carlyle took the nation's pulse and understood that the Crystal Palace was the beginning of a movement, rather than its finale. What was his advice? If the event produced noise, then he recommended silence. 'Silence above all, silence is very behoveful!' If not silence, then flight: and he travelled northward to Lancashire and Scotland to escape the exhibition-dominated city and its 'sanhedrin of windy fools'. He hoped that the Crystal Palace would be dismantled and taken 'quite away again' by the time of his return to London.[27]

'Such a year of nonsense here as was seldom seen ever in London years' was Carlyle's verdict to his brother, Alexander.[28] That correspondence continued the socio-economic criticism, as well, suggesting the ways that the 'this big Glass Soapbubble, and all the gauderies spread out in it' had harmed business and labour. 'England, I think, must have *lost* some 25 per cent of its year's labour by the job (the London shopkeepers are nearly bankrupt by the want of business).' Was this something more than an exaggeration of the oft-heard complaint that exhibitions were unfair competition for local tradesmen, creating, as it were, a protected bazaar within the host city? Perhaps it was.

The 'nonsensical talk, thought and speculation' at the Crystal Palace in 1851 was not, in Carlyle's vision, an aberration, but a revelation of this dismal new order, his famous 'cash nexus' writ large. The argument that lost labour and financial debt would never be recovered was a critique of the society and economy represented by the Great Exhibition. Did England lose 25 per cent of its labour because of the event? Not likely. Yet the boldness of Carlyle's exaggeration was intended to suggest the dramatic sea change in England signified by the exhibition.[29]

Other prominent figures within the mid-Victorian world of arts and letters shared some, if not all, of Carlyle's discomfort with the exhibitions as examples. Those cultural critics were often hostile to the new society created by the market economy, but that did not always translate into hostility towards the exhibitions. Charles Dickens and John Ruskin, among others, did not disagree with Carlyle's general sentiments. But, rather than dismissing the event and its participants, they found particular exhibits to study and celebrate.[30] Dickens flirted with Carlyle's stance when he admitted that Great Exhibition was 'too much'. He found the human mass and vast cosmos of exhibits excessive and tiring: 'I have only been twice; so many things bewildered me. I have a natural horror of sights, and the fusion of so many sights in one has not decreased it.'[31] Yet, he admitted to enjoying certain exhibits.

Charles Babbage: the frustrated exhibitionist

Although a strong advocate of the exhibitions for economic and intellectual purposes, even Charles Babbage found various reasons to complain. He voiced discontent about the role of government at the shows, the commissioners and the display of exhibits. In one case, Babbage argued that the government, or in his words, English 'statesmen', did not appreciate the importance of professional societies and thus the state did not engage them as much as it should have when organizing the Great Exhibition. He was not referring to the Royal Society of Arts, which provided much of the staff for that and future shows, but to other groups, comprising scientists and businessmen.[32]

Babbage provided his most systematic analysis of exhibitions and, in particular, the Great Exhibition, in *The Exposition of 1851; or, Views of the Industry, The Science and The Government, of England.* Two editions were published during 1851 and the volume was the subject of a lengthy essay in *The North British Review.*[33] Babbage had already achieved considerable renown by that time as the author of *The Economy of Manufactures*, his defence of political economy and factory production, and as the inventor of the Calculating Engine, or 'Difference Engine', an embryonic computer.[34] Babbage criticized the Great Exhibition ('this Diorama of the Peaceful Arts') as a way to shine his critical light upon larger problems, or take 'a more correct view of the industry, the science, the institutions, and the government of this country'.[35]

For example, the failure properly to integrate learned 'associations' and practical scientific exhibits at the Crystal Palace was evidence of the government's disregard for science and scientists. Commissioners had not encouraged scientific displays or the participation of scientists as organizers and exhibitors, thereby illustrating 'the position of science in this country'.[36] That was not an enviable position, in Babbage's view. By 1862, his train of thought had curved to include direct criticism of the commissioners as practical organizers. Were they showing disdain for his own exhibit, the famous 'Difference Engine'? Babbage thought so. He wrote with no small dose of sarcasm that the exhibit was 'placed in a *small hole* in a *dark corner*, where it could, with some difficulty, be seen by six people at the same time'.[37] In contrast, 'a trophy of children's toys, whose merits, it is true, the commissioners were somewhat more competent to appreciate', filled a prominent position in the exhibition halls at South Kensington.

What was at stake here, besides the pride of Charles Babbage? His anger found three targets: the continuation of patronage within English society which enabled some exhibitors to claim prominent places for their displays, and left others in the 'dark' corners; the continued lack of interest among the governing élite and its representatives, the commissioners, in practical science; and, in a slightly different twist, the commissioners' inability or reluctance by the second 'great' exhibition to treat exhibitions as money-making, commercial enterprises. Working-class and other radical commentators argued that the London International Exhibition turned a profit, albeit a corrupt one enjoyed only by the commissioners, speculators and the 'moneyed-interest'.[38] In contrast, Babbage saw a missed financial opportunity. 'Favouritism' and ignorance created an excessively rigid economy at the show, preventing the calculating machines and other potential money-generating exhibits from producing both public gratification and profit.

Two years after the show, Babbage suggested in his autobiographical *Passages from the Life of a Philosopher* that all of the working calculating machines could have been placed in one room, to which admission would have been charged. The experience might have included lectures, observation of mechanical drawings, and the sale of 'illustrations of machinery used for computing and printing Tables'. In one final slight upon the Commission, Babbage concluded that if its 'dignity' did not permit its members to make money from this court, then they could have announced that the proceeds of the tickets would be forwarded to 'the distressed population of the Manchester district'. There would then have been, in his view, 'crowds of visitors' to see the calculating machines in action. He wrote this with full knowledge that the commissioners had proven reluctant to contribute to the national relief effort in 1862.[39]

Babbage never seemed to lose his capacity to criticize exhibition commissioners, nor his faith in the exhibition as a form of education and exchange. As with the promise of political economy, consumers and producers were brought into direct contact at these shows. Babbage claimed at the time of the Great Exhibition that direct observation of craftsmen and contact between consumers and producers (individuals, classes and nations) 'removed the veil of mystery' about economic transactions.[40] Without commercial middlemen, prices and the experts' reports provided the filters between the two groups and demonstrated contemporary notions of the market's authority and power to improve taste, create value, civilize and establish social order.

But, alas, the executive commissioners at the Crystal Palace failed to realize the earthly paradise within their grasp by forbidding the attachment of prices, in Babbage's words 'the most important quality by which men judge of commodities'.[41] The absence of price was 'injurious both to art and to artists: it ... removes from the field of competition the best judges of real merit' and eliminated the method by which the public could 'form any just estimate of ... commercial value'.[42] Thus the evaluation of that merit and value now depended on non-market influences, such as aesthetic taste, utility, mere popularity, or the commissioners' official catalogues and essays. In the best of cases, Babbage admitted that published exhibition reports might act as prices, verifying the authenticity of displayed trade items and thus preventing dishonest exchanges and allaying fears of false advertising.[43]

The debate about pricing and selling objects at the exhibitions was part of the wider controversy over the nature of the cultural expert's authority and the power of the market to determine value. As experts and bureaucrats, did the commissioners draw upon the disinterested mind of a new aristocracy, or the retail mind of the businessman? Merchandise was enthroned by the authority of the state, the attributions by experts, and the power of the visitors' imagination at the exhibitions; however, were these reliable sources of value in a capitalist society, particularly one in which people might be influenced by irrational forces, such as advertising? Did they represent an authentic value?

Like the department stores of the near future, the exhibitions were making the fantastic observable and tangible. Irrational appetites were as much if not more of a force than the rational ones encouraged by Babbage.[44] Fantasy itself was a consumable commodity at exhibitions, making them what Walter Benjamin called 'sites of pilgrimages to the commodity fetish'.[45] Did this concern about what attracted visitors and why such things did so reveal deeper anxieties about political economy and economic behaviour during the era of apparent equipoise? Were many if not all of those concerns not resolved for observers and participants in 1851 and 1862? Ruskin noted in 1860 that the consumer often purchased what he 'wished for' rather than what he 'needed'.[46] Economic wealth and national equipoise might be possible through the manipulation of such 'visions, idealisms, hopes, and affections' at the exhibitions. The regulation of the purse was a regulation of the imagination inside the Crystal Palace, rather than Babbage's preferred regulation of the mind.

'The art and science clique': the state and its new cultural élite

Babbage was not alone in his criticism of the exhibition commissioners. Where he found incompetence and narrow-mindedness, others more commonly uncovered corruption and arrogance. As early as March 1850, over one year before the Crystal Palace officially opened, *The Mechanics' Magazine* was expressing discontent about the composition and behaviour of the executive committee charged with overseeing the event.[47] A 'low state of moral feeling' was found amidst its members, many of whom were, in the words of the editors, 'obscure individuals' from the Royal Society of Arts, 'people distinguished for nothing whatever in the world'. They put themselves forward to 'reap the benefits of the fraud practised on the Crown'. The Prince Consort had given his good name to the Commission, but he could hardly be expected to watch over the affairs with daily diligence.

As a result, the great event was in the hands of a 'pack of characterless nobodies', such as Cole, Matthew Digby Wyatt and Francis Fuller, examples of a new breed of cultural bureaucrats. 'Obscure' they might be, but now they represented their own élite 'interest', rather than that of the nation. The Crown was in danger of being 'sullied' by its alliance with such 'trickery and imposture' in the form of a commissioners' conspiracy. The commissioners were their own party, not disinterested public servants. The magazine's attitude towards such bureaucrats and experts, as well as their home, the Royal Society of Arts, hardly improved by the time of the London International twelve years later.[48]

Criticism of the exhibition commissioners at the time reveals uncertainties about the new forms and practitioners of intellectual, cultural and bureaucratic authority during the mid-Victorian era. After all, exhibitions were part of the wider project of perceiving and organizing Victorian England and its growing empire as immense administrative and informational challenges.[49] As state bureaucrats, entrepreneurs and showmen, the commissioners responsible for these expositions were at the centre of that project, using the shows to construct knowledge, as they did at new public institutions, such as the South Kensington Museum. Production and consumption of that knowledge, such as science and art displays, linked together England's various classes and regions and, simultaneously, developed connections between England and the outside world.

The construction of material culture and knowledge required commissioners and their staffs to bring objects and bodies out from private and enclosed space, such as homes and factories. They reconstructed and reclassified those Victorian 'things' with new meanings and value for shared public observation and consumption at the exhibition halls.[50] Commissioners oversaw that process as professional managers in a manner similar to that found among their commercial and industrial contemporaries. Exhibitions were a business and required the organizational techniques and expertise found in other large-scale Victorian-era projects, industrial firms among them, although in this case the commissioners produced knowledge and culture, not necessarily a tangible economic commodity.[51] They were among the first experts in Britain to apply modern scientific, economic and management techniques to the production of public culture, and they often did so as part of the more interventionist and active British state.

Exhibition commissioners were more often than not the same figures that the state called upon for science and art reforms, national educational policies, and the management of galleries, libraries and museums. Exhibitions offered a large, though temporary, venue for those mid-Victorians to achieve public authority, prestige and acceptance. These were moments in which the state and its cultural officers were revealed, making both accessible to advocates as well as critics, voices of support and voices of dissent. To a great degree, British, and even more so English, exhibition commissioners were examples of Samuel Taylor Coleridge's famous 'clerisy', or body of cultural experts responsible for cultivating ideas, maintaining intellectual life, forging a national culture and generally connecting the arts, professions and the people.[52]

The exhibition 'clerisy' produced knowledge, social categories and taste as a new cultural aristocracy. This was not only an administrative and informational act, since both the action itself and the resulting displays offered new languages of power and authority for the experts and the state. Exhibition commissioners and visitors were thus part of the more general nineteenth-century reorganization of public space and the bodies and commodities that occupied it. Commissioners and exhibitors uncovered bodies, relics, commodities, factory production and art, bringing them out from hiding behind household and factory walls for public display, evaluation and consumption. Such a public revelation brought deep, loud and sustained voices of dissent to bear on the form of exhibitions themselves, the ways in which they were managed by official commissions and the composition of those commissions. What was displayed and how workers were treated as exhibitors and visitors were also sources of debate.

For example, could those commissioners and their voluntary societies, such as the Royal Society of Arts, be trusted as a learned élite in the transition away from traditional authorities on scientific, artistic and economic questions? Among others, the editors of *The Mechanics' Magazine* did not think so. Their review of the Royal Society's annual exhibition held before the South Kensington show criticized the group's élitist stance and apparent lack of interest in applied models. The show did not fulfil the purpose of an exhibition; that is, it did not provide 'records of the nation's progress'.[53] There was only 'a quiet little collection got together somehow, to amuse the secretary and tickle the vanity of a few investors'. National shows required exhibition space and displays which only the government could provide. In this way, the weakness of the Society's exhibition was further proof of the need for public organization and funding of the upcoming London International and its separation from the élite, self-interested Royal Society.

Restless on the political Left, *The Bee-Hive* also found a similar target in the London International Exhibition's executive commission. Its leading editorial writer, 'Scourge', criticized the 'jobbery' and 'mismanagement' of the event, focusing on the ways in which the aristocratic and commercial classes benefited from the exhibition at the expense of the workers and the nation.[54] The 'monster booth of Kensington', as the writer nicknamed the show, revealed not only speculation and 'a vile, trading, huckstering spirit', or the drive of mid-Victorian capitalism, but also its ally within the state, 'the "art and science" clique'.

What was this cabal? The powerful combination of bureaucrats, officers and experts from the Department of Science and Art, the Royal Society of Arts, *The Times* and the circle around Prince Albert, most responsible for organizing and publicizing the exhibition. The *Mechanics' Magazine*'s unknown figures had now moved from outside to within the state, where they were highly visible. They had organized from that privileged position an event with more visitors and more days of operation than the Crystal Palace, but one with less profit and a series of 'discouraging' financial statements.[55]

That was the case because Scourge's 'clique' had organized the event for its own financial and political gain. Its members allowed contractors to ignore overtime pay for workers building the exhibition structure. At the very same time, those commissioners refused to contribute to the nation-wide relief fund for Lancashire. Readers were reminded that even the music-hall owners had donated to that fund. This was one more sign that the exhibition did not represent the interests of the nation and people, but the interests of an élite state, The Establishment, 'or parochial authorities of South Kensington'. Rich politicians and aristocrats got fat on the show, filling their 'well-lined pockets' with various schemes and 'dodges', while starving working-class families got thinner, both in South Kensington and Lancashire. The leading editorial about the show's closing concluded: 'Shame and disgrace upon these Commissioners that they so mismanaged their business, as to be unable to sacrifice even one day's receipts in the cause of charity!' for the North or for the widows and orphans created during the construction of South Kensington. Mismanagement and speculation tampered with 'the rights and wages of workmen' before, during and after the show.[56]

Exhibiting the nation? workers and the mid-Victorian equipoise

Additional critics of the exhibitions could be found on the opposite side of the political playing field from Carlyle and the economic one from Babbage: that is, among readers of *The Bee-Hive* on the Victorian Left, or, more specifically, within the radical, republican, socialist, artisanal and working-class press defending workmen's 'rights and wages'. The editors of such journals and newspapers often found economic or class-based targets among the commissioners and private organizers, as well as revelations of political economy's horrors in the way that workers were treated before and during the events. Those criticisms complemented the support given in their pages to striking workers at the exhibition construction sites. For example, *The Friend of the People*

sympathetically chronicled the working regulations and industrial actions by painters and glaziers as the Crystal Palace went up in late 1850
and early 1851.[57]

George Julian Harney's newspaper attacked the Palace's 'essentially
aristocratic' opening ceremony, preferring to see the exhibition 'opened
not in the presence of the richest, but of the worthiest of the nation,
selected by popular election, to represent not a class, but *all*'.[58] Hyde
Park could have been England's *Champ de Mars*. But exploitation and
capital, rather than enjoyment and labour, were the order of the day.
The reversal of the situation could only come about, concluded the
editorial writer, when the supremacy of labour and the sovereignty of a
republican nation replaced the 'flunkeyism ... the rule of masters, and
the royalty of a degenerate monarchy' on display at the Crystal Palace.

The Friend of the People also carried a series of open letters challeng-
ing the Great Exhibition's message about economic competition among
nations. Editors and correspondents urged that the event be turned in a
more internationalist and cooperative direction to exhibit 'those principles which would unite all nations in one common bond of brotherhood,
each contributing to the welfare of all'.[59] The spectacle might still serve
a nationalist purpose, after all, but one more in keeping with the
utopian nationalism of the 1840s. Who could turn their back on this
massive educational opportunity? Not the writers, editors and readers
of *The Friend*.

Hyde Park in 1851 might even be the most appropriate stage for
presenting non-violent reforms, such as the People's Charter. In that
vein, George Holyoake and other radicals published an open letter to
Robert Owen appealing to him to 'deliver a series of lectures' as part of
the commissioners' efforts to translate and distribute 'lectures on political and social subjects' during the show's season.[60] The socialist's
contributions could turn 1851 into a year to rival others in the radical
calendar, such as 1649 and 1793. Owen responded with his approval,
suggesting that 'the opportunity to disseminate important truths to
nations in a short period has never before occurred under such favourable auspices'.[61]

The Great Exhibition might provide for such radicals a large-scale
popular moment with 'favourable auspices' for the transformation of
English society in the aftermath of the political defeat of the Chartist
movement. It suggested the possibility of a fruitful union of direct
political action with educational and cultural practices, representing
labour as a class and idea. But what would be the nature of that
political action? Harney was reluctant to turn lectures, meetings and the
event itself into a moment of open revolt. Those sentiments echoed

pleas by other radicals, such as Feargus O'Connor, who noted the large concentration of police and soldiers in and around London at the time. The Irish Chartist advised readers to practise restraint to protect 'your liberty, your wives, and your children, and perhaps your lives'.[62] The exhibition was not the revolutionary moment. Instead, O'Connor advised patience, imploring readers 'not to be led away by the folly of others when the Exhibition takes place'.

Exhibitions were nearly peerless opportunities for observing and learning in the minds of others who also proclaimed themselves defenders of workers and artisans. The Mechanics' Magazine, for example, overcame its concerns about the International Exhibition's commissioners and provided detailed descriptions of activities and exhibits at the 1862 show. Regularly published 'Notes' from South Kensington included comments about the progress of the buildings, the official opening ceremony, machines in motion, colonial raw materials and exhibition publications.[63] The editors apparently agreed that the London International would be popular with its readers, who would either refer to the columns before, during or after their visit, or substitute the magazine for such a personal visit in the event that they could not enter the exhibition courts. The mechanical and industrial advantages to be gained were promised 'in spite of blunders, incapacity, and folly' on the part of organizers, contractors and commissioners.[64]

The educational experience worked best when workers and their families participated at the shows and observed displays first-hand. That was not always the case. It often seemed as if the commissioners were doing whatever they could to prevent working-class attendance. The Working Man supported the London International in 1862, but queried why '[t]he Commissioners seem determined to show that working men are not wanted at the Exhibition?'[65] The paper's editors found it more than ironic that Saturday admission charges were higher than those for weekdays. The five-shilling charge made the event rather expensive for the English working man, who, they argued, 'stands more in need of visiting the exhibition' than others, but who could only attend on Saturdays. The labourer studying other nation's exhibits would not only benefit English industry in general, but would also be enabled to 'contemplate the victories of labour, so as to rise in his own estimation'. That position was shared by the editors of The Mechanics' Magazine.

Exhibitions could celebrate both national wealth and working-class pride, but only if they were made available to the workers themselves. This argument integrated the working-class into the national community, into its sense of 'Englishness'. In this way, the exhibitions were perceived by some as potential celebrations of what scholars consider

'Radical' patriotism, or nationalism.[66] If the International Exhibition celebrated England, then, according to *The Working Man*, it should include the workers, the majority of citizens, as workers. In a working-class crafting of the mid-Victorian equipoise, the editors recommended that employers, railway companies and exhibition commissioners work together to offer not only reduced transportation and admission prices for workers, but a salary advance to cover expenses. 'The working man would then feel grateful, and at the same time, independent; and everyone would gain.'[67]

In this sense, *The Working Man* was suggesting the relevance of the exhibition experience to workers, but imputing to the commissioners either ignorance or malice in preventing those same workers from participating. The exhibitions could offer an alternative to the public house, as organizers such as Cole proclaimed, but only if the commissioners saw fit to reduce the high Saturday admission price to the more reasonable one charged on other days, so that the working man and his family could visit.[68] At one level, then, the editors were only asking that the celebrated spectacle be made available to the workers on the same terms and with the same opportunities that it had been for others during the working week.

But there were two noteworthy class-based additions to those mid-summer editorials, written at the height of the International Exhibition. In one case, the editors argued that admissions should be reduced for workers, who were 'the real power of the land', rather than for 'the *gentle* idlers and loungers', who could enjoy the other, one-shilling days that the admission schedule now offered.[69] In this way, the contributions of 'the million' might be allowed to take their fair share, rather than provide for the pleasures of 'the few', notably the 'idle' aristocrats. And *The Working Man* recommended the close scrutiny of the new machinery exhibits and other applications of science to production revealed to the public at South Kensington. Why?

Editors suggested that 'the great problem of labour is soon coming to a solution', in which the working man would be treated as another commodity and, perhaps, replaced. Thus the higher admission charge on Saturdays was making the working man invisible at the exhibition in the same way that new production processes would replace workers with machines in the factories of England's future, making labourers equally invisible at the workplace itself. If exhibitions mirrored, or in this case, prefigured a society without masses of workers, but one with self-acting machines in motion, like those exhibited in the courts, then was it not to be expected that workers should be made invisible as visitors?

Of machines and men: the equipoise of industrialism?

The Working Man's critique of the commissioners' decision to charge five shillings on Saturday had been transformed into a warning about the replacement of workers by machines and the subsequent decline in employment. Rather than suppressing 'The Machinery Question' that had captivated the preceding generation, or suggesting its resolution without contest, the exhibitions revealed it for the mid-Victorians, often in the controversial form of the scientific management of labour and the factory.[70] Machinery courts and reproduced factory environments filled the exhibition halls in 1851 and 1862 and did so in a way which iconized technology and obscured man.

At the London International Exhibition, 'Social Science' was celebrated in various forms, including machines in motion. The editors of *The Working Man* reminded their readers that

> We should be sorry if Social Science had no other conclusion to give us than that, for it appears very clear to us, that labour being less every day in request upon the market, there will be employment but for very few of us, and that the others will have to be put on the shelves to dry like loaves unsold at a baker's shop.[71]

We can envision with what foreboding such words echoed amidst starvation in Lancashire and calls for its relief throughout the land. They invited a different spin on the enthroning of technology found in official exhibition catalogues and the general press.

Exhibition officials and others promoting machinery turned to the shows to naturalize their vision of an industrial equipoise. In this case, industrialism was both ideology and practice; the machine as a metaphor for a new society accompanied the machine as a producer of power and commodities. The structure of the exposition provided the experience, language and legitimacy for this new industrial culture and society. Exhibition literature and the popular 'machines-in-motion' displays made connections between new technology, the organization of production in the factory and the social organization of the nation. As with all symbolic constructions of public culture, the displays of machines at the Crystal Palace and London International Exhibitions hid and mystified as much, if not more, than they revealed.

In doing so, the images of work at the exhibitions often complemented the images of factories and industrial labour in the popular press, novels and economic literature of the day.[72] Rows of machines in motion at the Great Exhibition replicated the idea and image of the new factories as a collection of 'self-acting machines', such as the archetypes studied by Andrew Ure and Babbage in their early works on manufacturing and political economy.[73] The commissioners applied Babbage's 'mechanical principles' when organizing exhibition space and offered Ure's 'perfection of automatic industry' in the machines-in-motion courts. Ure's frontispiece for *The Philosophy of Manufactures* shows the power-loom factory of Thomas Robinson in Stockport and it bears a nearly flawless resemblance to the popular cotton machines in motion at the 1851 exhibition. That symmetry reveals continuities in the representation of the new industrialism and in the ways that mid-Victorians imagined the factory as a metaphor for society. In both, only a few 'skilled artisans' operated the dominant, self-acting machinery.

Factories and exhibitions offered idealized visions of a self-regulating system without human agency and labour; that is, most urgently, without trade unions and industrial actions. Ure argued that 'self-acting machines' left the attendant with 'nearly nothing at all to do'; the factory system replaced human labour as a source of value with the machine's work.[74] This vision of the modern factory was more than a paradigm for society; it constituted a new social form and practice requiring obedience, regimentation, hierarchy and interdependence seemingly without individual agency or class 'interest'. It thus represented a powerful metaphor for the national equipoise by idealizing the relations between man and machine.

There was also a profound and painful irony in the way that factory space was constructed at the shows and in contemporary exhibition commentaries. Although the working man was made invisible, he was most certainly needed. One commentator about the Crystal Palace concluded that '[e]nchanted palaces that grow up in a night are confined to fairy-land'.[75] In 'this material world of ours, the labours of the brick-layer and the carpenter are notoriously never-ending' for 'palaces' such as those at Hyde Park and South Kensington. The process of erecting the exhibition buildings and organizing the displays housed within them presented to contemporary observers novel uses of new machinery in union with old forms of human work.

Some of those observers praised modern workers for building the dramatic and monumental exposition halls.[76] The exhibitions involved massive deployments of skilled and unskilled workers, most of whom laboured without the assistance of technology. Paxton's Crystal Palace, for example, included 300,000 hand-blown glass panes. Inside, visitors viewed artisanal needlework and hand-made cutlery and edge-tools from Sheffield.[77] These were exhibited amidst the mystifying whir of self-acting machines in motion. The labourers themselves were absent as labourers, even when they could afford to enter the exhibition halls. Workers and their families visited the exhibitions and they observed products and machines as representations of abstract work, rather than images of their own labour processes.

That was the case even though the clear majority of labour at the exhibition sites remained manual. This is not to ignore the fact that railways carried some displays and visitors to London and a handful of steam engines assisted with moving larger crates, exhibits and iron beams. Most shipping crates and exhibition objects were unpacked, moved and erected by workmen. Brute human strength organized most of the displays in England, although a limited number of steam cranes were used at South Kensington in 1862.[78] This was no small part of the labour at exhibitions. Workmen at the International Exhibition site moved and placed over 79,000 articles and packages before the show's official opening in 1862.[79] Among these packages were 'two enormously bulky' ones from Prussia containing a life-sized replica of a wood hut.[80] Exhibition work was not only tiring; it could also be dangerous. That condition was dramatically illustrated by the two workers who fell to their deaths in the race to complete the twin South Kensington towers before the London International Exhibition in 1862.[81] An assistant smith was also killed by a hammer blow while manually driving rivets into one of the girders.[82]

Such hand and animal labour continued to dominate production in England during those mid-Victorian years. More than half the demands for power in manufacturing in Burn's England were supplied by people and animals, as well as by increasingly efficient windmills and waterwheels.[83] The exhibitions presented to their millions of visitors a different picture of that economic order and the nature of work at its centre. The display and apparent embracing of machinery at the great exhibitions erased the common worker, elevated the machine in motion, and encouraged the anti-industrial sentiment popular among both Labour and Conservative critics alike.

A one-penny broadsheet published at the time of the Great Exhibition attacked 'the Glasshouse of Mammon' and called for an alternative celebration of labour, 'from whom all wealth proceeds'.[84] One of the lead editorials in *The Working Man* at the time of the 1862 London International proclaimed that the royal commissioners

> talk of giving medals and rewards to the exhibitors, whose produce will transcend the others in beauty, utility, economy, etc., *to the exhibitors*, that is to say, to those who, with the help of Mammon, have known how to purchase and to seduce the starving inventor, the houseless labourer, the ragged Working Man, to sell him the child of their genius or of their industry.[85]

The editors underscored the application of human power at the exhibition sites themselves and the persistence of hand power in the nineteenth-century workshops. They noted the slow growth of mechanization, and thus the apparent contrast between the Temples of Industry found at the expositions and the material conditions of the economy, most notably that of the working class.

Even the Whiggish *Leisure Hour* noted in the 1860s that exhibitions kept 'the real worker, who had performed the miracle of art or ingenuity ... entirely in the background'.[86] Working-class visitors (Watson's 'real' exhibition actors) came 'to see and to ponder on what has been *wrought* and *done*' at the 1862 London International, but generally viewed what had been wrought by machines and workers from the colonies and foreign nations.[87] English workers saw only machines and overseas artisans producing at the exhibition. Displays generally represented the value of traditional labour forms and social groups and the uses of modern technology, but rarely the common forms in England of unskilled and hand-powered work.

The Leisure Hour continued to criticize mid-Victorian exhibition commissioners and their 'Industrial Exhibitions' for ignoring the worker and his labour. Writing at the time of the 1865 Dublin International Exhibition, its editors suggested that at 'the grand national displays, in which peoples contended with peoples, ... employers, exhibition commissioners and other officials assumed credit for the workers' productions'.[88] The major international exhibitions represented 'unlimited capital leagued with the most consummate art' under the supporting wing of governments and states. The worker was in the 'background'.

Those editors had a solution to that dilemma. They championed specialized 'industrial exhibitions'. Among these was the one held at the Agricultural Hall in Islington a few years after the London International. The smaller show demonstrated 'the unassisted production of the working man' rather than the exhibits of 'prosperous tradesmen and manufacturers who work with the hands and brains of others'.[89] Later in the century, the London Trades Council sponsored similar National Workmen's Exhibitions as alternatives to the major expositions, thereby appropriating the form, but changing its meaning, participants and displays. Labour shows revealed 'the great advantages of excellence of production in all industries instead of the manufacture of slop-work' at the international exhibitions, which were 'a fraud upon the public and deeply injurious to the best interests of labour'.[90]

Conclusion: the legacy of discontent

Criticism of exhibitions from radicals and republicans, among others, continued during the nineteenth century. *Reynolds's Weekly Newspaper* considered the Colonial and Indian Exhibition in 1886 to be 'a wretched spectacle' intended to celebrate the union of capital and Crown at the expense of the English worker and colonial subjects.[91] Perhaps the show might reveal what 'the people can do', suggested the republican editors, 'in spite of bad government'. In that case, the exhibition would be more successful than previous ones, which promised peace, but were followed by years of war, or held out the promise of public collections, but which were turned into 'frequent junketings'. Those included 'the establishment of the Sheepshanks collection in an aboriginal hut' after the 1862 London International. The 1886 show celebrated aristocratic and royal 'idleness' in contrast to working-class labour. This was a seductive message and the republicans criticized trade union officials for being seduced away from the rank-and-file by the impressive spectacle and the favours of royalty.

Reynolds's Weekly was not alone in its attack on the popular Colonial and Indian Exhibition, which attracted over 5.5 million visitors.[92] The show was 'just a piece of commercial advertisement' for *The Commonweal*, the official journal of the Socialist League. Its editors, William Morris among them, toured South Kensington and found evidence of economic destruction in India and of the 'glory of the British arms gained in various successful battles against barbarians and savages'.[93] Readers were invited to visit the show and see 'the mercy of Colonists towards native populations' with the 'strong magnifying class' on display and '[t]he daily rations of an Indigo ryot and of his master under one glass case, with a certificate of the amount of nourishment in each, furnished by Professor Huxley'. Those and other exhibits realized the organizers' purpose: 'the exposition of the Honour, Glory, and Usefulness of the British Empire'. The opening ceremony's lengthy processional and 'Ode' by Tennyson were characterized as 'that farce of all farces' by *The Commonweal*. The Republican *Reynolds's Weekly* was no less critical of the event, characterizing it as an 'Imperial Prologue' to further expenditures on 'an army and navy and a costly civil service'.[94]

Expositions, like voluntary societies, factories, political economy, and the state itself, appeared to be self-regulating 'bee-hives' of mid-Victorian equipoise, seemingly without, but in fact permeated by, conflict, class, party and interest. Such experiences, however, offered a moment of social reconciliation and integration as a parallel to the cultural nature of the integrative, participatory nineteenth-century state, the market society, and the various social and legal disciplines discussed by W.L. Burn. Exhibitions invited participants to share an imagined and envisioned nation, intended, according to one observer in 1862, 'to bring painters from their studios, bookish men from their books, philosophers from their abysses of inner consciousness, gardeners from their artful–natural parterres, and foreigners from all quarters of the globe'.[95] Such varied interests and social groups could physically mingle, consume, observe and be observed at the exhibition.

That image suggested a national equipoise, but in doing so also revealed the fissures and tensions within that order, making the state, its commissioners and the practice of political economy open to criticism from various positions. Participation in the great exhibitions of 1851 and 1862 helped affirm the public roles and authority of the commissioners as new experts, strengthened the state's cultural power, and provided a participatory market. On the other hand, the events also provided opportunities for dissenting views to be expressed and, perhaps as importantly, focused. As Burn would have appreciated, authority made itself felt at the shows, but in doing so, also made itself vulnerable to criticism and dissent.

Part of the magic of exhibitions was their seeming inability to be described in a single image. One popular author queried at the time of the Great Exhibition:

> Who can describe that astounding spectacle? Lost in a sense of what it is, who can think what it is like? Philosopher and poet alike are agitated, and silent; gaze whithersoever they may, all is marvellous and affecting; stirring new thoughts and emotions, and awakening oldest memories and associations.[96]

Did the shows challenge the very representational skills of the Victorians with such stirring and awakening? Perhaps this was part of their mystification and power. On the other hand, each mystification contains its own demystification, and critics were very capable of finding systematic ways to contain and attack the exhibitions and their architects, the English state and the official commissioners. If the exhibitions expressed Burn's network of authorities, they also revealed its inherent tensions.

Exhibitions provide historical moments in which we can view the contested sinews holding society together. The great exhibitions of 1851 and 1862 were contests, then, for the hearts and minds of the mid-Victorians, rather than merely festivals of hegemony, progress, nationalism and rational recreation. Some critics even attempted to appropriate the exhibitions for their own alternative vision of England. Victor Kiernan once remarked that '[n]ations, like individuals, are only aware of themselves in any critical sense at times of intense experience'.[97] He referred to wars and rebellions, but we might extend his argument to include the intensity of organizing and visiting the 'great' mid-Victorian exhibitions at the Crystal Palace and South Kensington.

Notes

1. '1 May 1851', Joan Evans and John Howard Whitehouse, eds, *The Diaries of John Ruskin, 1848–1873* (Oxford: The Clarendon Press, 1958), p. 468.
2. Thursday, 1 May 1851, *The Life and Letters of Lord Macaulay, By His Nephew, George Otto Trevelyan, M.P.*, Vol. 2 (London: Longmans, Green, and Co., 1876), pp. 292–3.
3. W.L. Burn, *The Age of Equipoise: A Study of the Mid-Victorian Generation* (New York: W.W. Norton and Company, Inc., 1964).
4. Geoffrey Best, 'W.L. Burn: a recollection', *The Durham University Journal*, n.s. 36 (1974), pp. 1–3 and R.K. Webb, 'Review: *The Age of Equipoise*', *Victorian Studies*, 9 (1966), pp. 239–40.
5. The secondary literature on British, French and American exhibitions is now rather impressive. Readers can consult general works comparing shows across time and/or space, as well as more localized monographys on a specific exhibition or theme. For example, the Crystal Palace (1851) and London International (1862) Exhibitions are discussed in: John Allwood, *The Great Exhibitions* (London: Studio Vista, 1977); Jeffrey A. Auerbach, *The Great Exhibition of 1851: A Nation on Display* (New Haven, CT: Yale University Press, 1999); Robert Bain, 'Going to the Exhibition', Richard Staley, ed., *The Physics of Empire: Public Lectures* (Cambridge: Whipple Museum of the History of Science, 1994), pp. 113–42; Graeme Davison, 'Festivals of Nationhood: The International Exhibitions', S.L. Goldberg and F.B. Smith, eds, *Australian Cultural History* (New York: Cambridge University Press, 1988); Paul Greenhalgh, *Ephemeral Vistas: The Exposition Universelles, Great Exhibitions and World's Fairs, 1851–1939* (Dover, NH: Manchester University Press, 1988); Kenneth W. Luckhurst, *The Story of Exhibitions* (New York, The Studio Publications, 1951); John M. MacKenzie, *Propaganda and Empire: The Manipulation of British Public Opinion, 1880–1960* (Dover, NH: Manchester University Press, 1984).
6. Burn, *The Age of Equipoise*, p. 71.
7. The relationships between exhibitions and the various private and public spheres, such as civil society, are discussed in Debora Silverman, 'The 1889 Exhibition: The Crisis in Bourgeois Individualism', *Oppositions*, 8 (1977), pp. 71–91 and Tony Bennett, 'The Exhibitionary Complex', in Nicholas B. Dirks, Geoffrey Eley, and Sherry B. Ortner, eds, *Culture/ Power/History: A Reader in Contemporary Social Theory* (Princeton: Princeton University Press, 1994), pp. 123–54. These and similar studies draw upon Jurgen Habermas, *The Structural Transformation of the Public Sphere: An Inquiry into a Category of Bourgeois Society*, originally published in 1962, and various works by Michel Foucault, including *The*

Order of Things: An Archaeology of the Human Sciences (English translation 1970) and *Discipline and Punish: The Birth of the Prison* (English translation 1979).

8. Mary Poovey, *Making a Social Body: British Cultural Formation, 1830–1864* (Chicago: The University of Chicago Press, 1995).

9. *The Times*, 28 December 1872, p. 10. Watson also served as the Reporter on the Products of India for the India Office in London. For biographical information, see 'Dr. John Forbes Watson, M.A., M.D., LL.D.', *Journal of Indian Art and Industry*, 3 (1890), pp. 25–7.

10. John Forbes Watson, *International Exhibitions* (London: Henry S. King and Co., 1873).

11. Burn, *The Age of Equipoise*, p. 82.

12. Carlyle to Emerson, 8 July 1851, Joseph Slater, ed., *The Correspondence of Emerson and Carlyle* (New York: Columbia University Press, 1964), p. 468.

13. *The Friend of the People*, 7 December 1850, p. 2.

14. *Hansard's Parliamentary Debates*, 3rd series, 178, p. 1560.

15. 'Close of the Exhibition: Its Failure,' *The Bee-Hive*, 15 November 1862, p. 1.

16. Passing worries were voiced about various issues, such as post-1848 European revolutionaries flooding London and England, Pugin's display of a crucifix in the Crystal Palace, and the health and future of Hyde Park's trees. 'Some Various Panics During 1850–51', *Fifty Years of Public Work of Sir Henry Cole, K.C.B., Accounted for in his Deeds, Speeches and Writings*, Vol. 1, (London: George Bell and Sons, 1884), pp. 185–95 and Charles Babbage, *The Exposition of 1851; or, Views of the Industry, The Science and the Government of England*, 2nd edn (London: John Murray, 1851), pp. 28–30.

17. Babbage, *The Exposition of 1851*, pp. 42 and 129–31.

18. 'The International Exhibition: Its Purposes and Prospects', *Blackwood's Edinburgh Magazine*, 91 (1862), pp. 473–8.

19. Henry Cole, 'Reductions in the French Tariff', *Henry Cole Papers, Miscellanies, Volume 10, 1852–1860* (National Art Library, London), ff. 60b-61.

20. Thomas Richards, *The Commodity Culture of Victorian England: Advertising and Spectacle, 1851–1914* (Stanford, CA: Stanford University Press, 1990), esp. ch. 1.

21. Ibid., p. 18.

22. For a discussion of the 'Market' as an explicative and representative system, see Simon Gunn, 'The "Failure" of the Victorian Middle Class', in Janet Wolff and John Seed, eds, *The Culture of Capital: Art, Power and the Nineteenth-Century Middle Class* (Manchester: Manchester University Press, 1988), pp. 17–43.

23. 'A Letter to the Board of Visitors of the Greenwich Royal Observatory, 1854', *Sheepshanks Papers*, University of London Library, ff. 69 and 75.

24. Critics drew upon the cultural and intellectual traditions discussed in Stefan Collini, *Public Moralists: Political Thought and Intellectual Life in Britain, 1850–1930* (New York: Oxford University Press, 1991), and Raymond Williams, *Culture and Society: 1780–1950* (2nd edn, New York: Columbia University Press, 1983).

25. Thomas Carlyle to Alexander Carlyle, 10 October 1851, Edwin W. Marrs, Jr, *Letters of Thomas Carlyle to His Brother Alexander, with Related Family Matters* (Cambridge, MA: The Belknap Press of Harvard University Press, 1968), p. 684.
26. Carlyle to Emerson, 8 July 1851, Slater, ed., *The Correspondence of Emerson and Carlyle*, p. 468.
27. Carlyle to Emerson, 25 August 1851, Slater, ed., *The Correspondence of Emerson and Carlyle*, p. 473.
28. Thomas Carlyle to Alexander Carlyle, 10 October 1851, *The Letters of Thomas Carlyle to His Brother Alexander*, pp. 683–7. What a contrast to Macaulay, who attended the official closing ceremony and reflected that '[t]his will long be remembered as a singularly happy year, of peace, plenty, good feeling, innocent pleasure, national glory of the best and purest sort'. Thomas Babington Macaulay to Margaret Trevelyan, 14 October 1851, Thomas Pinney, ed., *The Letters of Thomas Babbington Macaulay, Volume 5: January 1849–December 1855* (New York: Cambridge University Press, 1981), p. 204.
29. Thomas Carlyle to Alexander Carlyle, 24 October 1851, *The Letters of Thomas Carlyle to His Brother Alexander*, p. 687.
30. John Ruskin, *The Opening of the Crystal Palace: Considered in Some of its Relations to the Prospects of Art* (New York: J.B. Alden, 1885).
31. Charles Dickens to Mrs Watson, 11 July 1851, *The Letters of Charles Dickens, Edited by His Sister-in-Law and His Eldest Daughter, Volume I, 1833 to 1856* (London: Chapman and Hall, 1880), p. 257.
32. Babbage, *The Exposition of 1851*, p. 12 and Derek Hudson and Kenneth W. Luckhurst, *The Royal Society of Arts, 1754–1954* (London: John Murray, 1954), esp. pp. 187–205.
33. Volume 15 (August 1851), pp. 273–94.
34. Anthony Hyman, *Charles Babbage, Pioneer of the Computer* (Princeton: Princeton University Press, 1982) and 'Babbage, Charles (1792–1871)', *Dictionary of National Biography*, Vol. 1 (New York: Cambridge University Press, 1921–22), pp. 776–8.
35. Babbage, *The Exposition of 1851*, pp. v–vi.
36. Ibid., pp. vii–viii and 189.
37. Charles Babbage, *Passages from the Life of a Philosopher* (London: Longman, Green, Longman, Roberts and Green, 1864), pp. 158–61. Emphasis in original.
38. *The Bee-Hive*, 15 November 1862, p. 1.
39. Babbage, *Passages from the Life of a Philosopher*, pp. 158–61.
40. Babbage, *The Exposition of 1851*, pp. 129–31.
41. Ibid., p. 21. Emphasis in original.
42. Ibid., p. 79.
43. Ibid., pp. 112–24.
44. Michael B. Miller, *The Bon Marché: Bourgeois Culture and the Department Store, 1869–1920* (Princeton: Princeton University Press, 1981) and Rosalind H. Williams, *Dream Worlds: Mass Consumption in Late Nineteenth-Century France* (Berkeley: University of California Press, 1982).
45. Walter Benjamin, 'Grandville, or the World Exhibitions', in Peter Demetz, ed. and Edmund Jephcott, trans., *Reflections: Essays, Aphorisms, Autobiographical Writings* (New York: Schocken Books, 1986), pp. 151–3.

46. John Ruskin, *'Unto this Last': Four Essays on the First Principles of Political Economy* (Lincoln: University of Nebraska Press, 1967), p. 78.

47. *The Mechanics' Magazine*, 2 February 1850, pp. 29–33 and 2 March 1850, pp. 168–9.

48. Richard Yeo, 'Science and Intellectual Authority in Mid-Nineteenth-Century Britain: Robert Chambers and *Vestiges of the Natural History of Creation*', *Victorian Studies*, 28 (1984), pp. 5–31.

49. Thomas Richards, *The Imperial Archive: Knowledge and the Fantasy of Empire* (New York: Verso, 1993) and Roy Macleod, ed., *Government and Expertise: Specialists, Administrators and Professionals, 1860–1919* (New York: Cambridge University Press, 1988).

50. Carol A. Breckenridge, 'The Aesthetics and Politics of Colonial Collecting: India at World Fairs', *Comparative Studies in Society and History*, 31 (1989), pp. 195–216 and Bernard S. Cohn, 'The Transformation of Objects into Artifacts, Antiquities and Art in Nineteenth-Century India', *Colonialism and Its Forms of Knowledge: The British in India* (Princeton: Princeton University Press), pp. 76–105.

51. For a nineteenth-century discussion of this new form of organizational authority, see Friedrich Engels, 'On Authority', in Robert C. Tucker, ed., *The Marx–Engels Reader* (2nd edn, New York: W.W. Norton and Company, Inc., 1978), pp. 730–33. Engels wrote this essay in 1872 and published it two years later.

52. The term was used by Samuel Taylor Coleridge as a label for cultural experts responsible for cultivating ideas, maintaining intellectual life, connecting the state and the professions, and forging a new Establishment. Theirs was a new gentleman class. See Samuel Taylor Coleridge, *On the Constitution of the Church and State* (1830); Peter Allen, 'S.T. Coleridge's "Church and State" and the Idea of an Intellectual Establishment', *Journal of the History of Ideas*, 46 (1985), pp. 89–106 and Ben Knights, *The Idea of the Clerisy in the Nineteenth Century* (New York: Cambridge University Press, 1978).

53. 'An Exhibition of the Society of Arts', *The Mechanics' Magazine*, 12 April 1861, pp. 243–4.

54. *The Bee-Hive*, 15 November 1862, p. 1.

55. *The Bee-Hive*, 4 October 1862, p. 7.

56. *The Bee-Hive*, 15 November 1862, p. 1.

57. For example, *The Friend of the People*, 7 December 1850, p. 8 and 14 December 1850, p. 8.

58. *The Friend of the People*, 10 May 1851, pp. 189–90. Emphasis in original.

59. *The Friend of the People*, 29 March 1851, p. 123.

60. *The Friend of the People*, 1 February 1851, p. 59.

61. *The Friend of the People*, 1 March 1851, p. 92.

62. 'To The Working Classes', *The Northern Star*, 19 April 1851, p. 1. There are two interesting footnotes on the relationship between Harney and exhibitions: he applied for a position with Owen Jones at the rebuilt Crystal Palace in Sydenham, turning to Louis Blanc for the necessary letter of introduction, and, several years later, wrote to Engels that he looked forward to attending the Colonial and Indian Exhibition at South Kensington. Harney extended his stay in London for that purpose. See

Louis Blanc to G. Julian Harney, 10 March 1854 and G. Julian Harney to Frederick Engels, 26 August 1886, *The Harney Papers*, Frank Gees Black and Renee Metivier Black, eds (Assen: Van Gorcum and Company, 1969), pp. 12 and 312–13.

63. For example, 'Notes on the International Exhibition', *The Mechanics' Magazine*, 21 February 1861, p. 116; 'The Opening of the International Exhibition', 2 May 1862, p. 291 and 'The International Exhibition: The Western Annexe', 9 May 1862, pp. 308–9.

64. *The Mechanics' Magazine*, 18 April 1862, p. 270.

65. *The Working Man*, 1 July 1862, pp. 173–4 and 1 August 1862, pp. 197–8.

66. Victor Kiernan, 'Working Class and Nation in Nineteenth-Century Britain', Harvey J. Kaye, ed., *History, Classes and Nation-States: Selected Writings of V.G. Kiernan* (New York: Basil Blackwell, Inc., 1988), pp. 186–98 and Margot Finn, '"A Vent Which Has Conveyed Our Principles": English Radical Patriotism in the Aftermath of 1848', *Journal of Modern History*, 64 (1992), pp. 637–59.

67. *The Working Man*, 1 August 1862, p. 198.

68. Henry Cole, 'National Culture and Recreation: Antidotes to Vice', *Sir Henry Cole Papers, Miscellanies, Volume 17, 1845–1875* (National Art Library, London), 55 AA 62, ff. 300–305.

69. *The Working Man*, 1 August 1862, p. 197.

70. For discussion of the various views concerning early nineteenth-century political economy, machinery and industrialism, see Maxine Berg, *The Machinery Question and the Making of Political Economy, 1815–1848* (New York: Cambridge University Press, 1980) and Robert Gray, *The Factory Question and Industrial England, 1830–1860* (New York: Cambridge University Press, 1996).

71. *The Working Man*, 1 July 1862, p. 174.

72. Gray, 'The Factory Imagined', *The Factory Question*, pp. 131–59.

73. Andrew Ure, *The Philosophy of Manufactures: or, An Exposition of the Scientific, Moral and Commercial Economy of the Factory System of Great Britain* (London: Charles Knight, 1835) and Charles Babbage, *On the Economy of Machinery and Manufactures* (London: John Murray, 1846).

74. Ure, *The Philosophy of Manufactures*, pp. 7 and 21.

75. *Reminiscences of the Crystal Palace, 1852* (National Art Library, London), 400.A.114, p. 29.

76. 'The International Exhibition: Its Purposes and Prospects', pp. 473–5.

77. Raphael Samuel, 'The Workshop of the World: Steam Power and Hand Technology in mid-Victorian Britain', *History Workshop*, 3 (1977), pp. 57–8.

78. 'Testimony of Sir Henry Cole, 9 July 1867', *Report from the Parliamentary Selection Committee on the Paris Exhibition, 1867, Volume I: Reports by Executive Commissioner; with Appendices*, English Parliamentary Papers, 1868–69, [xxx]. Pt i. 1., p. 37.

79. *Report of the Commissioners for the Exhibition of 1862, to the Right Hon. Sir George Gray, Bart., G.C.B., etc., etc.* (London: George E. Eyre and William Spottiswoode, 1863), p. l.

80. *Illustrated London News*, 15 March 1862, p. 269.

81. *The Morning Chronicle*, 10 January 1862, p. 3, 17 January 1862, p. 3 and 25 January 1862, p. 4.
82. *The Building News*, 8 (1962), p. 97.
83. Dolores Greenberg, 'Energy, Power, and Perceptions of Social Change in the Early Nineteenth Century', *American Historical Review*, 95 (1990), p. 697.
84. *Voices from the Workshop on the Exhibition of 1851* (National Art Library, London), 400.A.103–104.
85. 'The Great International Exhibition of 1862', *The Working Man*, 1 June 1862, p. 142. Emphasis in original.
86. *Leisure Hour*, 14 (1865), pp. 31–2.
87. *Leisure Hour*, 11 (1862), p. 72. Emphasis in original.
88. *Leisure Hour*, 15 (1865), pp. 31.
89. Ibid., p. 32.
90. 'Extracts from the Minute Books of the London Trades Council relating to the National Workmens Exhibition, 8 December 1892', pp. 7–8, Trades Union Council Archives, London.
91. *Reynolds's Weekly Newspaper*, 9 May 1886, p. 4, 26 September 1886, p. 4 and 21 November 1886, p. 4.
92. *Report of the Royal Commission for the Colonial and Indian Exhibition, London, 1886*, Parliamentary Papers [c. 5083], xx. 1., p. xlvii and *Journal of the Royal Society of Arts*, 44 (1887), p. 375.
93. *The Commonweal, The Official Journal of the Socialist League*, 2 (1886), pp. 49–50.
94. *Reynolds's Weekly Newspaper*, 9 May 1886, p. 4.
95. 'At the Great Exhibition', *Cornhill Magazine*, 5 (1862), p. 666.
96. Samuel Warren, *The Lily and the Bee; an apologue of the Crystal Palace* (Edinburgh: William Blackwood and Sons, 1851).
97. Victor G. Kiernan, 'After Empire', *Imperialism and its Contradictions*, Harvey J. Kaye, ed. (New York: Routledge, Inc., 1995), p. 198.

CHAPTER TWO

Equipoise and the object: the South Kensington Museum[1]

Tim Barringer

On 17 May 1899, Queen Victoria, making her last public appearance, laid the foundation stone for a magnificent extension to the South Kensington Museum. Reviewing the history of an institution which she felt symbolized her husband's efforts for the public good in the 1850s, she pronounced herself to be:

> pleased that the priceless collection of treasures which the munificence of private persons and the Public Spirit of Parliament have brought together will always be associated with my name and that of My Dear Husband ... I gladly direct that this Institution shall be styled 'the Victoria and Albert Museum' and I trust that it will remain for ages a Monument of discerning Liberality and a source of Refinement and Progress.[2]

This act of renaming inaugurated a triumphant and frankly imperialist phase in the museum's history, expressed through the splendid façade designed by Aston Webb, completed in 1909. From the turn of this century onward, the status of the 'V&A' as an international museum of the fine and applied arts was never in question, and most histories of the institution have insisted on a teleological narrative, tracing the growth of the museum's present collections, and often expressed through anecdotal accounts of triumphant campaigns of purchasing and acquisition.[3] The institution which now styles itself 'the world's greatest museum of the fine and decorative arts' is descended, however, from the South Kensington Museum, a very different, and in many ways more fascinating cultural formation. The museum was founded in 1852 and in 1857 opened on the present site in South Kensington.

There are considerable evidential problems involved in exploring the history of museums, which claim to provide a perspective that stands outside of time, a fixed, final ordering, a transcendental taxonomy which has been discovered rather than constructed.[4] Museums have, indeed, traditionally been understood as revealing immanent truths rather than putting forward narratives which themselves will change with time. Museum curators of the Victorian era, busy like their successors with the care and study of objects in the collections or with prizing money out of government and private donors, were not concerned with documenting the history of their own actions, and sometimes deliberately obscured the record for political reasons. These factors, combined with the destruction of files deemed unimportant by the Public Records Office, have left little evidence of discussions concerning aims and policies beyond the published papers and official reports.[5]

Perhaps it is provocative, in a collection which places a question mark after Burn's characterization of the period, to use the phrase 'the mid-Victorian moment' to imply that there is some coherence in a span of time which runs, in South Kensington terms, slightly longer than Burn's period, from the opening of the Great Exhibition in 1851 to 1873, the date of retirement of the museum's first superintendent, Henry Cole. Can anything be gained from discussing a quarter-century of rapid change as a unit of time with enough coherence to mark it off from other, distinct periods; and if so, can the history of a fledgling museum offer any useful form of commentary on these wider developments? In this chapter I argue that key social, political and aesthetic developments of the period find expression in the history of the museum. Speaking in very broad terms, the mid-Victorian period can surely still be seen as a moment of ascendancy for middle-class interests. However, a key social development was the founding of important links between skilled labourers – 'the aristocracy of labour' – and the middle class, an alliance which involved qualified middle-class acceptance of moderate trade unionism, and of many attempts to provide educational opportunities for respectable artisans. Work by Crossick and Gray has established the importance of institutions such as the Volunteers in establishing and cementing bonds between skilled labourers and the urban middle classes.[6] These developments provide a context for viewing South Kensington as a reformist institution whose class address was specifically focused on the skilled artisan. The close and crucially important involvement of Prince Albert in the project, in conjunction with a group of middle-class educationalists, civil servants and design reformers, also adds an interesting case study of 'equipoise' between members of different classes. Furthermore, this period also saw (in spite of rhetoric to the contrary) an increase in state intervention in many areas of life.

Painting with the broadest of brushstrokes, one might suggest in addition that the mid-Victorian moment was marked by a near fanatical interest in the making, distribution, exchange and display of things. As *The Times* noted on 13 October 1851: 'Just now we are an objective people. We want to place everything we can lay our hands on in glass cases, and to stare our fill.'[7] In a period dominated by a widespread belief in unhindered economic progress through free trade, the commodity held a position of huge importance which was also accorded to a repository of commodities, such as the South Kensington Museum. As the period progressed, however, the ideology of free trade came to fit uneasily with an increasingly prominent ideology of imperialism underpinned by protectionism. The display of colonial objects at South Kensington, culminating in 1886 with the Colonial and Indian Exhibition, marks the dominance of a protectionist and imperialist attitude. A steady shift from educational and didactic functions to the provision of popular imperial spectacle can be detected from the early 1860s to the 1880s. Whatever the chosen sphere of their circulation, from 1851, the notion of London as a central clearing house for goods, capital and commodities, including works of art, became more firmly established. London, positioned at the heart of a burgeoning empire, operated as a hub for people and things from across the world; yet amid such diversity, British systems and taxonomies – whether of objects, as at the Great Exhibition, or of people, as in the case of ethnologies like James Cowles Prichard's *The Natural History of Man* or Henry Mayhew's *London Labour and the London Poor* – existed to provide order.[8] Furthermore, Britain's national role was presented as being that of maintaining order in the world, and addressing evils such as slavery (while policy was in fact rigorously tied to the protection of perceived national and commercial interests). Certainly, London's role as the centre of world-wide trade and finance offered a panoramic, if not a panoptic, view of the material production of the world, which was to be replicated in the South Kensington Museum.

There can be no question that the mid-Victorian moment was inaugurated by a single event, the Great Exhibition of the Industry of All Nations, held in the Crystal Palace in Hyde Park, London, in 1851. Under the active patronage of Prince Albert, its chief organizer was a bureaucrat and design reformer, Henry Cole, who by 1851 had already distinguished himself in the postal service and had reorganized the Public Records Office. Cole, a quintessentially mid-Victorian figure, born in 1808, looms large in this chapter in his later role as the first director, or 'general superintendent' of the South Kensington Museum. Cole was profoundly influenced in his youth by utilitarianism, contriving a meeting with Jeremy Bentham shortly before his death. Many of Cole's notions concerning the functioning of the state and its institutions, along with so much of the governmental activity of mid-Victorian Britain, was premised on assimilated Benthamite ideas. His notion of the museum as a free-acting mechanism for instilling improved principles of taste into a broad swath of the population owes something to Benthamite theory.

The display at the Crystal Palace in 1851 was based on the concept that all human life and culture could be represented by exhibiting manufactured objects and their components.[9] Over a hundred thousand exhibits were divided into four categories: raw materials, machines, manufactures and fine arts. On display were the wares of thirty-two nations from Europe, America, Africa and the Far East, and prominent among the commissioners, chaired by Prince Albert, was a strand of rather idealistic free-trade internationalism. Housed in an innovative and progressive building by Joseph Paxton, the Great Exhibition embraced an eclectic mixture of historicizing styles, most notable in Augustus Welby Northmore Pugin's Medieval Court, with its collection of household items and monuments in the Gothic style. In many ways the character of the South Kensington Museum was closer to the Great Exhibition's extraordinary *mélange* of the commercial and didactic than it was to the great art museum into which it was eventually transformed. Like the exhibition, the museum was to focus on innovative technical solutions to contemporary design issues while offering the art and design of the past as providing a vocabulary of stylistic sources. One of the major conclusions drawn from the exhibits of 1851, especially by Cole and his circle, was indeed that while British machinery and entrepreneurship were dominant, there was a clear need to improve the quality of product design in order for the British economy to compete effectively with rival nations. It was accepted that objects exhibited in 1851 could usefully be preserved as examples of good practice, and a government grant of £5000 was awarded for their acquisition. Among the objects purchased were those considered by the selection committee to represent the best in British manufacture, such as A.W.N. Pugin's *Gothic Armoire* (London, V&A), while other acquisitions were typical of the highly ornate (and since much reviled) style of so many of the modern objects exhibited in 1851 and of the workmanship of European competitors considered to be superior to British productions. An example is Antoine Vechte's *Poet's Shield* (London, V&A).

When the exhibition unexpectedly made a profit of £186,000 on ticket receipts owing to the massive visitor figures, it became possible to apply some of the reformist principles which had underpinned the display in more permanent form. While two of the leading commissioners of the exhibition, Henry Cole and Lyon Playfair, campaigned respectively for improvements in art and design education and in technical education, it seems to have been the chairman of the exhibition's commissioners, Prince Albert, who provided the most ambitious ideas. The linkage of art and science, which underpinned the South Kensington project, was felt by Albert to provide the wherewithal for man to 'conquer nature to his use; himself a divine instrument'.[10] In a memorandum which indicates the grandiosity of his ambitions, Albert advocated in 1851 the purchase of land on which to build not museums as such, but institutions based on the classification of objects adopted in the catalogue to the Great Exhibition: raw materials, machinery, manufactures and plastic art. Each of these would contain a library and study rooms; lecture rooms; exhibition space; and rooms for 'conversation' and commercial meetings. The intention was to appeal to manufacturers, promulgating the latest scientific and commercial information, while also attracting the working man. A garden would occupy the centre of the square formed by these institutes. Though none of these plans – which Cole recognized as idealistic and impractical – was to come directly to fruition, major elements of Albert's blueprint were eventually realized in the South Kensington Museum. Most important among these, perhaps, is the notion of the close proximity of collections of objects and facilities for teaching and lecturing – in short, the educational role of the museum for an audience which notionally embraced both middle and working classes.

Cole's main interest was in the reform of public taste through the improvement of design, an agenda which he had pursued as a journalist and by example, through the production of Felix Summerly's Art Manufactures. In 1852 he was invited to head a government Department of Practical Art, with the explicit project of reorganizing art and design education. The next year, with the amalgamation of this body into the larger Department of Science and Art, Cole headed the art section, while Lyon Playfair, also an exhibition commissioner, headed the science section. Cole believed that what went on in schools of art and design should be dictated by industrial considerations: the upshot of the Great Exhibition was taken to be that Britain's prosperity depended on an improved quality of design in manufactured objects. In 1853 Cole issued a manifesto which was eventually to guide the art schools and the South Kensington Museum throughout the mid-Victorian moment. The three main objects of the Department were, he wrote:

> 1st, General Elementary Instruction in Art, as a branch of national education among all classes of the community, with the view of laying the foundation for correct judgement, both in the consumer and the producer of manufactures; 2nd, Advanced Instruction in Art ... ; and lastly, the Application of the Principles of Technical Art to the improvement of manufactures, together with the establishment of Museums, by which all classes may be induced to investigate those common principles of taste, which may be traced in the works of excellence of all ages.[11]

While there is much of interest in Cole's educational work,[12] it is this last
point which concerns us here. Cole's vision of a museum was quite
different from those other national institutions, already thriving, which
had been based on great collections acquired by the nation: Sir Hans
Sloane's gift of antiquities of 1753 lay at the heart of the British Museum,[13] whereas the National Gallery was based on the Angerstein
collection of old master paintings.[14] Connoisseurs' cabinets would yield
their precious secrets only to those sufficiently educated; Cole's museum
was itself concerned to educate. Pugnacious as ever, Cole did not wait
long to open his didactic museum for teaching the principles of taste. At
his disposal were some objects left over from a small museum the department had put together for the use of students in the 1840s, and the
purchases from the Great Exhibition.[15] Once again Cole's sure touch with
the royal family came into play when through Prince Albert he persuaded
the Queen to allow the department and its fledgling museum to occupy a
vacant royal palace, Marlborough House. It was known as the Museum
of Manufactures and, as watercolours of the interiors of the galleries
made in 1856 show, much of the museum was given over to a dense
installation of decorative arts objects, including a considerable amount of
Sèvres, Meissen and oriental porcelain on loan from the Royal Collection
and elsewhere, and some objects which remain in the V&A collection
today.[16] The catalogue claimed: 'The Museum is intended to contain not
only works of art selected as fine examples of design or art workmanship,
but others chosen with a view to an historical series of manufactures'.[17]
This concept of a historical series, a complete taxonomy of high-quality
manufactured goods, indicated a massive collecting project which was
never systematically pursued, as the museum veered more towards collecting historical examples of the decorative and fine arts in the subsequent
decades.[18] But one peculiar feature of the museum when it opened in
1852 related very closely to Cole's didactic notion of affecting industrial
design. This was the 'Gallery of False Principles', a title which, it seems
likely, refers to Pugin's famous work, *The True Principles of Pointed or
Christian Architecture* of 1841.[19] Pugin had argued that 'all ornament
should consist of enrichment of essential construction of the building',
which might just as well apply to decorative art objects.[20] Although we
do not have a representation of the gallery as such, it has been possible to
identify many objects which appeared in it. Among them were wallpapers
with perspective views, including one representing the Crystal Palace;
more extraordinary is R.W. Winfield's table gas lamp in the form of a
convolvulus.[21] Discovered in the 1970s in storage, uncatalogued and
unrecognized, this extraordinary object certainly carries naturalism up to,
if not beyond, the limit. Described in the catalogue as 'one of a class of

ornaments very popular but indefensible in principle', it qualified for the chamber of design horrors not least because of the wonderful possibility of bending down to smell the enamelled metal flower and having your nose severely burned by a flame of gas. Like the other objects in the gallery, it was a demonstration by false example, showing how not to do it. Contemporaries were quick to satirize Cole's rather heavy-handed didacticism in so blatantly bullying his public about good and bad taste. In a story in Charles Dickens's magazine *Household Words* called 'House Full of Horrors', Henry Morley introduces Mr Crumpet of Brixton, a South London suburb at that time populated mainly by the *nouveau riche*, who describes a visit to Marlborough House:

> I had heard a Chamber of Horrors was there established and I found it, and went through with my catalogue. It was a gloomy chamber, hung round with frightful objects, in curtains, carpets and clothes, lamps and what not. In each case the catalogue told me why such a thing wasn't endurable and I found in the same place also, on equally good authority, in black and white, a few hints on what the correct principles of decoration are in each class of ornament.[22]

The acquisition of good taste was traumatic, though, for Crumpet continues:

> I could have cried, Sir, I was ashamed of the pattern of my own trousers, for I saw a piece of them hung up there as a horror ... I saw it all; when I went home I found that I had been living among horrors up to that hour.[23]

The attack on imitative naturalism mounted by Cole and Redgrave seems to have been successful, and not only in bludgeoning Mr Crumpet into embarrassment over the coral reef represented on his handkerchief and the birds of paradise and pagodas on his wallpaper: the catalogue of the 1862 International Exhibition includes a noticeable reduction in imitative naturalistic decoration.[24]

But the question of who was being addressed, the producer or the consumer, the working classes or the middle classes, was unclear. Cole would doubtless have argued that all classes could benefit from his prescriptions. At Marlborough House, efforts had been made to make the museum accessible to a wide public: admission was free on two days a week, while three days were set apart for the department's pupils to study the collections.[25] There was also a circulating museum, which sent touring exhibitions around the country, with the intention of 'having a useful influence on the special manufactures of their respective localities', and encouraging small local museums – a feature of the museum's life which continued until 1979.

In 1855 Cole was given the go-ahead to plan the removal of the department from Marlborough House to this undeveloped area between the suburb of Brompton and the more fashionable residential area of Kensington, which was fast being developed. Enthusiastically adopting Prince Albert's original idea for a complex on the site, Cole initially had to make do with a temporary prefabricated structure made of iron in which to house the Marlborough House collections, and construction began in 1856. Instantly christened the 'Brompton Boilers' because of its utilitarian appearance, the building was never really appropriate for the display of art objects and what Cole called manufactures.

One aspect of the museum's mission was to promote good design, and more broadly to encourage the pursuit of increasing general standards in education among artisans and skilled labourers. In this it was, as I suggested at the outset, a typically mid-Victorian project, standing alongside the London Working Men's College, founded by F.D. Maurice, where Ruskin and Ford Madox Brown taught drawing, and numerous mechanics' institutes and adult education projects around the country. The museum was an important part of this education mission, indeed, perhaps the most important part. The department's *First Report*, drafted by Cole, claimed:

> A museum presents probably the only effectual means of educating the adult, who cannot be expected to go to school like the youth, [yet] the necessity for teaching the grown man is quite as great as that of training the child. By proper arrangements a museum may be made in the highest degree instructional. If it be connected with lectures, and means are taken to point out its uses and applications, it becomes elevated from being a mere unintelligible lounge for idlers into an impressive schoolroom for everyone.[26]

In this passage are inscribed some of the dominant discourses of the mid-Victorian moment. The museum aimed to instil a culture of self-education and self-help into the artisan community and to improve the profitability and competitiveness of industry by doing so. Like the most ambitious schemes of utilitarian philosophers such as Jeremy Bentham, who had deeply impressed Cole as a young man, and whose thinking was encapsulated in much legislation of this period, the museum was expected to operate as a kind of machine, a self-regulating mechanism, whereby the raw material of artisans was fed, or fed itself, into the entrance, and educated designers would issue from the exit. The flaw in this scheme was that there were few artisans to be found in South Kensington: indeed, one of the perceived virtues of the site was its leafy suburban character, its distance from smoky industries, from the mass working populations of the East End and from the rookeries and slums of central London. Unlike later schemes, such as the South London Art Gallery and the Whitechapel Art Gallery, Cole's Kensington empire was not aiming to bring culture into the darker areas of the city.[27] Rather, the artisans were expected to make the trip to South Kensington, and much was made of the invigorating walk across the park from central London. When the 'Brompton Boilers' were taken down in the 1860s to be replaced by permanent structures, they were transported to Bethnal Green, then, as now, an area of relative deprivation in the East End of London, where they formed a branch museum. Meanwhile, some efforts were made to counter the problem of South Kensington's location, including the installation of gas lamps in the permanent buildings of the new museum, and late openings to facilitate visits after work.[28] The arrival of the underground railway in 1868 increased visitor numbers, but the fare-paying passengers were mainly well off and representations of the interior of the museum tend to feature middle-class figures. None the less, Cole felt that for the working man a visit to the museum could replace the depredations of a visit to the pub. In 1857 he set forth his vision of the social mission of the museum:

> The working man comes to the museum from his one of two dimly lighted rooms, in his fustian jacket, with his shirt collar a little trimmed up, accompanied by his threes, fours and fives of little fustian jackets, a wife in her best bonnet, and a baby, of course, under her shawl. The look of surprise and pleasure of the whole party when they observe the brilliant lighting in the museum shows what an acceptable and wholesome excitement this evening entertainment affords ... Perhaps the evening opening of the Public Museums may furnish an antidote to the gin palace.[29]

Night openings of a very few selected galleries once a week have recently been reintroduced at the V&A, but the imposition of compulsory admission charges in October 1996 surely represented a comprehensive abandonment of the museum's original rationale, however patronizing and manipulative the language in which that was expressed may seem when transposed into a late-twentieth century context.

The spectacle confronting the visitor to the 'Brompton Boilers' was very different to that which today's visitor might expect from an art museum. Most prominent were the educational collections, covering subjects from building materials to fish culture, geography and geology to lace-making and oriental ceramics. Although the overall effect was chaotic, there was, predictably, an elaborate attempt at a taxonomy to impose discipline on a bewildering diversity of material culture – an unruly empire of things. The collection was divided into nine categories:

Objects of Ornamental Art, as Applied to Manufactures; an Art Library; British Pictures, Sculpture and Engraving; Architectural Examples; Appliances for Scholastic Education; Materials for Building and Construction; Substances used for Food; Animal Products; Models of Patented Inventions; Reproductions by means of Photography and Casting.[30] This list reinforces my earlier comment that the museum in its early years was closer to the 1851 exhibition than to the V&A as we now know it. Little is known at present about the scientific elements of the museum, which were removed to the new Science Museum, on the other side of Exhibition Road, at the turn of the century. The same goes for the Museum of Patents, which presumably exhibited models and drawings of patented machinery.[31]

More is known of the collection of casts and reproductions: here the museum was pioneering in its use of photography and plaster and electrotype casts to provide a library in two and three dimensions of the world's great masterpieces of architecture, sculpture and the decorative arts. In contrast to later museological practice, these objects emphasize the educational role of the museum over the connoisseur's fetishization of the original and unique object, and the V&A's casts narrowly avoided destruction in the 1960s. Luckily, the majority of the collection of casts have survived, and they are now reinstalled in one of the most spectacular Victorian spaces in London. Henry Cole instigated an international convention in 1867 in which heads of state agreed to exchange of casts of major sculptures;[32] casts, traditionally associated with art-school education, provided vital access to the works of plastic art which Cole felt would inspire designers to a new quality of historicizing design. Electrotype copies of metalwork, too, were considered of the highest importance, though these are now relegated to a museum store.

Permanent buildings were gradually erected on the site throughout the 1860s and 1870s,[33] utilizing innovative techniques of construction and covered with iconographic figuration and lettering. The building itself can be considered as a massive and complex text, a large-scale three-dimensional manifesto for the reform of design. The masterpiece of Francis Fowke, the seconded Royal Engineer who was the site's main architect, is probably the lecture theatre block, dating from the 1860s. The pediment contains a mosaic, designed by Reuben Townroe and executed by Minton, Hollins and Co., representing the Great Exhibition, with the outline of the Crystal Palace clearly visible. The symbolic marriage of art and science at South Kensington is symbolized by a steam locomotive occupying the left corner and symbols of music, architecture and painting in the right.

The interior of the museum was even more overwrought with didactic detailing than the exterior. Most extraordinary and controversial was the elaborate west staircase, designed by another follower of Sykes, F.W. Moody.[34] In spite of repeated attempts during the twentieth century to remove it as a gross aesthetic embarrassment (the fate of much of the cultural production of the 1850s and 1860s), the ceramic staircase survives, completely encased in Minton's Della Robbia ware. As usual there is a complex iconographic scheme including a mural of *The Pursuit of Art by Man*.

Other facilities underlined the institution's educational mission: a large lecture theatre was built, although the ambitious scheme for an allegorical ceramic mosaic by E.J. Poynter, for which a design survives, was never executed. Also built at the end of the mid-Victorian period was the library, completed in 1883. This was intended to provide a reference collection of material on the fine and decorative arts, and has continued to be available for consultation by students and designers ever since. The production of a universal catalogue of books on the arts, a grandiose project which seems to have reached only proof stage, reflects a typically mid-Victorian concern with categorization and taxonomy.[35]

Refreshment rooms – without alcohol – were also a necessity, but here too the interior was itself didactic, with panels extolling the virtue of labour. There was also a grillroom, for more substantial fare, decorated with ceramic tiles designed by E.J. Poynter and painted by the female students of the Schools, for whom such labour was considered appropriate by the authorities.[36] Most daring and far-sighted was the museum's decision in 1865 to commission the firm of Morris, Marshall and Faulkner to decorate the third dining room.[37] This key example of an early William Morris interior remains virtually unchanged and certainly promoted the agenda of design reform.

Increasingly, the building became a metonym for the economic might, cultural ambition and technological prowess of the Victorian state. This culminated in the elaborate, prefabricated iron and glass structure of the South Court, intended to display items on loan, designed by Francis Fowke and decorated in a neo-Renaissance style by Godfrey Sykes. As at the Crystal Palace, there was a balance between the modernity and technological sophistication of the structure and the historicism of the interior design. The South Court was originally to be called the 'Lord President's Court' and was intended to memorialize those political grandees – the Presidents of the Board of Trade and the Lords President of the Committee-in-Council for Education – who had been the ultimate paymasters for the massive growth of the Department of Science and Art and who had (despite frequent misgivings) made possible the ambitious schemes of Henry Cole and his associates. Large portrait medallions of the Lords President, worked in mosaic, were mounted on the end walls of the South Court. These curious, ceramic icons of establishment self-congratulation occupied a shadowy realm beneath the balconies at each end of Fowke's structure: staring out above the notional audience of educated artisans, the patriarchal heads appear as architectural features, in contrast to the transitory nature of portraits painted in oil, implying perhaps the unshakeable permanence of the mid-Victorian *status quo*, equipoise frozen in stone.

The symbolic geography of the South Court culminated in the raised gallery above the central corridor. Affording spectacular views on both sides, it contained cases in which were arranged some of the museum's finest treasures, notably medieval goldsmithwork and metalwork. At the end of the gallery was mounted a posthumous mosaic roundel of Prince Albert designed by Sykes, approved by Queen Victoria in 1863 and installed in 1865. The presence of what amounts to a shrine to the Prince's memory gave this area its name: the Prince Consort's Gallery. If the museum is a metonym for the mid-Victorian state, then in this court the benign influence of the constitutional monarch and her public-spirited consort is embodied at its very centre.

The South Court was completed by the commission in 1868 of Frederic Leighton, already a significant painter in the ranks of the Royal Academy, to provide two frescoes on archetypal South Kensington subjects, *The Industrial Arts applied to Peace and to War*.[38] Completed with the aid of South Kensington students only in 1886, the frescoes marked the culmination of the institution's rise to status as a great museum and a public celebration of mid-Victorian state-funded decoration. However, Leighton's work, influenced by French and Germanic academic classicism and by the Aesthetic movement, remained strictly within the tradition of the fine, rather than the decorative, arts, and wantonly refused to provide the kind of robust, moralizing allegory with which the museum buildings were embellished. With the arrival of an Aesthete and (by the time he had finished the frescoes) President of the Royal Academy, the museum was on its way to becoming a shrine of fine and decorative rather than industrial art.[39]

After the retirement of Cole in 1873, the museum, under the direction of Philip Cunliffe-Owen, became absorbed in the administration of spectacular temporary exhibitions on the adjacent site. More than a million people attended each of these annually in the 1880s, on subjects such as Health and Fisheries. Most spectacular was the Colonial and Indian Exhibition of 1886, in which aggressive pomp and circumstance accompanied huge displays of imperial produce and plunder. Victoria herself appeared, and was portrayed by the *Graphic* 'Twixt East and West' and the geography of South Kensington mapped out in miniature the geography of empire. South Kensington's quest for popular education with the intention of promoting national prosperity through free trade had given way to the provision of popular spectacle and a concentration on the material benefits of empire, and the art museum had begun to pursue the connoisseur's twin ideals of taxonomic completeness and art for art's sake, eschewing the utilitarian basis for the collection's existence. The mid-Victorian moment was ended.

Notes

1. I would like to thank Rafael Cardoso Denis for many stimulating discussions of these issues and comments on an earlier draft of this chapter.
2. Quoted in J. Physick, *The Victoria and Albert Museum: the History of its Building* (London: Victoria and Albert Museum, 1982), p. 214.
3. There is no adequate history of the South Kensington and Victoria and Albert Museum, though the history of its building is described in detail in Physick, *Victoria and Albert Museum*. The only attempt at an introductory survey and history of the collections is A. Summers Cocks, *The Victoria and Albert Museum: The Making of the Collections* (Leicester, 1980). Some of the material discussed in the present chapter appears in a more extended discussion in Tim Barringer, 'The South Kensington Museum and the Mid-Victorian Moment', in Howard Creel Collinson, ed., *Victorian: Style of Empire: Selected Proceedings of the Decorative Arts Institute of Canada* (Toronto: Royal Ontario Museum, 1996), pp. 23–47. A highly perceptive but idiosyncratic history of the museum appears in the autobiography of one if its most charismatic directors: Sir John Pope-Hennessy, *Learning to Look: An Autobiography* (London: Heinemann, 1993). Useful essays on the subject are collected in Brenda Richardson and Malcolm Baker, eds, *A Grand Design: The Art of the Victoria and Albert Museum* (New York, Harry N. Abrams, 1997).
4. Craig Clunas has raised these issues in a sophisticated exploration of the history of the major London collections of Chinese art in a different form in Tim Barringer and Tom Flynn, eds, *Colonialism and the Object* (London: Routledge, 1998), pp. 41–57.
5. On related issues see Charles Saumarez Smith, 'Museums, Artefacts and Meanings', in P. Vergo, ed., *The New Museology* (London: Reaktion, 1989), pp. 6–21.
6. Robert Q. Gray, *The Aristocracy of Labour in Victorian Edinburgh* (Oxford: Oxford University Press, 1976), G. Crossick, *An Artisan Élite in Victorian Society: Kentish London 1840–1880* (London: Croom Helm, 1978).
7. Quoted in Andrew H. Miller, *Novels Behind Glass: Commodity Culture and Victorian Narrative* (Cambridge: Cambridge University Press, 1995), pp. 51–2.

8. James Cowles Prichard, *The Natural History of Man* 3rd edn, (London: Hypolite Ballière, 1848), Henry Mayhew, *London Labour and the London Poor*, published serially 1850–52; published in 4 vols (London: Griffin Bohn, 1861).

9. See Thomas Richards, *The Commodity Culture of Victorian England: Advertising and Spectacle, 1851–1914* (Stanford: Stanford University Press, 1990).

10. [Prince Albert], 'Speech given at a Banquet given by the Right Hon. the Lord Mayor [of London], Thomas Farncombe, to Her Majesty's Ministers, Foreign Ambassadors, Royal Commissioners of the Exhibition of 1851 and the Mayors of one hundred and eighty towns, at the Mansion House', reprinted in *Principal Speeches and Addresses of His Royal Highness the Prince Consort* (London: John Murray, 1862), p. 112.

11. *First Report of the Department of Practical Art* (London: HMSO, 1853), p. 2.

12. Janet Minihan, *The Nationalisation of Culture* (London: Hamish Hamilton, 1977); N. Pevsner, *Academies of Art, Past and Present* (Cambridge: Cambridge University Press, 1940), pp. 233–55; A. Rifkin, 'Success Disavowed: the Schools of Design in the Mid-Nineteenth Century', *Journal of Design History*, 1, 2 (1998), pp. 89–102; R. Denis, 'The Brompton Barracks: War, Peace and the Rise of Victorian Art and Design Education', *Journal of Design History*, 8 (1995).

13. Sir John Pope-Hennessy, who was successively Director of both institutions, has made the following illuminating comparison: 'The Victoria and Albert Museum was a post-Industrial Revolution museum; it was designed, that is to say, for a world not entirely unlike our own. The British Museum, on the other hand, was a pre-Industrial Revolution museum, whose roots went back to the seventeenth-century tradition of antiquarianism', Pope-Hennessy, *Learning to Look* (1991), p. 206.

14. *The National Gallery: Illustrated General Catalogue* (London: National Gallery, 1986), p. x.

15. Some of these were stored at Kensington Palace until 1857; further research is needed to establish precisely which came to Marlborough House.

16. In the first year of the Museum, '42 vases illustrating the early style of the Royal Manufactory at Sèvres' were lent by the Queen: 'Loans to the Museum for Public Instruction', *First Report*, p. 287.

17. 'Catalogue of the Museum of Manufactures', published as Appendix V of *First Report*, p. 233.

18. Although the emphasis gradually shifted from manufactures to the fine and decorative arts, the collection grew at a terrific pace in its early years. As early as 6 September 1852, Cole was of the opinion that 'when sufficient space is provided, a more minute subdivision will probably be desirable', *First Report*, p. 230.

19. The late Clive Wainwright pointed out this connection in a lecture given to the seminar of the RCA/V&A M.A. Course in the History of Design in March 1994; his thesis is more thoroughly rehearsed in Clive Wainwright, 'Principles True and False: Pugin and the Foundation of the Museum of Manufactures', *Burlington Magazine*, CXXVI (1095), (June 1994), pp. 362–3.

20. A.W.N. Pugin, *The True Principles of Pointed or Christian Architecture*

(1841), vol. 1, quoted in A. Saint, 'The Fate of Pugin's True Principles', in Paul Atterbury and Clive Wainwright, eds, *Pugin: A Gothic Passion* (London: Victoria and Albert Museum, 1994), p. 273.

21. See the catalogue entry by Eric Turner in B. Richardson and M. Baker, eds, *A Grand Design*, pp. 123–4.

22. H. Morley, 'House Full of Horrors', *Household Words: A Weekly Journal Conducted by Charles Dickens*, vol. 4, no. 141, 4 December 1852, pp. 265–6.

23. Ibid., p. 266.

24. Barbara Morris, *The Inspiration of Design: the Influence of the Victoria and Albert Museum* (London: Victoria and Albert Museum, 1986), p. 21.

25. Minihan, *The Nationalisation of Culture*, p. 114.

26. *First Report*, p. 30.

27. On these initiatives see G. Waterfield, ed., *Art for the People: Culture in the Slums of Late Victorian Britain* (London, 1994), and F. Borzello, *Civilising Caliban: The Misuse of Art, 1875–1980* (London, 1987).

28. On this issue see Borzello, *Civilising Caliban*, pp. 41–2.

29. H. Cole, *Fifty Years of Public Work* (London, 1884), p. 292, quoted in Louise Purbrick, 'The South Kensington Museum: the Building of the House of Henry Cole', in M. Pointon, ed., *Art Apart: Art Institutions and Ideology across England and North America* (Manchester: Manchester University Press, 1994), p. 83.

30. British Parliamentary Papers, *Report from the Select Committee on the South Kensington Museum; together with Proceedings of the Committe, Minutes of Evidence, and Appendix* (London: Reports from the Committees, XVI, 11, 1860), quoted in Purbrick, 'The South Kensington Museum', p. 69.

31. Louise Purbrick's pioneering work on this subject was presented verbally at the Mobil Research Seminar in Victorian Studies, Victoria and Albert Museum, March 1994.

32. M. Baker, *The Cast Courts* (London: Victoria and Albert Museum, 1982). See also M. Baker, 'The Establishment of a Masterpiece: the Cast of the Portco de la Gloria in the South Kensington Museum, London, in the 1870s', in *Actas Simposio Internacional sobre 'O Portico de Gloria e a Arte do seu Tempo'* (Santiago de Compostela, Galicia, 1988), pp. 479–87.

33. A full account of this part of the building appears in Physick, *The Victoria and Albert Museum*, ch. VII.

34. Physick, *The Victoria and Albert Museum*, pp. 124–9.

35. Department of Science and Art, South Kensington, *Universal Catalogue of Books on Art: Comprehending Painting, Sculpture, Architecture, Decoration, Coins, Antiquities &c.* (London, 1870) [proofs only, London: published by Chapman and Hall and at the Office of Notes and Queries: National Art Library].

36. Physick, *The Victoria and Albert Museum*, pp. 139–41.

37. Ibid., pp. 131–5.

38. See Richard Ormond, *Leighton's Frescoes* (London: HMSO, 1975), Tim Barringer, 'The Leighton Gallery at the V&A: The Context, Conservation and Redisplay of the South Kensington Frescoes', *Apollo* (February 1996), pp. 56–64.

39. For a fuller account of this argument see Tim Barringer, 'Leighton in Albertopolis', in Tim Barringer and Elizabeth Prettejohn, eds, *Frederic Leighton: Antiquity, Renaissance, Modernity* (New Haven and London: Yale University Press, 1998), pp. 135–68.

CHAPTER THREE

Spectacular failures: Thomas Hopley, Wilkie Collins, and the reconstruction of Victorian masculinity

Sheila Sullivan

> Competent men withal, whether their spheres be wide or narrow, prominent or obscure ... leave their impress on the world ... what we call manly men
>
> William Landels, *How Men are Made* (1859)

In August 1864, Thomas Hopley, educator, writer and convicted felon, published an extraordinary pamphlet, *A CRY to the LEADING NATIONS OF THE WORLD FOR JUSTICE: and for the SOULS OF MY WIFE AND CHILDREN* (hereafter *Cry*). Dedicated to that patron of reform causes, Lord Brougham, Hopley's *Cry* offered itself to the public as both an authentic account of a criminal conspiracy and a form of action which, by rousing 'throughout the land ... a cry of "Shame"', would not only repair its author's private situation, but also restore to the nation a much-needed masculine authority.[1] Those unfamiliar with Hopley's story may yet find something familiar in this description of his project; for his text displays a clear debt to the sensation novel which was, even as Hopley wrote, becoming the defining sign of modern conditions.[2]

Like so many of sensation fiction's nominal heroes, Thomas Hopley represented himself as man whose sense of domestic security had been shattered. His pamphlet tells the story of that loss, outlining the theory that, while he was serving his sentence for manslaughter, his loving wife, Fanny, was tricked into breaking up the family home.[3] Figured in his own words as a man betrayed by those closest to him, Hopley thus joins a line of contemporary characters, including Mary Elizabeth Braddon's Robert Audley and Ellen Wood's Archibald Carlyle, who cannot keep disorder outside the doors of the respectable home. But Hopley's *Cry* is not finally about male ineptitude. Like the story of Walter Hartright in Wilkie Collins's *The Woman in White*, it makes a spectacle of failed masculinity only to assert a new kind of gendered authority.[4]

In the past twenty years, critical responses to the nearly simultaneous discovery, somewhere around 1860, of the sensation novel and the sensationalism of mid-century British culture have made much of the relation between sensation and 'ideologies of gender and femininity'.[5] It is hard not to see the fictional genre's concern with female transgression as registering certain anxieties about capitalism and the gendered structures that underwrote it. It seems equally obvious that our own fascination with the culture's most sensational gendered transgressor, the middle-class criminal woman, is also a historical phenomenon, reflecting an array of political and professional imperatives. Yet what becomes most clear when we read Hopley's pamphlet against its literary counterparts is that no account of sensation's fascination with dangerous women can be complete without some recognition of its deep interest in the failures of supposedly normal men.[6]

Once we become conscious of this concern, we find it everywhere: confessions of masculine inadequacy in medical journals and novels, sermons and economic treatises. But why do mid-Victorian readers and writers take such pleasure in the spectacle of male failure, and why, in particular, does a privileged class embrace such representations of its own condition? I will argue that sensational narratives of male failure are part of a wider effort to establish a new model of gendered authority. More specifically, they facilitate the construction of a form (and ideology) of identity, the professional, which is gradually freed from its mooring in specific jobs to become the qualities that allow Englishmen to exercise power from a variety of positions.[7] This version of professionalism promises to stabilize troubling relations among authority, class and gendered identity by resolving the differences between subjects into one difference – that of socially useful competence.

In considering a moment when an apparently dominant class represents itself in crisis, this essay at once takes for granted what John Kucich calls the 'divisiveness of privileged groups'[8] and identifies its particular relation to the project of reassessment this book is engaged in. For Thomas Hopley appears in the early pages of W.L. Burn's seminal study in his guise of criminal pedant, as a figure for the 'dark side' of 'the mid-century'.[9] And it is Burn's method of handling disturbing characters and trends that seems most to distinguish his work from the wave of recent scholarship devoted to deviance, disorder and marginality. Looking back on the early 1960s from what seems to be an immense distance, one can only be struck by the scrupulousness with which Burn admits the complexities of individual and classed relations to dominant ideologies. Both Burn's choice of materials (he uses an impressive range of literary and cultural sources) and his willingness to see his period as one lacking 'a single coherent line of thought'[10] seem oddly prophetic of the more generalized rejection of master narratives we have come to associate with critical theory's impact on the disciplines of literature and history.

It is only when we come to Burn's discussion of the 'forces which regulated and disciplined society' that we begin to see what it means to move from telling stories of equipoise to anatomizing pockets of anxiety.[11] Burn identifies a set of mechanisms through which, he claims, mid-century Britain struck a balance between regulation and liberty; but his idea of balance turns out to be an oddly arithmetic one. He notes destabilizing impulses only to discover the measures and countermeasures by which those impulses were effectively neutralized. In this account, the balance that is Burnian 'equipoise' at once admits incoherences and resistances and renders them insignificant, allowing the writer to recognize 'innumerable grounds for individual dismay' and even signs of 'national anxiety' while insisting that what mattered was not their presence but the 'vigorous effort towards their solution'.[12] He is, finally, interested in the strategies by which normality is produced rather than in the relationship between the normal and the abnormal, the regular and the deviant.

What I would like to suggest here is that any effort to reconsider the 'age of equipoise' must of necessity involve rethinking the structural principles that have shaped the last several decades of writing about mid-nineteenth-century England. As inheritors of the post-modern suspicion of the naturalness of the normative, critics and historians have turned eagerly to the investigation of marginal subjects associated with the subversive side of culture. In the process, we have found it all too easy to dismiss normality, to accept as a simple function of power the process by which, to borrow Burn's words, England's surface came to seem 'reasonably firm and reasonably clear' by 1860.[13] Thus my concern with Thomas Hopley, a man who must grapple with his own deviance to lay claim to an identity we often see as an unambiguous register of reality, can be seen more broadly as a way of thinking through the apparently contradictory impulses that have dominated historical and literary narratives of *the* mid-century condition. As the very public spectacle of Hopley's efforts to normalize his own failures reveals, the problem for individual subjects in the late 1850s and 1860s was a problem of managing a set of relations – between deviance and normality, authenticity and fiction, classed masculinity and femininity – at a moment when those relations were constructed by the nation as both deeply troubled and the only legitimate ground of authority.[14]

The undisciplined home

If the high Victorian public increasingly saw the sensationalizing of culture as a problem, they most often associated that problem with the sex whose job it was to maintain the home. By the end of the 1850s, they were awash in evidence, gleaned from divorce courts, popular novels and criminal trials, that women's transgressions were threatening both the ideal and the reality of domesticity. As I have already noted, however, this vision of gendered danger was almost always accompanied by recognition that something was wrong with masculinity as well.[15] New forms of womanhood and new forms of manhood, or at least the possibilities and problems of producing a new kind of man, shared the same public stages in 1860 because they had become conceptually inseparable.

Whether they represented a new type of gendered subject or a twisted version of more traditional models of femininity, the dangerous women of these decades embodied forces whose very presence in the home constituted a form of pollution. Destined by birth for a respectable position, Eliza Linton's Girl of the Period packaged herself for the marriage market by dressing and talking like a fashionable prostitute, raising the spectre of an unseemly sexualization of middle-class privacy. Even more disturbing were figures like Mary Elizabeth Braddon's fictional Lucy Audley and Scotland's all too real Madeleine Smith. Skilled in concealment and manipulation, they looked like everything one might desire in a womanly woman. Yet, as their careers demonstrated, the very qualities which defined the domestic ideal could become the tools that destroyed it. Even where the right sort of woman was in her place, then, the regulatory guarantee associated with that placement was changing; by the 1860s, feminine domesticity was becoming a suspect cultural anchor indeed.[16] During the same decade, a series of commercial and bank frauds threatened to recast the gendered narrative of entrepreneurial adventure as a story of over-reaching appetite, bringing the naturally aggressive expression of masculinity, what the right sort of men do outside the home, under suspicion.[17] England was forced to consider whether there was any necessary connection between disturbing trends in economic relations and masculinity itself. Was the financial bandit a dangerous exception or a natural adaptation of the manly man? Was it possible to distinguish between the desires that drove the giant of commerce and those that corrupted the speculative criminal?

If the crimes of a Madeleine Smith or a Lady Audley represented femininity distorted by biological weakness and social circumstances, the crime wave among respectable men suggested a dangerous instability in the ethical and social values associated with traditionally male qualities.[18] David Mourier Evens's 1857 study of commercial crime, *Facts, Failures, and Frauds*, describes men like Michael Sadleir (MP, forger and suicide) and George Hudson (railway magnate and fraud) in terms which, scant years before, would only have been used to characterize positive achievement.[19] They triumph in 'an almost titanic period of warfare ... and accomplishment' acting with unparalleled swiftness and cool acuity.[20] Even figures the author criticizes more openly, like the criminal clerk Walter Watts, manifest what might seem to be an estimable capacity for self-help.[21] But unlike the rising artisan, the white-collar criminal did not follow a well-worn path upward. He is, as Charles Dickens points out, an innovator.

> Criminals ... are great practical demonstrators ... the fraudulent bankrupt has a use in pointing out the traps and pitfalls of trade; the forging bank clerk directs the attention of men to the blindness of business professions, and the inutility of so-called business checks.[22]

Where the dangerous classes hide from those they prey upon, these men work openly among their victims, as theatre magnates, purveyors of commercial paper, seekers after 'a monopoly on the trade in metals'.[23] They are everywhere business is. A dwelling place, whose structure is effectively fixed, can be secured with enough effort, but the swiftly developing field of commerce always offers new points of entry. Men who exploit these opportunities are particularly troubling for a nation whose faith in *laissez-faire* principles is more and more complicated by a desire to regulate markets, stabilize currency and control competition. They are full of male energy, but at what cost to society?

Stories of the criminally womanly woman and the dangerously manly man posit and construct a third term, the man of insufficient power whose failures create the space in which both criminal agencies flourish. *Facts, Failures, and Frauds* insists, for example, that clerks can turn their £200 per year jobs into fortunes because they operate in an 'inexcusably lax system' run by 'men of straw'.[24] Similarly, Braddon's Lucy Audley succeeds because the men around her are either helpless victims of their own investment in a gendered ideal or aimless creatures like Robert Audley, the briefless barrister.[25] Triangulating the causes of disorder, sensationalism stresses the fragile interdependence between gendered spheres, gendered performances, and public and private orders.

The narratives this vision give rise to require the revelation of what has been hidden, but they also encode suspicions about revelatory practices that give another twist to public debates about the culture of sensation.[26] A *Chambers Journal* article on the murder of young Francis Seville Kent begins by noting

> It is in this case ... almost certain that some member of a respectable household – such as your's reader or our's – which goes to church with regularity, has family prayers, and whose bills are punctually settled, has murdered an unoffending child.[27]

In other words, the crime is sensational because it exposes respectability as a façade. Yet the text's work in articulating that truth is anything but comforting. While the exposure of what has been hidden might be expected to create a new security, the *Chambers* author ends with a question/statement that suggests otherwise.

> Under what roof, then, can it be certified that no crying wickednesses are being committed daily and nightly! What paterfamilias is so secure in his household that the consideration of such a case as this affects him with no terror![28]

If reading about the Kent case scares men into doubting their own felicity (and, in light of this question, who of the masculine among us could be totally secure?), publication of this report will spread a nervousness that militates against the security of all husbands and fathers.[29] Such expressions of 'anxiety' clarify the nature of the crisis of masculinity articulated in the discourse of sensation: can men assert power without falling into the gendered excesses which threaten national stability or anatomize failure without increasing the consciousness of inadequacy that eats away at masculine certainty?

The next two sections of this essay read Wilkie Collins's *The Woman in White* and Thomas Hopley's polemic on his appearance in the divorce court in the context of these questions. Shifting away from the earlier Victorian commitment to silence about the tensions that structure private life and the exercise of public power, both narratives demonstrate how the trope of masculine failure becomes an occasion for the display of a newly professionalized model of male authority and identity.

The disciplined man

Despite its title, *The Woman in White* is a novel about men, a novel concerned not only with 'the proper regulation of innate male energy', but with the fear that such energy is being drained out of respectable men.[30] That terrifying possibility reverberates throughout Collins's preface, and is explicitly thematized in the story of Walter Hartright's evolution from weak drawing-master to masterful detective-narrator. Linking Walter's initial passivity with the disorder that explodes around him, *The Woman in White* makes it clear that male failure and domestic crime are mutually dependent phenomena.

Many recent critics of the novel have followed D.A. Miller's lead and organized their readings around the seminal moment when Anne Catherick, asylum escapee, steals up to Walter Hartright on the road to London. The moment she touches his arm, he freezes, paralysed by the intimate encounter. Yet this haunting moment need not immobilize us as completely as it does Walter. If, on some level, sexual panic is being enacted here, the immobility apparently produced by erotic demand precedes the encounter. From its very first words, Walter's narrative stresses the hero's weakness. He turns even writing, the quintessential act of power, into a tortured exercise in incapacity: 'I trace these lines self-distrustfully with the shadows of after-events darkening the pages I write and still I say, what could I do' (p. 50).[31] Walter's repeated denials of agency ('I can hardly say that I thought at all' (p. 14)] and power ('I am only a drawing master' (p. 14)) and identity ('Was I Walter Hartright?' (p. 18)) are traces of the demand that structures his inadequacy. Registering the tension between what individual men can do and what society expects of men, his paralysis raises the possibility that contemporary society is producing good men who are incapable of exercising power properly.[32]

That possibility is given a social dimension in Walter's initial position, somewhere between a gentleman, a professional and a servant. A man in this state lacks authority, but he is also unmanned in a more literal sense. While the odd status of Walter's female counterpart, the governess, simultaneously erases and eroticizes the female subject, the dependent male is 'admitted among beautiful and captivating women much as a harmless domesticated animal is admitted among them' (p. 89).[33] Unable to participate in the family life of his class, Collins's hero is also castrated, denied a share in the heterosexual potency that is his 'rightful' heritage. *The Woman in White* presents Walter's ambiguous social position, his lack of sexuality and his anxiety as related symptoms. However, it complicates its diagnosis of masculine failure by postulating a prior cause for its hero's inadequacy. Readers of the Revd William Landels's 1859 pamphlet, *How Men are Made*, would have recognized Walter's real problem as his inability to transcend circumstance.[34] In Landels's version of gendered nature, man is defined as what 'is not molded by others'.[35] Manly men deny social limits because they possess an 'internal force which resists and masters'.[36] Walter's failure to achieve Landelian manhood is thus seen most clearly in his exile from the nascent economy of professional identity which promises that men can, without violating codes of manners or law, remake the cultural and social prison of their current condition.

Walter displays his resistance to this gendered ideology almost immediately. When, early in the novel, his friend Pesca proposes that the young man rise through a prudent marriage and hard work to 'Walter Hartright, MP', Walter freezes.

> No sooner had I read the memorandum than I felt an inexplicable unwillingness within me to stir in the matter ... Though I could not conquer my own unaccountable perversity, I had at least virtue enough to be heartily ashamed of it. (p. 45)

Hartright's unaccountable resistance might be seen as symptomatic of sensationalism's use of male intuition as a form of providential design. But the language of the passage, its stress on perversity and shame, suggests a deeper resistance. *The Woman in White* employs a grammar of class and sexual disempowerment to establish the proper expression of gendered energy as man's true challenge. In a world in which men of all classes are becoming ever more subject to regulations which limit the exercise of traditional forms of male power, masculinity must be at once controlled and, if it is to provide a unifying social ground, cut loose from the mere circumstances of life.

The novel's interest in the problematic intersection of potency and virtue goes beyond Walter; it is manifested as well in the attention given to such oddly classed and gendered figures as Count Fosco and Frederick Fairlie. Like Fosco, with his feminine delicacy and his obvious sexual power, Fairlie's 'languid fretful voice', his little 'womanish kid slippers', and his equivocal relations with his valet suggest that the novel associates failed manliness with either or both improper sexual performance and ambiguous class status. But *The Woman in White* finally defines true male power less as an attribute of the properly classed or sexed self than as what secures individual energies in reproducible form. To stabilize the cycle of private relations, one must be able to ensure the future, and Fairlie fails to master the tools of social reproduction: wills, settlements and marriages. When men cannot transcend death by creating fixed value, they cannot guarantee the stable meanings that are History and Property. That failure not only opens the way for the conspiracy against the Limmeridge estate and fortune; it ushers in a future of unending plots and endless anxieties.

The Woman in White's obsessive mapping of varieties of masculine inadequacy indicates Collins's fascination with the consequences of the historical breakdown between class identity and gendered authority. Economic movement and the shift from a class to a professional society mean that more and more men will occupy positions which are not secure in the traditional sense and which must still be the province of men. There are also compelling reasons in the 1860s, ranging from fears about the resistant animality of man to worries about population, to try to elide connections among sexuality, sexual activity and masculinity.[37] Like Landels and the writers on white-collar crime, Collins desires a masculinity independent of imprisoning social circumstances while fearing the disorder that might accompany that gendered power. What is important about this apparently contradictory desire is what it does to the idea of a stable structure of male identity: men cannot escape from the forces which are pathologizing masculinity until they recognize that true manliness is something that must, in Landels's words, be made.

A novel which calls itself the story of what man's 'resolution can achieve' and yet begins with a hero who has no resolution at all clearly postulates manliness as a goal rather than a bedrock of identity. And by the time *The Woman* ends, Walter has indeed been 'made' a man, gaining wealth, status, even a son. Yet it is Walter's ability to control not only his narrative ('my position is defined – my motives are acknowledged') but everyone else's as well ('I shall relate both narratives, not in the words ... of the speakers themselves, but in the words of the ... studiously simple abstract which I committed to writing') that is designated as the precondition of those other successes (p. 457). Before Walter can secure a place in the middle class or function as a heterosexual subject, he must become man enough to control his life story through a mastery of publication.

Careful readers of the novel will note an irony here. Collins's formal affirmation of man's capacity to be remade depends on something *The Woman in White* does not represent. Walter's reconstruction occurs outside the novel's pages and beyond the public space of the nation. It is textually present only in Marian's fever dream of a man journeying through pestilence, native attack and shipwreck, and in Walter's own version of his transformation. 'In the stern school of extremity and danger', he says, 'my will had learnt to be strong, my heart to be resolute, my mind to rely on itself. I had gone out to fly from my own fate. I came back to face it as a man should' (p. 427).

We know that Walter is cured by working in an outpost of empire. We also know that his experience neither transforms impotence into explicitly sexual energy nor bestows on him the riches that would cure social insecurity. Rather he is masculinized by exercising his domestic skills in the service of the state.[38] Graduating from mounting watercolours to making 'excavations ... among ruined cities', classifying and preserving the traces of other civilization, Hartright becomes one of the experts on whom the empire depends. Though danger and a certain lawlessness seem necessary to his transformation, Walter's new masculinity is tempered by the fact that it originates in the assumption of a position associated not just with expertise but with some nascent quality of professionalism.

Refusing to represent the process of gendered reconstruction, *The Woman* focuses instead on its meaning and effect. Because Hartright's agency is constructed from outside the sphere of private interest – he gives up the idea of marrying Laura before he leaves – and away from the struggle for success – believing Laura to be married there is no gain to him in the search for justice – it possesses the tempering distance that connects it with professionalism. That disinterest distinguishes Walter from Count Fosco, separating his appropriation of other stories from the criminal's effort to do the same.[39] In this formulation, the new professional man is associated not with getting on, but with the control of women's bodies and stories. Walter thus justifies his exposure of the private and his control of the feminine in the same terms: both are responses to a necessity rooted in national utility, and insulated by a series of controls from the hungers associated with entrepreneurial appetite.[40]

At this point, Walter's history collides with the novelist's. As Collins tells us in the Preface, he too operates in a feminized sphere and in a market economy that threatens to make him either servant or machine. No less than his hero, then, he must resist and master his circumstances, taking control of the private for penetration, striation and publication.[41] To that end, the novel offers itself as a form of experience whose workings on the private psyche, like those of the empire, simultaneously escape representation and foster the hidden springs of manly energy. The author's claim to professionalism thus depends upon his ability to contain this simulacrum of stimulating experience in a structure controlled enough to model the mastery of public forms which all new men need if they are to be useful to the nation.[42] It is this combination of utility and competence which separates Collins, in his own self-construction, from the popular women writers he otherwise resembles and makes his work a cultural restorative rather than a pathological symptom.

Making a spectacle of oneself

Like that of the fictional Walter Hartright, Thomas Hopley's future depends on producing an authoritative text of his life. To repair his marriage and secure his livelihood, he must provide the public with a compelling explanation for his failure in both areas. Echoing the rhetoric and structure of sensation fiction, Hopley's pamphlet clarifies the role that popular literature plays in constructing the matrix through which Victorian male subjectivity is formed, emphasizing the distance between the cultural promise of professionalism (a category open to all properly regulated subjects which also regulates the competition between men) and the limits it imposes on real historical subjects.[43]

A schoolmaster of advanced views, Thomas Hopley had long been interested in infants' and women's education. He published and lectured extensively in both fields, pointing to his school as evidence of his authority on matters domestic.[44] In 1860, Hopley was found guilty of manslaughter in the beating to death of one of his pupils, young Reginald Cancellor.[45] His wife, Fanny, defended him publicly until the time he was to be paroled: she then filed for a separation, claiming that Hopley had abused her physically and emotionally throughout their marriage. Acting as his own counsel, Hopley argued that whatever happened between the two of them was condoned by his wife.[46] The court agreed and refused to grant the separation. Immediately after the verdict, Fanny disappeared with the couple's children and Hopley published his cry for justice.[47]

Even before the final act in the Hopley drama, then, the case was a popular sensation.[48] Combining crackpot reform theories, domestic dirt and accusations of physical violence, it played itself out in one of the most sensationalized forums of the early 1860s, the divorce court, and its popular avatar, the divorce court news reports. As if that were not enough, Hopley was technically, as *The Times* pointed out, 'A Ticket-of-Leave man', a phrase that invokes both contemporary debates on law reform and the popular dramas that focused on the convict's return to society.[49] In short, Hopley's case became interesting to the public as part of a cultural intertext, or metanarrative, that can only be seen as sensational.

Like Collins's fictional story of masculinity under siege, Hopley's *Cry* makes a spectacle of its hero's troubles. It employs the sensational narrator's strategy of direct address to make our response to that sight the measure of whether this act of publication succeeds: the reader must determine if 'there has been planned and perpetrated an awful plot of perjury' (p. 3). Hopley's appeal 'to the nation as a jury' (p. 5) echoes Collins's claim that what we read resembles a story 'as the Judge might once have heard it' (p. 34). And Collins's explanation of why Walter goes to the public instead of the courts – 'the law is still ... the pre-engaged servant of the long purse' – is matched by Hopley's presentation of himself as a man competing with powerful social forces. He is, he tells his readers,

> Ignorant of the ways of law courts, unpracticed [sic] in the art of eliciting evidence, unaccustomed to plead, unable to afford the guidance of counsel, unable to defray the expenses of such witness as, if summoned, could have helped me rebut these cruel charges. (p. 6)

Speaking from the deviant position of felon and accused wife-beater, Hopley struggles to reconstruct his life in terms which render him first familiar and then acceptable to a respectable audience.

To that end, Hopley crafts a personal narrative that identifies his apparent failures of authority with those of the sensation hero. Domestic reformers of the decade operated in a sphere feminized by its association with servants and women. Seeking to escape that association, ambitious educators tried to define the care of the young as a science.[50] Given the demands of the modern world, children were simply too vital a national resource not to be subjected to systematic discipline: 'A grand revolution in educational systems seemed to be the prime want of the world.'[51] As a practitioner of this new science, Hopley's class was as open to question as his masculinity. His wife's 'betrayal' thus translated a double vulnerability into a double failure. That she fled from him after the trial suggested his inadequacy as a husband and father. That she put him on trial at all, after Hopley had supposedly succeeded in transforming her from a woman whose 'education ... had been **entirely neglected**' (p. 13) into the perfect partner, raised doubts about his professional performance. Hopley's *Cry* thus appears to reiterate the sensational strategy of linking private criminality, female transgression and male weakness.

As a man with a public history, Hopley could not, however, repudiate that connection by simply replotting his life. He could not represent his movement into the role of husband as part of the story of gendered cure. He was already married with children. Nor could he claim that his impotence arose solely from his position; he did not want to deny his record of success. To the extent that it tells the story of a man who has already resisted and mastered his circumstances once, Hopley's text makes visible what fictional narratives disguise when they concentrate on heroes whose alienation and repair come before their entry into man's estate. Male authority, once it becomes something to be achieved, can never be entirely stable.

To make matters more complicated, Hopley's text identifies a causal connection between criminal disorder and the emergence of new types of masculinity. Hopley's profession, with its inherently critical relation to conventional domestic arrangements, gave him the power to transform his wife from one who 'knew nothing of poetry, botany, the beautiful mysteries of nature' (p. 12) into a fit companion. But it also threatened traditional canons of masculine work and the conventional ideology of separate spheres. Understood in this fashion, Hopley's appearance on the horizon of history marks the end of an order of dominance based on men's unthinking possession of women, and on their refusal to acknowledge the national significance of the domestic sphere. As traditional men, Fanny's brothers responded to this shift first with rage, and then with conspiracy: 'As by degrees she unfolded the powers of her mind ... they ... grew more and more embittered ... Their antipathy seemed to have risen to a mania' (pp. 61 and 65). Conventional masculinity here becomes the true source of crime, the attack on Hopley an assault on the emerging future. Embracing the uncertainty at the heart of the sensational discourse of masculinity, Hopley's story defines resistance and peril as the condition of England's new men. It is the pressure of new masculinities that awakens all men to the knowledge of being within history, a revelation that simultaneously presages a new order and activates disorder.

Where *The Woman in White* focuses on individual efforts to escape from the paralysing intersection of cultural mandates and gendered convention, then, Hopley's *Cry* turns our attention to the resistance that accompanies transformations of masculinity. In both cases, however, the beleaguered man's assertion of his authority hangs in the balance until he can establish control over the meaning of his life, the shape of his life story. For Hopley, that meant controlling the evidence which made him a laughing-stock in court, his wife's letters. Hopley's cure thus depended, just as Walter's did, on his ability to appropriate private relations for public use. He had to prove that he had not been duped by his wife's manipulation of gender codes. He had also to demonstrate that no excess of masculinity, as embodied in any criminal behaviour of his own, had destroyed his home. And he could only do those things by using the public space of the pamphlet to reread the private communications which structure marriage.[52] 'But let us now see what my wife has asserted ... not, as present, under fearful threats or cruel family pressure ... but when under the sole influence of her private feelings' (p. 13).

Those feelings are, he argued, as visible in the greeting with which a letter of August 1860 begins, the first 'received by me after the trial'

(p. 13) – 'My own most dearly loved and loving husband' – as they are in the last ones he receives – which start out 'My very dear husband' (p. 84). He also noted that Fanny signed her letters the same way during all the years of their separation: your ever devoted little wifey. Hopley pounded away at these points, invoking literary, legal and common-sense standards to support his claim that there is 'nothing more beautifully tender ... more wifely and womanly, than the language of these gentle letters' (p. 26). Like his readers, this husband and man of business had to take such expressions as evidence of sincere feeling.

> Does not that letter – do not all her letters show her to have been, up to that period, a faithful, loving, devoted wife? ready to join her lot with her husband's ... anxious to carry out his ideas and wishes upon his liberation, earnest for that liberation as the one thing longed for? (p. 85)

If Fanny's consistency and her words did not reflect real intentions, they could only be the product of that mastery of gender and linguistic codes which belongs to criminal genius. Freeing us from the burden of choosing between the unlikely and the unthinkable, Hopley's text provides a comforting third alternative. We can see his wife as the real victim. Though she was the chief witness against him, she was not the source of this conspiracy. With her husband away in prison, Fanny and her children were rather the 'helpless victims of designing people', of the male family members who set her 'on the broad and deadly road' of domestic crime (p. 6). In Hopley's hands, the story of gendered failure was transformed into a tale of the resistance encountered by professional pioneers.[53]

But Hopley's claim to that status required one more thing. His text had to be disinterested, had to demand 'public attention' on 'public grounds' (p. 4). According to Hopley, the success of his accusers showed how easily institutions which depended on the control of information, such as courts and newspapers, could be manipulated. How was one to know what to believe in the world of respectable fraud and unhappy families? Whether true or false, revelations about what the private could hide threatened the peace by disturbing any unselfconscious performance of normality, producing an environment of suspicion, which could not be disciplined in traditional ways. As we can see in both Victorian courtrooms and novels, such revelations testified to, and created a gap between, appearance and reality: they encouraged the dangerous assumption of a deeper privacy hidden in every marriage and family and enlarged the audience willing to see respectability shattered. Hopley could therefore establish the link between self-exposure and professional duty only by identifying his immensely personal revelations with public necessity. His *Cry* seeks to produce this unity of goods by eliding the distance between reader response as an aesthetic and emotional fact and reader response as a metonymic for social action. The text's ability to rouse throughout the land 'a cry of Shame' is not just the means of restoring to Hopley 'my wife and children'; it is also a way of resisting the manipulative abuse of publication. If readers were roused properly, their outrage would send his family home; but that arousal would also help reconstruct them as men in control of the workings of their own culture.

> If such things can be done in England and not excite feelings of the warmest moral indignation, then 'England's greatness' is a myth; her 'moral power' a mockery; her 'home firesides', mere hearths of treachery; her 'largeness of heart', cold cruelty; her 'religion', blasphemy. (p. 124)

The idea of a compelling revelation of mystery is folded in on an ideal of aesthetic affect, conflating the author's success with the culture's cure. The author's authority depends on creating a national feeling which testifies to his version of truth, and that feeling in turn repairs the damage done by the criminal manipulation of appearances.

This version of the sensational cure foregrounded a range of problems that fictional sensations often obscured. A simple summary of Hopley's story of the plot against him reveals, for example, how much the tools of his persecutors resembled his own. Both published hidden relations, sought to control the text of the feminine and fell back on a standard of judgement perilously close to an aesthetic one. A vituperative *Saturday Review* attack on Hopley reminds us of the difficulties of stabilizing an authority determined by its affect. The court's finding of condoned cruelty could merely, as the *Saturday Review* observed, demonstrate that Hopley possessed the power he attributed to his attackers.[54] What he said about his wife loving him and honouring his work meant nothing if Hopley totally controlled her feeling and her thinking. Repossessing the words of Hopley's wife, the article insisted that what they really evinced was crime; in this reading, Hopley the hero became Hopley the abuser and his wife a woman 'completely mastered ... by her torturer'.[55]

The cure of masculinity cannot, as this response makes clear, reinstate a simple connective relation among authority, gender, power and order. Placing every reader on their honour to return a verdict uninfluenced by favour or prejudice, Hopley's *Cry* makes visible the distance between narratives about the power of narrative and the historical process by which texts work in the world. How can individual judgements, differences, desires be erased in a spontaneous and unified demand? Would not a text so controlling render the appearance of uniformity disturbing? What does it mean to say that if things such as these can be done in England then England's greatness is a myth? How can feeling repair the wreckage of a marriage or punish criminal con-spiracy?

As *The Woman in White* veiled and wrote over the process of mascu-line revision, Hopley's *Cry* also imagines a male cure manifested primarily in the struggle to establish the proper relation between public and private, to determine what should be given to the public eye. The power associated with this struggle is dislocated from traditional sources (sexual or class identity), and defined primarily as the disinterested control of revelatory texts and manipulable bodies. The man who would be guard-ian of modern order is thus given to himself, comes to know and imagine his condition, in narratives that claim dominion over an entire class of subjects on the grounds that their exploitation threatens the systems by which order is guaranteed. As one rhetoric of manhood was replaced by another, stressing both resistance and self-mastery, the cul-ture gestured towards an ideal of transcendental masculinity; its articulations of that ideal, however, could only reiterate the comforting and appalling fact that male authority is never grounded in itself.

Professional masculinity

Sensational stories of England's new man entail a complication of mas-culinity in the context of a public discourse of gender as problem. If masculinity was not to be acted out in old ways, as aggression, move-ment, uncontrolled appetite, and not necessarily to be enacted in familiar theatres, the bedroom or the marketplace, it had to be rethought. To the extent that, as Harold Perkin and others have argued, there was 'a contraction of opportunities for social climbing' after the 1850s, or at any rate that the deceleration of economic growth might be perceived as a loss of cultural energy, narratives of private disorder solved by the progress into professionalism affirmed that opportunities still existed, opportunities whose perils and complexity would be a proving-ground for masculinity.[56] The fact that such narratives tended to take as their starting-point spectacles of failure, even martyrdom, linked the popular strategies of sensationalism to the more élitist problematizing of mascu-linity that we see in such figures as Carlyle, Kingsley and Pater.[57] In that sense, sensational narratives of new women and new men represent only one strand of a larger mid-century concern with establishing new conditions for displaying and writing manhood.

Historically, these stories seem to prefigure fiction's turn to the hyperprivate and hyperpublic space of empire. The works of Rider Haggard and Rudyard Kipling take as their subject, for example, man's movement into a space whose distance makes it both more public and less supervised (or private) than anything that could be imagined at home. The popularity of such stories near the end of the century hints at a further complication of the gendered matrix in which manliness and professionalism were being brought together. The novel of adventure could do without the criminal woman, but the shift from narratives of a feminine sphere saved by masculinizing to fictions of a sphere supposedly exterior to the feminine and more enthralling than the now feminized public sphere exposed new pressures on ideologies of manhood, and the difficulty of separating male action from sexual energy.

It would be interesting to trace the relations between the various waves of popular stories which make heroes out of the beleaguered or paranoid male; but I have focused here instead on a discourse which identifies the production of a stabilizing and valuable masculinity with a form of identity in which sexuality and class are supplanted as the true sources of effective male performance. As we can see in Hopley and Collins, the high Victorian fascination with spectacles of male failure marks a point at which traditional gendered constructs, the changing expectations of individuals and classes, and new national concerns with the regulation of public activity collided. Defined as much by the apparently limitless expansion of credit, business opportunities and access to textual authority as by the concern with the criminality hidden in all women, the 1860s produced a range of narratives which represented the revision of gendered subjects, rather than cultural or political change, as the key to securing an orderly society. If England were to stabilize the public or business world, it would have to improve its businessmen.[58] In this context, the general ideology of professionalism formulated in these texts makes perfect sense. It provided a category of authority which is open, hypothetically, to all classes because it replaced the markers of class identity with the supposedly neutral ones of competence, disinterest, mastery of publication and so on. Such an identity was, by definition, something that one could struggle for without threatening national order.

But if sensational narratives of failed masculinity provided an example of how, in principle, the professional ideal was being 'extended to everyone', we must also recognize that the individual's ability to use 'persuasion and propaganda', the tools by which professional disciplines legitimated themselves, was limited in fundamental ways.[59] Reading Hopley's Cry against Collins's novel, we are made painfully aware of the hidden registers of gender and class, which structure this supposedly unmarked ideology. The fact that professional disinterest is defined primarily as the desexualized/deprivatized control of women's bodies and stories marks it as an essentially male prerogative. The fact that male authority is associated with the control of textual affect, and thus with the creation of sympathy between authors and publics, means that the appearance of power provides no real guarantee of legitimacy. Even men who rise and prosper can be defined, by the voice of the male public, as criminal manipulators rather than manly men. Even more disturbingly, and this problem is most visible in Hopley's *Cry*, the regulated self (and the regulating texts) that professionalism presupposes is difficult to separate from middle-class status and ideology. Regulation involves a masking of desire, a denial of the relation between work and remuneration, a dependence on the approbation of a selected group of peers, and the cultivation of a style of authority which, in practice, either limit its application to those who are already middle-class or impose on those who wish to succeed the burden of approximating middle-class manners and morals.

This essay has tried to stress the role that literary structures played in articulating and individualizing the narratives of male identity available to a diverse range of subjects in mid-nineteenth-century Britain. These structures unquestionably reflected and served a cultural mandate to produce a more regulated masculinity; however, they also provided at least the fiction of new, and in some ways more democratic, modes of power, a fiction which, if we take seriously the popularity of the sensational, had wide appeal. It is, finally, at this point that I would like to bring my narrative back to the problem of equipoise set up in the introduction. For Burn's essentially static model of equipoise makes it difficult to consider the making of either individual or national identify as a dynamic process in which the normal is as contested, problematic and protean as the abnormal. Much of what Burn does with the concept of equipoise is, as he implies in his final chapter, done with an eye to maintaining the idea of period or generational difference.[60] But in producing a story of cultural condition, which focuses on the interplay of forces, he produces a history which takes the human experience of culture for granted. The great power of Hopley's story is that it reminds us of all that is lost when we do that.

Notes

1. Thomas Hopley, *A CRY to the LEADING NATIONS OF THE WORLD FOR JUSTICE: and for the SOULS OF MY WIFE AND CHILDREN*

(London, 1864), p. 4. All further references to the text will appear in the
body of the essay.

2. Criticism of the 1860s consistently represents the popularity of sensational novels as merely one example of a wider, and more disturbing,
public appetite for sensation. For a brief introduction to this kind of
analysis, see Margaret Oliphant, 'Sensation Novels', *Blackwood's*, 91
(1862), pp. 564–84, H.L. Mansell, 'Sensation Novels', *Quarterly Review*,
113 (1863), pp. 481–514, and the anonymous review 'Sensation Literature', *The Englishwoman's Journal*, 6 (1862), pp. 14–20.

3. Fanny sues for a legal separation right before Hopley is released from
prison; but he actually writes the pamphlet only after he wins their much-
publicized legal battle and she disappears with the couple's children.

4. Wilkie Collins, *The Woman in White* (New York: Penguin, 1964); all
further references to the novel will appear in the body of the text.

5. Ann Cvetkovich, *Mixed Feelings* (New Brunswick: Rutgers University
Press, 1992), p. 25. See Richard Altick, *Deadly Encounters* (Philadelphia:
University of Pennsylvania Press, 1986), pp. 3–5, for a good summary of
the by-now standard argument about the significance of the Victorian
construction and use of sensation as a critical term.

6. Not all recent critics ignore this concern. Both D.A. Miller, *The Novel
and the Police* (Berkeley: University of California Press, 1988) and Joseph
Litvack, *Caught in the Act* (Berkeley: University of California Press,
1992) recognize, for example, that sensational self-consciousness is linked
to a reconstruction of masculinity. However, their analyses tend to focus
on the text's role in policing male sexuality, reinstating the notion that the
relation between gender and sexuality is a given. They also have a difficult time not reproducing the erasure of the feminine that they describe
and that sensation heroes practice.

7. Gloria Clifton's study of the Metropolitan Board of Works, *Professionalism, Patronage, and Public Service in Victorian London* (Atlantic
Highlands, NJ: Athlone Press, 1992), suggests that activities and positions can begin to be professionalized without the institutional frameworks
or job-specific status often associated with professionalization, through
an attitude, a set of assumptions about life choices, and so on.

8. John Kucich, *The Power of Lies: Transgression in Victorian Fiction* (Ithaca,
NY: Cornell University Press, 1994), p. 282.

9. William L. Burn, *The Age of Equipoise* (New York: W.W. Norton & Co.,
1964), p. 42.

10. Ibid., p. 127.

11. Ibid.

12. Ibid., p. 331.

13. Ibid., p. 332.

14. My sense of the importance of thinking about masculinity and femininity
together, as part of a discourse of gender, has been influenced by a
number of theoretical considerations of the subject; however, my most
obvious debt is to Judith Butler, *Bodies that Matter* (New York and
London: Routledge, 1993), who has insisted on the need to understand
that both the masculine and the feminine have been regulated by the
'policing and shaming of gender', p. 238.

15. Martin Kayman, *From Bow Street to Baker Street* (New York: St Martin's

Press, 1992), sees suspicion bleeding from the female criminal to the male detective, p. 191, while Cvetkovich remarks on the extent to which masculine weakness haunts Braddon's story of the beautiful fiend, Lady Audley: *Feelings*, pp. 56–65.

16. Mary Poovey, 'Speaking of the Body', in *Body/Politics* (New York: Routledge, 1990), argues this point, pp. 42–4.

17. If it seems odd to us today to connect business scandals with the sensation novel, Victorian readers clearly felt differently. Fraud, forgery and other financial transgressions are everywhere in Trollope, Eliot, Collins, Reade and Dickens. Among the lesser-known sensation texts published in 1860, Mary Elizabeth Braddon's *The Serpent on the Hearth: A mystery of the New Divorce Court* explores this connection in excruciating detail, moving between boudoir, country house, divorce court and the city. *Serpent*, published anonymously, connects a range of domestic disorders with financial crime, offering as its icon of pervasive corruption a melodramatic portrait of the famous fraud Michael Sadleir whose suicide it imagines as faked, one last triumph for the king of scams. The heroine's father, also a forger and a thief, explains his fall by saying that he would rather be a 'great criminal than a mere crawling knave', p. 10.

18. Although it takes as its subject the entire 'modern' phenomenon of white-collar crime, George Robb's fine *White Collar Crime in Modern England* (Cambridge: Cambridge University Press, 1992) tends to support the claim that the anxiety about business immorality in the 1860s had its roots, at least in part, in disturbing similarities between masculine competitiveness and criminal manipulation.

19. David Mourier Evens, *Facts, Failures, Frauds: Revelations, Financial, Mercantile, Criminal* (London, 1857). A writer for a variety of specialized publications, Evens's own career manifests the impulse towards professionalism. He is one of the growing number of men who seek to position themselves as experts in the field of financial services by providing reliable information to consumers and financial players; such experts play a role in efforts to historicize the interactions of the state, the national market and larger social forces.

20. Evens, *Frauds*, p. 9.

21. Ibid., pp. 75–8.

22. Charles Dickens, 'Convict Capitalists', *All the Year Round*, III (1860), p. 202.

23. Evens, *Frauds*, p. 157. Though they tend to focus on major transgressors, texts like Evens's (and there are a number of them) imply by their structure (and sometimes even assert directly) that criminality is everywhere in the world of respectable work, particularly in the area of finance. The more development, change and energy they associate with a professional field, the greater the pressures/temptations to go wrong.

24. Evens, *Frauds*, p. 78; Dickens, 'Convict', p. 202.

25. To the extent that Lucy's power is associated with her use of a discourse of true womanhood, she does indeed depend on men's wilful passion for their own imaginative constructions. See, for example, Cvetkovich, *Feelings*, pp. 45–50 and Lyn Pykett, *The 'Improper Feminine'* (London and New York: Routledge, 1992), pp. 91–3.

26. The public representation of this case shares the basic structure that I

have already described; see reports in *The Annual Record*, *The Law Times*, etc. Like novelists, real-life Victorian detectives and reporters initially traced disturbances in the home back to women, proffering scenarios in which stepmothers are wicked, and nursemaids kill to cover their own errors, whether of duty or morality. Enquiries initially focused, for example, on two pieces of women's underclothing, Elizabeth Gough's breast flannel and Constance Kent's nightgown, whose sudden visibility provides a convenient, though unarticulated, metaphor for the secrets that conventional femininity may cover. But those scenarios always seemed to require a contributory cause. As coverage of the Kent case shows, no hypothetical solution to the murder at Road Hill could disguise the fact that the man in the case, the victim's father, was either a murderer himself or the agent, by way of a failure of paternal knowledge and power, of a terrible criminality.

27. 'Worse Than We Seem', *Chambers Journal*, 14 (1860), p. 307.
28. 'Worse', p. 307. As we can see in this quote, the writer's work begins to display certain qualities associated with the white-collar criminal. Although the moral character of the forger, a man who simultaneously depends on and undermines the nation's commitment to the authority of forms, may differ from that of the writer, the effects of their actions become disturbingly similar when the latter publishes truths that dispel the certainty associated with knowledge.
29. The sensation novel plays with this problem of textuality more indirectly. The new woman who threatens the middle-class family has, for example, often learned her performance of femininity from popular books: Lucy Audley's 'style' of domestic management bears a distinct relation to the conduct prescribed in Sarah Ellis's *Wives of England*, while her version of femininity owes much to bad French novels. Similarly, both Robert Audley and *The Moonstone*'s Franklin Blake lack masculine energy in part because of excessive indulgence in foreign fiction.
30. Herbert Sussman, *Victorian Masculinities* (Cambridge: Cambridge University Press, 1995), p. 3.
31. Unlike Cvetkovich, *Feelings*, I think it is something besides Walter's womanly 'incapacity to control his own body' that permits him 'to rise to power without appearing to aspire to it', p. 75.
32. These pressures threaten to turn the domestic, at once the origin of individual identity and men's traditional escape from the distorting pressures of history and social circumstances, into something as 'alien and alienating' as a foreign landscape (Cvetkovich, *Feelings*, pp. 93–4).
33. In the respectable fiction of this decade, at least. But since Victorian pornography makes use of sexually active male servants and later novels clearly recognize connections between class antagonism and erotic choice, it would be interesting to explore the prohibition against this model of relations. Where men do marry up, as in Gaskell's *North and South*, the 'hard' masculinity of the rising man seems inextricable from its absolute separation from the home.
34. A Baptist preacher, Landels publishes a number of books on masculinity and modern business, including *Business is Business* (London: James Clark & Co., 1876), and *How Men are Made* (London: J. Heaton & Son, 1859).

35. Landels, *Men*, p. 11. The relation between masculinity and freedom is a matter of vital concern at mid-century. Catherine Hall's *White, Male and Middle-Class* (New York: Routledge, 1992) positions the Eyre trial in the public debate over the nature of 'proper British manhood', p. 277. Hall suggests that, for most high-Victorian male readers and writers, 'a man's individuality, his male identity, was closely tied to independence', p. 257.

36. Landels, *Men*, p. 11.

37. Frank Mort, *Dangerous Sexualities* (London and New York: Routledge & Kegan Paul, 1987), uses the hydraulic model of male sexuality to explain why the high-Victorian emphasis on conserving energy made it increasingly difficult to fit aggressive heterosexuality into new ideologies of manliness, pp. 76–9.

38. Jenny Bourne Taylor, *In the Secret Theatre of the Home* (London and New York: Routledge, 1988), and Miller, *Novel*, similarly see sensationalism's formal struggles, the war over who narrates and represents others' testimony and evidence, as one of the ways that the story undermines and affirms 'a gendered, middle-class subjectivity' (Taylor, *Theatre*, p. 26).

39. Fosco too is a great appropriator of the feminine, of Anne Catherick's body, Laura Fairlie's life and Marian Halcombe's diary. But his mastery is always linked with the desire for personal gain, which marks it and him as criminal.

40. Burn's claim that publicity was one of the 'most notable agencies of social discipline', *Equipoise*, p. 233, seems especially interesting in this context, particularly given his characterization of the newspaper as a public forum for private checks on the exercise of authority, p. 238. But I would also want to emphasize the fact that publicity was increasingly a tool by which professional men legitimated their intrusions into realms traditionally defined as private, including such delicate spaces as the middle-class bedroom.

41. In that sense, as the Preface and Preamble to *The Woman in White* suggest, the sensational revision of the private is always constituted as a textual and performative act through which both individual and national stories can be reconstructed.

42. Clearly authors' efforts to access professionalism rhetorically can be connected to a variety of more concrete professionalizing moves, including active engagement in copyright law reform, the creation of professional societies (including Besant's Society of Authors), and the emergence of intermediaries such as publishers' readers and literary agents. John Feather, *A History of British Publishing* (London and New York: Croom Helm, 1988), provides valuable insight into this history, pp. 173–9. But this essay is concerned primarily with what might be called a 'style' of professionalism and with the idea that this style could transcend the specifics of a job and be realized as a set of qualities or characteristics under individual control.

43. Packed with letters, testimonials and footnotes, Hopley's *Cry* text restages Hopley's defence in the divorce court, though not in a single narrative line. It offers evidence, letters and documents, but not to contest a lost legal battle. And it frames itself with a preamble and an introduction that put the troubling act of publication, the exposure of a sordid private world, on trial. Considered in isolation, these choices might seem odd,

but they would surely be less peculiar to an audience trained by texts such as *The Woman in White*.

44. Hopley interested himself in a variety of reforming causes, eventually creating for himself a career in education. A relentless self-promoter, he used the lecture platform and pamphlet publication to legitimate the model school he opened and ran with his wife. Entering the education discussion by way of class-oriented concerns with the nation's health, Hopley's professional status depended in large part on establishing that physical health and sanitation were central to a theory of comprehensive education, a model that should be applied to all English children.

45. Not surprisingly, Hopley's marginal, though visible, construction as the professional alternative to parental, or private, regulation of the family was contested. Socially conservative organs, such as *The Times* and *The Saturday Review*, gleefully seized upon the death of Cancellor to identify Hopley as a hypocrite and fanatic whose lunacy was manifested in the desire to theorize what was natural. These responses suggest that, however self-serving Hopley's representations of himself were, something about his efforts to colonize the family for professional activity was genuinely threatening.

46. The divorce court struggles to define condonation, and the related concept of revived injury, throughout the 1860s and 1870s, producing a series of decisions which seem to reflect a growing awareness of the forces that might compel women to seek to appear complaisant in horrific marital situations while striving to maintain the idea that forgiveness was an essentially gendered quality, signifying weakness in men and virtue in women. See James Hammerton, *Cruelty and Companionship* (London and New York: Routledge, 1992), and Mary Shanley, *Feminism, Marriage and the Law in Victorian England* (Princeton: Princeton University Press, 1989).

47. One might see Hopley's text as an effort to use, in Burn's terms, the discipline of publicity against the discipline of the law. Burn's take on legal disciplines works against what he sees as the overly legislative focus of Dicey's *Law and Opinion* by taking seriously the expansion of enforcement agencies and the development of administrative law. But Burn is still bound to Diceyian structures of thought, assessing shifts in terms of their relation to *laissez-faire* and/or collectivist policies. He mentions 'public opinion', pp. 156–7, as a vital force in the transformation of the law, and briefly discusses points at which the law affects the development of particular professions; but he is primarily concerned with articulating this discipline as one whose patchiness must be supplemented by domestic and social disciplines. I would argue, structurally, for a much more intimate relation between law and publicity, and for a much more significant relation at mid-century (with the emergence of expert witnesses, the reconstruction of ideas of intellectual property, significant changes in legal procedure and legal education) between the law and the emerging discourse and practice of professionalism.

48. Lacking many of the usual sources of interest, illicit sexuality or high position, the Hopley divorce is thus still widely covered; the rather staid *Times* publishes, for example, several reports of the trial, concluding with a longer editorializing piece on the case which was printed on page 11

(marking it as of interest to those who did not regularly read the divorce court reports). Hammerton briefly discusses the problem of publicity associated with the creation of the divorce court, *Cruelty*, p. 103.

49. 'Hopley vs. Hopley', *The Times*, 15 July 1864, p. 11.

50. Thomas Hopley's *An Introductory Lecture on Education* (London, 1857) clearly registers the educator's need to associate his work with the rising professions. Reform is a matter of applying 'well-established scientific principles to practical education', p. 9. Here again Hopley's story marks an interesting intersection of Burn's concerns with my own. Hopley's incessant pamphleteering would seem to connect him to the private users of publicity that Burn makes central to the discipline of publicity. But it also provides, as the careers of men such as Hopley, Banting and hundreds of small businessmen suggest, an arena for a form of activity in which advertisement, professional justification and the production of knowledge are constantly mixed, and whose rhetoric provides vital clues to understanding how individuals managed the inherently contradictory registers of those activities.

51. Hopley, *Introductory Lecture*, p. 7.

52. They are to the author what the woman's body is to her doctor, a corpus of signs whose nominal controller must be deposed as authoritative explicator of its own meaning.

53. Like Robert Audley's stepmother and Pip's benefactor, it is Hopley's enemies who transform the surface of his domestic life into a mask for something unpredictable, even fundamentally unknowable. Hopley's *Cry* thus turns the myth of male helplessness into a narrative of criminal conspiracy; it is not so much that modern experience enfeebles as it creates the conditions under which the unawakened or unready man can be stripped of control.

54. It is interesting that the court's decision and statement of the case do in some way support Hopley's narrative. As *The Times* of 19 July 1864 notes in 'Hopley vs. Hopley', Mrs Hopley's letters create a 'case' for condonation, and even this very critical voice seems more comfortable explaining their content by 'the strange force and nature of feminine attachment' than by female hypocrisy, fear, or any criminal force in Hopley, p. 11.

55. 'The Hopley Case', *Saturday Review*, 23 July 1864, p. 114.

56. Harold Perkin, *The Rise of Professional Society* (London: Routledge, 1989), pp. 425 and 410–11.

57. James Eli Adams, *Dandies and Desert Saints* (Ithaca: Cornell University Press, 1995), argues compellingly that the figures of the dandy and the professional share an affiliation with the gentleman, an affiliation grounded in a disinterestedness that implies a negation of economic self-interest, p. 192. Similarly, as I have argued here, the sensational hero's inadequacy is figured initially in terms of a lack, sexual and social, which is repaired not in traditional ways, but through an appeal to an ideal which itself denies the legitimacy of a power rooted in those arenas.

58. Robb, *White Collar*, makes a similar point in his discussion of mid-century responses to white-collar crime; despite evidence of systematic and systemic abuses, professionalization and self-control rather than new

laws were the preferred solutions to the problem of respectable criminality, pp. 169–70.

59. Perkin, *Rise*, p. 6, p. 8.
60. Burn, *The Age of Equipoise*, pp. 329–30.

CHAPTER FOUR

Democracy and the mid-Victorians

Roland Quinault

In *The Age of Equipoise* W.L. Burn argued that in the mid-Victorian period 'the old and the new, the elements of growth, survival and decay, achieved a balance which most contemporaries regarded as satisfactory'.[1] Burn did not invent the idea that the mid-Victorian period was an era of balance; he simply re-employed a long-established concept. The idea was implicit in Sidney and Beatrice Webb's *History of Trade Unionism*, first published in 1894, and was explicitly used by G.M. Young in his influential book *Victorian England: Portrait of an Age*, which originally appeared in 1936. Young claimed that in the 1850s, after thirty years of alarms and agitations, the state 'swung back to its natural centre'.[2] Since W.L. Burn was not employing an original idea, he did not feel obliged to demonstrate its general validity. His coverage of mid-Victorian Britain in *The Age of Equipoise* was not comprehensive, but focused mainly on social and legal issues. He also concentrated, by his own admission, on the rural and professional, rather than on the urban, industrial and proletarian spheres of Victorian society.[3] Burn also ignored events and conditions in the non-English part of the United Kingdom and all foreign influence on Britain. Furthermore, he included 'next to nothing of the party politics of the period' since he left out the two chapters which he had drafted on the subject.[4] Yet both his time-frame and his idea of equipoise were largely political in their conception.

Burn started his survey in 1852 – a date which enabled him to exclude the political and economic traumas of the later 1840s. He ended his survey in 1867 – the year of the second Reform Act, which many contemporaries feared had destroyed the balance of the constitution. Burn referred, in *The Age of Equipoise*, to Lord Robert Cecil's 1858 essay on 'The Theories of Parliamentary Reform', but not to its central thesis: that the enfranchisement of the working classes would upset the balance of the constitution. Cecil believed that 'The principle ... of constitutional perfection was to check every class by another class' and he opposed the enfranchisement of the working classes on the grounds that 'their number was such that every other class would be swamped'.[5] Cecil's concern with constitutional balance was equally evident when he opposed the 1867 reform bill:

> The long periods of political repose which communities enjoy from
> time to time are due ... to the establishment of an equilibrium
> between the Conservative and the innovating force ... The two
> forces are complementary to each other; the paralysis of either
> makes the other ruinously strong.[6]

Burn adopted, consciously or unconsciously, Cecil's concept of equilibrium as a balance between two equal opposing forces, and he contrasted the stasis of the 1850s and early 1860s with the eras of change which preceded and followed this period.

Burn's concept of equipoise implied that there was general consensual support for the *status quo* in the mid-Victorian period. This view reflected a widely held assumption that the period 1852–67 was a time of economic prosperity and political conservatism, when there was little popular protest or agitation for parliamentary reform. This generalization contains a degree of truth, but it is a far from complete picture of a complex era, which displayed diverse and often contradictory characteristics.

There was much prosperity in both industrial and rural Britain in the 1850s and 1860s, but it was very unevenly distributed, both geographically and chronologically. There were significant, if short, economic recessions, at the start of the 1850s and in the later 1850s and mid-1860s. Despite the repeal of the Corn Laws in 1846, wheat prices rose significantly in the mid-1850s, boosted partly by the Crimean War and by growing demand. This led to a rapid increase in English agricultural rents and profits which did not directly benefit the rural working class. Living conditions for both rural and urban workers generally remained poor, especially with respect to accommodation and sanitation. Some industries and towns did not share in the general economic prosperity of the period. The silk-weaving industry in Coventry, for example, was decimated by cheap French imports after Cobden had negotiated the Anglo-French commercial treaty in 1860.

Although Great Britain was the most prosperous country in Europe during the mid-Victorian period, very large numbers of its citizens emigrated overseas. This exodus was most apparent in the rural areas of southern England and in the depressed industrial districts. Most British emigrants went to the United States or to British colonies like Australia and New Zealand, where there were generally better job prospects and higher wages. There was an even larger emigration from Ireland, where the state of the economy and the standard of living were far worse than in Britain. The 1850s in Ireland witnessed the grim aftermath of the great famine: land clearances which depopulated the countryside and led hundreds of thousands to leave their homeland.

Most emigrated to the United States, but hundreds of thousands of the poorest Irish took the shorter and less expensive trip to Britain. This increased congestion and health problems in cities and industrial areas, especially in Lancashire.

The British political system during 'the age of equipoise' was certainly conservative in some respects, at least by subsequent standards. The governments of the period were greatly influenced by public opinion, referred to as 'pressure from without', but their fates were determined at Westminster by 'pressure from within'. None of the ministries which fell from power between 1852 and 1867 were rejected by the electorate, but all of them were defeated in the House of Commons. That was the fate of Derby's ministries in 1852 and 1859, of Aberdeen's ministry in 1855, Palmerston's in 1858 and Russell's in 1866. The first premier who resigned directly as a result of defeat at a general election was Disraeli in 1868. General elections in the mid-nineteenth century were hardly general, since during the 1840s and later 1850s there were no contests in over half of all the constituencies.[7] The freedom of electors to choose their own representatives was further restricted by the very high cost of contested elections, which did not significantly decline until after the 1872 Ballot Act. General elections also carried less moral authority since the great majority of men (and all women) were unable to participate in them.

Parliament and government were undemocratic in a religious sense as well. Despite the repeal of the Test Act in 1828, and Roman Catholic emancipation in 1829, the parliamentary élite remained overwhelmingly Anglican. Roman Catholics formed a large proportion of the 103 Irish MPs, but they were virtually excluded from the ranks of the British MPs and the House of Lords. Nonconformists had many representatives in the Commons, but none in the Lords. The Cabinet, moreover, remained exclusively Anglican. The first avowed nonconformist to become a Cabinet minister was John Bright in 1868 and the first Roman Catholic to do likewise was Henry Matthews in 1886. The privileged status of the Church of England in religion, education and the state was not seriously undermined by legislation until after the second Reform Act. As late as 1868, Disraeli told the Queen that the disestablishment of the Church would be 'a revolution and an entire subversion of the English constitution'.[8] Thus in the religious sphere, it was not an age of equipoise, but an age of Anglican ascendancy.

The conservatism of the British establishment in the period did not, in itself, guarantee consensual support for the *status quo*. Indeed, there was a surprising amount of popular protest in mid-Victorian Britain, by comparison not only with the subsequent period, but also with the preceding period. During the Chartist agitation, in the late 1830s and 1840s, there had been widespread *fear* of disorder, but the actual incidence of violent disorder had been very limited in scale, location and duration. Despite a few well-known episodes, like the Bull Ring riots in Birmingham and the Newport 'rising' in Wales, the vast majority of Chartist meetings and demonstrations, like that at Kennington Common in April 1848, passed off peacefully, as their organizers intended. There were very few serious confrontations between the Chartists and the law-enforcement authorities.

By contrast, the years between 1852 and 1867 were surprisingly disturbed. The period witnessed the last classic food riots outside wartime, although they were generally confined to the more remote rural areas, like the West Country, which had still not been connected to the national rail network. There were also many disturbances by factory operatives in industrial areas and by miners in the coalfields. Severe outbreaks of religious rioting occurred in several cities, such as the anti-Catholic riots in Salford and Birmingham. There were also election riots in many small constituencies, like those at Kidderminster, in 1857, which strengthened Robert Lowe's conviction that the lower classes were unfit to vote. In fact, it was the continued exclusion of the great majority of men from the franchise which encouraged them to voice their political feelings by direct action. The lack of parliamentary reform precipitated violence in other ways as well. The small size of many electorates and the absence of local polling booths meant that intimidation around the hustings could significantly affect the outcome of an election. Some mid-Victorian riots impinged directly on the consciousness of the London establishment. The tranquillity of Hyde Park, the favoured recreation ground of the upper classes, was disturbed by Sunday trading riots in 1855, the Garibaldi riots in 1862 and the reform riots in 1866.

The mid-Victorian period was also marked by a prolonged, if rather intermittent, popular agitation for parliamentary reform. It is true that no major measure of *British* parliamentary reform was enacted between 1852 and 1867, but such major reforms generally had a long gestation period. The thirty years of popular reform agitation which led up to the second Reform Act was no longer than the time it took to secure the repeal of the Corn Laws in 1846 or the abolition of slavery in 1833. Between 1852 and 1867, moreover, there were far more attempts by MPs at Westminster to reform the representative system than there had been during the two decades after 1832. The 1848 revolutions on the Continent gave a stimulus to the Chartist movement in Britain, which prompted the leaders of the Whig, Tory and Peelite parties to agree, in principle, to a further extension of the franchise.[9]

The Irish Reform Act of 1850, which has been overlooked by all save a few Irish historians, widened the Irish county franchise and more than doubled the Irish electorate.[10] The Irish Reform Act stimulated the activities of the English reformers. In 1851 Locke King told the House of Commons that 'the same principle which had been applied to Ireland ... of placing the borough and county franchise on the same footing, ought to be extended to England also'.[11] In 1852, the Whig Prime Minister, Russell, drafted a reform scheme but his government was soon succeeded by a Tory ministry led by Derby and Disraeli, who contemplated their own measure of reform. They were, in turn, succeeded by Aberdeen's coalition of Whigs and Peelites and in 1854 Russell introduced a reform bill which he was so confident he could carry that he commissioned a portrait of himself holding the bill.[12]

In the event, it was mainly external, rather than internal, developments, which delayed the passage of reform for another thirteen years. In 1854, the outbreak of war with Russia obliged Russell to announce the withdrawal of his reform bill with tears in his eyes. For the next four years, the Crimean War, the Indian Mutiny and a war with China preoccupied the governments of Aberdeen and Palmerston. When the war ended, the reform issue quickly returned to the forefront of the political stage. John Bright began a new campaign for reform in the Midlands and the north of England and in 1859 Derby's minority government introduced the first Conservative reform bill. This was regarded as too moderate by most MPs and it was superseded, in 1860, by a Liberal bill sponsored by Palmerston's new ministry. Palmerston was not personally keen on reform, but as Robert Cecil observed, 'nobody dares resist it'.[13] Once again, however, reform was postponed largely because of external events. A second war with China was closely followed by the American Civil War which lasted until 1865. The unification of most of Italy in 1860 and Prussia's wars with Denmark in 1864 and with Austria in 1866 provided further distractions which delayed the enactment of reform.

The continuance of the reform campaign, despite numerous parliamentary set-backs, reflected the prevalence of democratic sentiments in many sections of the population. This was encouraged by the progress of democracy abroad, as much as by radicalism at home. In the 1850s the British electoral franchise was much more restricted than that in France and less extensive than that in Germany. The 1848 Revolution in France led to the introduction of manhood suffrage, equal electoral districts and payment of members – three of the six points demanded by the British Chartists. In 1850, some French voters were disenfranchised, but in 1851 Louis Napoleon revived manhood suffrage, which became an integral part of the political system of the Second Empire. In Prussia, there was a modified version of manhood suffrage for the popular chamber, which allowed a wider public participation in elections than was the case in Britain.

The comparative tardiness of British franchise reform has been overlooked by historians such as Norman Gash, who have assumed that Britain had nothing to learn from foreign countries. Yet mid-Victorian politicians often discussed parliamentary reform in an international context. When the manhood suffrage electorate in France endorsed Napoleon III's Second Empire, Sir Robert Inglis, a high Tory, concluded that franchise extension was not so dangerous after all.[14] Cobden's initial distaste for French democracy was overcome by Napoleon III's support for the 1860 Anglo-French commercial treaty. John Bright, from the start of his reform campaign, in 1857, stressed that other countries were democratizing rapidly and leaving Britain far behind. In 1866, he told Charles Villiers that franchise extension in Germany and other countries made it impossible 'that 84 out of 100 of our countrymen should be content to be excluded from the franchise'.[15] In 1867 the North German Confederation adopted universal male suffrage – a much more extensive franchise than that created in Britain by the second Reform Act. This prompted the British Reform League to send its congratulations to Bismarck.

The attitude of mid-Victorian intellectuals to democracy was deeply influenced by Alexis de Tocqueville's *Democracy in America*, which was published in France in 1835 and immediately translated into English. De Tocqueville was convinced that the rise of democracy was irresistible and his prediction seemed to be borne out by the 1848 Revolutions on the Continent. Thomas Carlyle wrote in 1850:

> For universal democracy has declared itself the inevitable fact of the days in which we live ... and here in England, though we object to it resolutely in the form of street barricades and insurrectionary pikes ... the tramp of its million feet is in all streets and thoroughfares, the sound of its bewildered thousandfold voice is in all writings and speakings, in all thinkings and modes and activities of men.[16]

Gladstone's interest in democracy was also aroused by reading de Tocqueville, whom he later praised as 'the Burke of our age'.[17] De Tocqueville had equated the word 'democracy' mainly with the ascendancy of the middle classes, but by 1848 the word was being used, as Henry Maine noted, 'very much with its ancient meaning, the government of the Commonwealth by the Many'.[18] In 1861, John Stuart Mill, in his *Considerations on Representative Government*, distinguished between two different kinds of democracy:

The pure idea of democracy, according to its definition, is the government of the whole people by the whole people, equally represented. Democracy as commonly conceived and hitherto practised, is the government of the whole people by a mere majority of the people exclusively represented. The former is synonymous with the equality of all citizens; the latter, strangely, confounded with it, is a government of privilege, in favour of the numerical majority, who alone possess practically any voice in the State. This is the inevitable consequence of the manner in which the votes are now taken, to the complete disfranchisement of minorities.[19]

Mill was a radical Liberal, but his Tocquevillian fear of the tyranny of the majority was shared by the high Tory Robert Cecil. Robert Cecil was one of the most articulate and outspoken opponents of democracy in the mid-Victorian period. Paul Smith has accounted for Cecil's attitude by reference to his reading and shy personality.[20] But Cecil's opposition to democracy, which was shared by most of the contemporary political élite, was prompted by familial and financial, rather than individual, considerations. He feared that a democratic government would expropriate the wealth of families like his own. In 1860, for example, Cecil argued that there was a close connection between Gladstone's Budget, which raised income tax to 10d. in the pound, and the Liberal government's reform bill. He declared that the incidence of taxation was 'the vital question of modern politics'. He believed that artisans cared for democracy only because they hoped that it would end inequalities in wealth:

The struggle between the English constitution on the one hand, and the democratic forces that are labouring to subvert it on the other, is now, in reality, when reduced to its simplest elements and stated in its most prosaic form, a struggle between those who have, to keep what they have got, and those who have not, to get it.[21]

Cecil claimed that 'Wherever democracy has prevailed, the power of the State has been used in some form or other to plunder the well-to-do classes for the benefit of the poor.'[22] He supported this statement by reference to modern America and France, but his argument was an old one, which harked back to Aristotle's *Politics*. During the parliamentary debate on the 1866 Liberal reform bill, Cecil asked Gladstone, who was a noted classical scholar, 'whether he cannot find in the range of ancient literature much that will teach a man to dread democracy?'[23]

Cecil's fear of democracy was also linked with his fear of revolution. He collected many books on the French Revolution of 1789 and wrote several articles on its historiography. In 1858 he claimed that the 'symmetrical reformers' who advocated the principle of one man, one vote were the 'children of Abbé Sieyès and the doctrinaires'.[24] He believed that the history of France in the 1790s proved that democracy led to tyranny rather than to individual freedom.

Cecil's fear of French-style revolution was widely shared, despite the relative prosperity and security of mid-Victorian Britain. The continental revolutions of 1848 and 1830 were still fresh in the public memory, while in the late 1850s and early 1860s, the political *status quo* was dramatically challenged in Italy, India, the United States, Mexico and Poland. In Ireland, the emergence of revolutionary fenianism illustrated that even in the United Kingdom there were some who rejected the methods (if not the objectives) of constitutional reformers. Many contemporaries believed that the instability of the age had its origin in one cardinal event: the first French Revolution.

The leaders of mid-Victorian Britain had grown up in the shadow of the French Revolution, which, even in the 1830s, 'was still the fecund mother of potent dreams and also of potent nightmares'.[25] Brian Harrison, in an apt analogy, has noted that 'The memory of the Terror haunted educated early Victorians just as Belsen and Auschwitz haunt the modern intellectual.'[26] The French Revolution was the subject of a rapidly growing number of historical accounts, not only in France, but also in Britain. Thomas Carlyle's *The French Revolution* – which stressed the activities of the revolutionary sans-culottes – exercised a powerful influence over Charles Dickens, who published his *A Tale of Two Cities* in 1859. This introduced the 'horrors' of the French Revolution to a new and extensive popular readership.[27]

Mid-Victorians regarded the French Revolution not as past history, but as unfinished business. Disraeli, for example, in his famous 1864 'apes and angels' speech at Oxford University, referred to 'that mighty movement popularly called the French Revolution, which has not yet ended, and which is certainly the greatest event that has happened in the history of man'. He claimed that the revolution had changed every political constitution in Europe.[28] Disraeli's interest in the French Revolution was shared by Gladstone, who added to his knowledge of the subject by reading de Tocqueville's *L'Ancien Régime* in 1861 and Michelet's *Histoire de la Révolution* in 1866. When Gladstone introduced the Liberal Reform Bill in 1866, Disraeli reminded him that in 1831 he had claimed that a much more moderate reform bill would subvert the social and political order. Gladstone acknowledged his volte-face, but pointed out that Disraeli had also changed his stance since he had endorsed the French Revolution in his 1833 poem, *The Revolutionary Epick*.

The shadow of the French Revolution hung over the parliamentary debates on reform in the mid-1860s. When Gladstone supported the principle of franchise extension, in 1864, he stressed that he was opposed to any 'sudden and sweeping measure ... which might deserve the epithet of revolutionary'. He reminded MPs that most of them had been brought up under the influence of 'those lamentable excesses of the first French Revolution, which produced here a terrible reaction, and went far to establish the doctrine that the masses of every community were in permanent antagonism with the laws under which they lived'. But Gladstone believed that times had changed, that the ghost of the French Revolution had finally been laid, and that therefore it was now safe to advocate this proposition:

> That every man who is not presumably incapacitated by some consideration of personal unfitness or of political danger is morally entitled to come within the pale of the Constitution. Of course, in giving utterance to such a proposition, I do not recede from the protest I have previously made against sudden, or violent, or excessive, or intoxicating change.[29]

Gladstone gave the impression, despite his emphatic opposition to revolutionary change, that he had embraced the natural rights ideology associated with the French Revolution. This alarmed *The Times*, which thundered:

> This is the language of sweeping and levelling Democracy, of men who have emancipated themselves from the divine right of Kings in order to fall into the equally dangerous fallacy of the divine right of multitudes ... It is Equality against Liberty, Theory against Practice, abstract dogmatism against experience, confusion between the ends and the means.[30]

Robert Lowe, who wrote for *The Times*, declared that Gladstone's arguments in favour of the enfranchisement of working men amounted 'to that assumption of the *a priori* rights of man which formed the terror and ridicule of that grotesque tragedy, the French Revolution'.[31] Lowe dismissed the argument that a large reduction of the borough franchise would settle the reform question by recalling the many occasions when the French Revolution was declared to have ended, only for 'the ground ... to sink again next day!'[32]

Since French democracy was associated with the excesses of the revolution, many British reformers dwelt on the more peaceful democratic example of the United States. Both Cobden and Bright admired American democracy and Lowe accused Bright of wanting to 'Americanize' British institutions. Yet the electoral system of the United States in the mid-nineteenth century fell a long way short of representative democracy, both at the state and federal level. The federal franchise was generally wider than the British parliamentary franchise, but suffrage qualifications varied widely from state to state. Both African Americans and native Americans were generally excluded from the franchise, as were unnaturalized immigrants, who were a large and increasing proportion of the population. In the United States in the 1860s, the proportion of adult males with the vote was less than half that in France after the revolution of 1848. Both Cobden and Bright admitted that the United States did *not* have manhood suffrage. In 1858 Bright described the American electoral system as *household* suffrage, equal electoral districts and the ballot, which was what he wanted for Britain.

In the United States a 'democrat' was a party man and most American politicians avoided using the term 'democracy'. This was especially true of the early Republicans, like Abraham Lincoln. Although it has been claimed that Lincoln regarded democracy as a religion, he never used the word in his speeches, not even in his 1864 Gettysburg Address.[33] On that occasion, he famously referred to 'Government of the people, by the people, for the people', which echoed Mill's recent definition of 'pure democracy'. But neither on that, nor on any other occasion did Lincoln explicitly associate the concept of popular government with the principle of 'one man, one vote'. Lincoln's reluctance to embrace 'democracy' was echoed by Congress. When the Capitol, in Washington DC, was enlarged and embellished in the 1850s and 1860s, the new dome was decorated with Brumidi's fresco of the 'Apotheosis of Washington'. Democracy was not represented in the Capitol building until Bartlett's frieze 'The Apotheosis of Democracy' was completed in 1916.[34]

Despite the limitations of the American franchise, it was more extensive than the British franchise in the mid-Victorian period. That fact, together with the American rejection of a hereditary monarchy and aristocracy, prompted British Conservatives to describe the United States as a democracy. Robert Cecil, for example, called the US 'the first modern instance of the application of the democratic theory to the government of a large state'.[35] He regarded the outbreak of the American Civil War in 1861 as a defeat for democracy since 'Democratic change now lacks the one recommendation that has power with the English mind – practical success.' Cecil claimed that the course of events in America had prompted MPs to lose their recent enthusiasm for parliamentary reform.[36]

The British appetite for democratization, which was lessened by the outbreak of the American Civil War, was quickly revived in 1865 by the victory of the North. Bright hailed the defeat of the Confederacy as 'the event of our age' and observed that 'the friends of freedom everywhere should thank God and take courage'.[37] In the following year, Russell's

Liberal government introduced a new reform bill, which Gladstone defended by reference to North America:

> Recent events which have taken place on the other side of the Atlantic have demonstrated to us how, by enlarging the franchise, augmented power can be marshalled on behalf of the government and increased energy given to the action of a nation.[38]

The victory of the North encouraged British radicals to revive the reform campaign. *Essays on Reform*, published in 1867, was peppered with references to the US and admiration for American democracy was voiced in radical papers like *Reynolds's News* and *The Bee-hive*. This sentiment assisted both the return of reform to the centre of the political stage in 1866 and its triumph in 1867.

Nevertheless, Disraeli insisted that the 1867 Tory reform bill was not a democratic measure:

> We do not ... live and I trust it will never be the fate of this country to live under a democracy. The propositions which I am going to make tonight certainly have no tendency in that direction.[39]

Disraeli claimed, indeed, that the bill was designed to maintain the traditional equipoise of the constitution:

> If there are checks and counterpoises in our scheme, we live under a constitution of which we boast that it is a Constitution of checks and counterpoises. If the measure bears some reference to existing classes in this country, why should we conceal from ourselves ... the fact that this country is a country of classes, and a country of classes it will ever remain.[40]

Many of the safeguards in the Bill were, however, removed during its passage through the Commons, so that the bill became, in the words of Asa Briggs, 'far more democratic than Disraeli, or indeed, most of his opponents, had ever intended'.[41] Yet even after the passage of the reform bill, Disraeli denied, in a major speech at Edinburgh, that the new form of household suffrage had established democratic government.[42] In 1872 he told Lord Derby that the 1867 Act 'only restored to the working classes the electoral privileges which they had before 1832 in the boroughs where scot-and-lot vote existed'. He noted that although the total of registered electors in the UK was not much more than a quarter of all adult males, 'this is the system which by opponents on both sides is said to be a near approach to universal suffrage!'[43]

In the longer term, however, the consequences of the 1867 Reform Act were more democratic than Disraeli realized.[44] Robert Cecil's fears that reform would prove to be 'a leap absolutely in the dark', which would 'bring democracy to us, if not at once, at least by stages', proved largely justified.[45] When Cecil was prime minister, in the late Victorian period, even he accepted that the weight of political power had shifted irreversibly towards the masses. Conservatives no longer sought equipoise between the classes; they sought, instead, to traditionalize the masses. The age of 'Tory democracy' had arrived.

Notes

1. W.L. Burn, *The Age of Equipoise: A Study of the Mid-Victorian Generation* (London: George Allen and Unwin, 1964), p. 17.
2. G.M. Young, *Victorian England: Portrait of an Age* (London: Oxford University Press, 1960 edn), p. 78.
3. Burn, *The Age of Equipoise*, p. 7.
4. Ibid., p. 9.
5. *Hansard*, 3rd series, 153 (1859), c. 479.
6. 'The Conservative Surrender', *Quarterly Review*, 123 (1867), p. 557.
7. J. Vincent and M. Stenton, eds, *McCalmont's Parliamentary Poll Book 1832–1918* (Brighton: The Harvester Press, 1971 edn), p. xix.
8. W.F. Monypenny and G.E. Buckle, *The Life of Benjamin Disraeli, Earl of Beaconsfield* (2 vols, London: John Murray, 1929 edn), II, pp. 371–2: Disraeli to the Queen, 1 May 1868.
9. Roland Quinault, '1848 and Parliamentary Reform', *The Historical Journal*, 31 (1988), p. 845.
10. K. Theodore Hoppen, 'The franchise and electoral politics in England and Ireland 1832–85', *History*, 70 (1985), p. 208.
11. *Hansard*, 3rd series, 94 (1851), c. 853.
12. The painting, by Sir Francis Grant, was exhibited at the Royal Academy in 1854.
13. Lord Robert Cecil, 'The Budget and the Reform Bill', *Quarterly Review*, 107 (1860), p. 542.
14. *Hansard*, 3rd series, 99 (1852), c. 279.
15. Quoted in G.M. Trevelyan, *The Life of John Bright* (London: Constable, 1913), p. 364.
16. Thomas Carlyle, *Latter-day Pamphlets* (London, 1850), pp. 7–8.
17. M.R.D. Foot and H.C.G. Matthew, eds, *The Gladstone Diaries III 1840–47* (Oxford: Clarendon Press, 1974), pp. 24 and 39. W.E. Gladstone, 'Kin Beyond The Sea', in *Gleanings of Past Years* (London, 1879), p. 203.
18. Sir Henry Sumner Maine, *Popular Government* (Indianapolis, IN: Liberty Classics, 1976 edn), pp. 90–92.
19. John Stuart Mill, *Considerations on Representative Government* (London, n.d.), p. 126.
20. Paul Smith, *Lord Salisbury on Politics* (Cambridge: Cambridge University Press, 1972), pp. 29–30.
21. Cecil, 'The Budget and the Reform Bill', p. 523.
22. Ibid., p. 524.
23. *Hansard*, 3rd series, 183 (1866), c. 1523.

24. Lord Robert Cecil, 'The Theories of Parliamentary Reform', *Oxford Essays*, IV (London, 1858), p. 67.
25. George Kitson Clark, *Peel and the Conservative Party: A Study in Party Politics 1832–41* (London: Cass, 1964 edn), pp. 320–21.
26. Brian Harrison, 'The Sunday Trading Riots of 1855', *Historical Journal*, 8 (1965), p. 219.
27. J.M. Roberts, *The French Revolution* (Oxford: Oxford University Press, 1978), pp. 149–50.
28. Monypenny and Buckle, *Life of Disraeli*, II, p. 107.
29. *Hansard*, 3rd series, 175 (1864), c. 324.
30. *The Times*, 12 May 1864.
31. *Hansard*, 3rd series, 178 (1865), c. 1424.
32. A. Patchett Martin, *Life and Letters of the Rt. Hon. Robert Lowe Viscount Sherbrooke* (2 vols, London, 1893), II, p. 293: Lowe to Henry Sherbrooke, 7 May 1866.
33. Roy P. Basler, ed., *Abraham Lincoln: His Speeches and Writings* (Cleveland, OH: The World Publishing Company, 1946), p. 42.
34. See Thomas P. Somma, *The Apotheosis of Democracy 1908–16: The Pediment for the House Wing of the United States Capitol* (Newark, DE: University of Delaware, 1995).
35. [Lord Robert Cecil], 'Democracy on its trial', *Quarterly Review*, 110 (1861), p. 250.
36. Ibid., p. 284.
37. R.A.J. Walling, ed., *The Diaries of John Bright* (London: Cassell, 1930), p. 289: entry for 23 April 1865.
38. *The Times*, 7 April 1866.
39. *Hansard*, 3rd series, 186 (1867), c.7.
40. Ibid., c. 25.
41. Asa Briggs, *Victorian People* (London: Penguin, 1965 edn), p. 293.
42. *The Times*, 30 October 1867.
43. John Vincent, ed., *A Selection from the Diaries of Edward Henry Stanley, 15th Earl of Derby (1826–93)*, Camden fifth series, 4 (1994), p. 103: entry for 30 March 1872.
44. See John Davis and Duncan Tanner, 'The Borough Franchise after 1867', *Historical Research*, 69 (1990), pp. 306–27.
45. Cecil, 'The Budget and the Reform Bill', pp. 539–40.

CHAPTER FIVE

Equipoise and the myth of an open élite: new men of wealth and the purchase of land in the equipoise decades, 1850–69

David Brown

Professor Burn's argument in favour of labelling the period 1852–67 'an age of equipoise' depended on the existence of several influences for social cohesion, such as rising living standards and the abeyance of 'forces of disruption' and, more relevantly to the present purpose, the dominance of a relatively closed landed élite. He argued that entry into the landed élite continued as it had done for centuries and accepted that it was an ambition shared by leading members of the bourgeoisie. At the same time he believed that this mobility was limited in extent and that the class structure of the 1850s was more rigid than that of the 1950s. Certainly Burn did not consider whether bourgeois infiltration of the aristocracy accelerated during his period of study and if this contributed to equipoise.[1] In this, Burn was conspicuously overlooking the prevalent view in his era that most leading businessmen or their descendants acquired land because of its value as a status symbol and in successive generations often neglected or abandoned their business careers, a haemorrhaging of talent which Sir John Habakkuk argued had ruinous consequences for Britain's economic performance after 1870. The apotheosis of such thinking was marked by Martin Wiener's *English Culture and the Decline of the Industrial Spirit* of 1981.[2]

Many historical economists, most notably Donald McCloskey, have challenged the claim of entrepreneurial failure;[3] Bill Rubinstein[4] and later Lawrence and Jeanette Stone[5] have also questioned what the Wiener thesis was saying about the purchase of landed estates. This has led to an active debate, particularly between Rubinstein and Michael Thompson, who has maintained the view that most of the super-wealthy in the period up to 1880 continued to buy landed estates of above 2000 acres. Although Habakkuk in his latest book now contends that only a minority of new men of wealth bought landed estates, he still believes that 'it remained the ambition of the wealthiest of the new rich to join this landed élite'.[6] All this has formed part of a much larger debate about the nature of the landed élite and the reasons for its survival. On one hand, there are those who would agree with Burn's view of a relatively closed élite. The Stones, for example, extend it to the whole period between 1540 and 1880. Rubinstein would not go as far as that, but he does believe that there was an increased disinclination of new men of wealth to buy land between 1832 and 1885 which contributed to 'the apogee of the landed aristocracy as a ruling class ... significantly more closed to newcomers than its predecessors fifty or a hundred years before'. An alternative view, proposed by P.J. Cain and A.G. Hopkins for the period from 1688 to 1914, suggests that the aristocracy formed an alliance with the business interests of the City of London from the late eighteenth century, an alliance which provided the basis for Britain's economic and imperial success.[7]

The purpose of this chapter is to examine whether the 'equipoise decades' were ones of relatively little movement into the landed élite and if this was a major reason for the social stability Burn believed characterized the period. Based on interim results of the first comprehensive study of all purchases by the 'new wealthy' between 1780 and 1879, it will first examine the decennial rate of purchase of landed estates by 352 new men of wealth between 1780 and 1879 to see whether the equipoise decades stand out as exceptional. Then it will focus more narrowly on the land market in the two equipoise decades, 1850–69, to give some idea of the volume and nature of purchases made during the period and to relate the results to current debates, particularly about the relationship between the aristocracy and the bourgeoisie. Finally, it will address the issue of the myth of an open élite and the reasons for the British aristocracy's ability to maintain its supremacy until the end of the nineteenth century.

Before starting to examine the level of land purchase in Britain by new men of wealth, some consideration is needed of the size of landed estate which such men required to become landed gentlemen. Rubinstein has employed a limit of 5000 acres on one occasion and 2000 acres (the criterion for inclusion adopted by John Bateman in his *Great Landowners of Great Britain* of 1883) on another, and has criticized those who prefer a limit of 1000 acres. However, John Beckett in his study of the English aristocracy distinguished three bands within the landed élite which, taken together, suggest a much lower level than either of Rubinstein's.[8] Beckett defined the aristocracy as being composed of owners of over 3000 acres with a commensurate rental (in 1873 terms), who thereby enjoyed a national significance. Owners of 1000 to 3000 acres formed the squirearchy, who each dominated a parish or two and had a regional significance. Finally, there were the owners of landed estates between 300 and 1000 acres, the landed gentry, whose influence was largely limited to their immediate country.

Such a division is obviously not hard and fast, and other potential measures of status could be adopted – such as the education of the children of new men of wealth at élite schools, the intermarriage of new wealth with old wealth, the acquisition of either positions of status (such as a parliamentary seat, a title or a place on the magistrate's bench) or of the trappings of status (such as mansions). While each one is an important indicator, they are all flawed in one way or another. Take as an example one frequently used indicator, the ownership of a title. Many substantial landowners never entered the nobility, or, like the Earls of Leicester and Yarborough, only did so after a very long period. On the other hand, 21 per cent of the peerage in 1883 owned under 2000 acres and so by Beckett's definition were not aristocrats. While these other indicators are useful, the most significant measure is the acquisition of a landed estate, as by definition it formed the basis of the traditional élite. Furthermore, using Beckett's bands, some precision can be achieved in assessing the extent to which a new man of wealth entered the landed élite.

As an illustration of the merits of this approach, some consideration of what it meant to be a landed gentleman is worthwhile. Like members of all élites, the landed élite are identifiable by their conspicuous behaviour. They own a mansion in a landscaped park. They enjoy landed pursuits, especially hunting and fishing; they are the leaders of local society, exercising patronage and philanthropy. On their property they build model cottages, chapels and schools and they are often called 'the squire'. They marry persons in the same social group. In other words, they behave like landed gentlemen. To do so they do not always need 2000 acres, never mind 5000. Indeed, as Beckett's bands suggest, many long-established and highly respectable landed families would not break through the lower barrier. To take one local example, there were six long-established families in an eight-mile radius of Tamworth on the borders of Staffordshire and Warwickshire who fail to gain entry into Bateman and yet were members of the local landed élite, serving as magistrates, poor-law guardians, political activists and in general behaving like landed gentlemen, who thus easily found their way into *Burke's Landed Gentry*, ranging from the Reverend George Inge of Thorpe Constantine with 1607 acres through F.S. Pipe Wolferstan of Statfold with 1404 acres down to C.W. Repington of Amington Hall with 718 acres.[9]

Therefore, as Rick Trainor noted for the Black Country,[10] and Colin Owen remarked of the Burton 'beerage',[11] many businessmen who bought estates of less than 2000 acres were 'gentrified'. They did live in mansions situated in parks and often had home farms. The wealthier ones bought or rented Scottish shooting lodges to participate in what had always been a symbol of landed privilege – game.[12] Others, like Benjamin Gibbons, the inheritor of a Black Country ironmaster's fortune, spent heavily, indulging their love of foxhunting. They endorsed the prevailing hierarchical system of society, becoming magistrates or officers in the local yeomanry. Many moved in landed circles and the wealthier ones intermarried with the aristocracy. In their rural estates, they were often philanthropic if not downright paternalistic. Again, like the Wolferstans and Repingtons, they often gained entry into *Burke's Landed Gentry*. Even if they continued their business activities, most purchasers had entered landed society. Thus the *Dictionary of Business Biography* describes the businessman, Edward Hermon, as living 'the life of a country gentleman' on 900 acres at Wyfold Court in Oxfordshire bought at the end of the equipoise era, although he also used this as a place of business.[13]

There were those who bought land for other reasons than simply the acquisition of status. For example, Mary Rose argued that Robert Hyde Greg bought property largely as a diversification. Again, William Hanbury Sparrow bought over 9000 acres of land in the ten years after the repeal of the Corn Laws, both to pursue an interest in farming and to prove to Tory protectionists that agriculture could still pay. Nevertheless, their descendants often used these purchases to become country gentlemen, as did two of the Gregs and two of the Hanbury Sparrows; indeed, Robert Hyde Greg himself spent a large sum in rebuilding Coles in Hertfordshire as a mock Elizabethan mansion in a 140-acre park in 1847.[14] Moreover, purchases of land as pure investment fell in line with rents during the nineteenth century. George Palmer had invested over £100,000 on 3651 acres by 1878 while continuing to live near his biscuit works at Reading but found, like some others, that his investment did not pay in cash terms. Nevertheless, one of his sons found it a useful social investment, using the estate as a base to become a Tory MP and a knight.[15] More alert businessmen than Palmer must have recognized that by the late 1860s (with 'land hunger' driving up prices so that purchases paid under 3 per cent return even at the high rentals of the time) land was not a viable long-term economic investment; it could only pay if quickly resold at a profit. The fact that there were those who continued to buy and retain land shows that this was often a social investment, especially as nearly all of these purchases included a mansion or the site for a mansion.

Although there have been studies of the purchases of landed estates by the new wealthy, they have either been impressionistic (like Habakkuk's) or partial studies either of their activities in individual counties (like Stone's or Knapp's[16]) or by samples of the very wealthy (like Michael Thompson's); no comprehensive study has ever been undertaken. Therefore, following Michael Thompson's advice 'not to venture into uncertain cultural waters until the firm ground of material evidence has been explored',[17] such a study has been started. By May 1996, 682 new men of wealth had been identified who bought landed estates of over 1000 acres and £1000 rental in the United Kingdom between 1780 and 1880. The purchasers have been broken down into the three categories identified by Beckett, and various details about their probate estates, source of wealth and so on have been included. Those like Henry Perkins, who bought land clearly as a speculation or with no intention of residing upon their estate, have been excluded. Subsequently, a closer examination of the equipoise decades for the purpose of this chapter was undertaken, producing a group of 423 men of wealth (many not in the May 1996 list).[18]

From these 682 'new-wealth' purchasers, the precise date of purchase of just over a half can be determined absolutely. A decennial breakdown of these 352 purchasers produces the result shown in Figure 5.1. This suggests that, at least in terms of estate purchase, the élite may have been becoming more open after 1830, not less, as Rubinstein argued. More specifically, the equipoise decades, far from seeing a decline of upward social mobility, as Geoffrey Best claimed, actually saw an acceleration of the process.[19] Indeed, in the conditions operating after 1846, such a picture is what one would anticipate. As Thompson demonstrated over forty years ago, the land market was expanding at this time, as some established landholders decided to sell land either due to debt problems or fears over the long-term profitability of land after the repeal of the Corn Laws; William Hanbury Sparrow was able to buy estates cheaply for exactly these reasons.[20] Moreover, only a few existing aristocrats were in the market for such estates – either those who were selling outlying estates to consolidate their holdings (like the Earl of Lichfield in Staffordshire) or those using 'new wealth' derived from mineral or urban rents (like the Duke of Cleveland's purchase of the 6000-acre Battle Abbey estate in 1857, or the Duke of Northumberland's extension of his estate commented upon by Burn himself).[21] The increasing rarity of such purchases in the face of the growing financial muscle of the bourgeoisie was commented upon by the leading Lancashire estate agent Thomas Fair in 1864: 'the old families [would] soon be unable to compete with the fortunes of men of commerce'.[22] Although a few estates were dispersed,

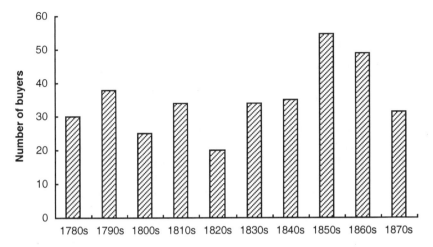

5.1 Estate purchase by new men of wealth in the United Kingdom, 1780–1879

usually by sale to the sitting tenants, such morcellement characterizes the sale of estates after the onset of the Great Agricultural Depression. The demand for land by new men of wealth was such that although more estates were in the market, the price of purchase was rising, reaching a high point just after 1870, a phenomenon described by later commentators as 'land hunger'.[23]

Focusing now more closely on the narrow period of 1850–69, further research from the 'domestic occurrences' section of the *Gentleman's Magazine*, the *Estates Gazette* 1858–70, county directories, various editions of *Walford's County Families* and the return of owners has yielded a group of 423 new men of wealth who were buying landed estates in the United Kingdom during this period. This includes men who had begun their purchases before 1850 or continued to do so after 1870, but only their purchases between these two dates have been included. The research attempts to distinguish sources of 'new wealth', although such neat categorization is very difficult as many new men of wealth had their fingers in many pies. For example, several cotton manufacturers also became merchants or bankers or invested in railways.[24] Nevertheless, as far as possible they have been categorized by what seems to be their main economic activity. Furthermore, although their entrance into the ranks of the landowners can be dated precisely in many cases, in others estates were assembled piecemeal over the period and these have been separately distinguished. Finally, where purchase prices were known, these figures have been included. To give some sense of the approximate cost of the other estates, thirty years' purchase of their rental value (excluding mineral or urban estates where possible) in the 1873 return has been calculated. This rough and ready expedient probably understates the true purchase price as mansion house estates were fetching more than this figure over much of the period. Ideally a more precise multiplier, representing the average years' purchase for each year, would have been used; but the only series, calculated by Norton, Trist and Gilbert in 1889, is unsuited to this purpose for two reasons. First, it is based on such a small sample that it can only give some idea of the general drift of prices and it is probably wise to follow Thompson's example of averaging these figures over at least a three-year period. More critically, it consists of 'purely agricultural land', excluding 'fancy property'; as nearly all of the estates counted here included a mansion, they would be excluded from this series.[25]

Several trends emerge from this study. First, these figures prove that there was a considerable volume of land purchase made by new men of wealth during the period. Using the thirty years' purchase formula, these 423 purchasers together paid £43,351,050 for 1,853,807 acres – on average each was paying £102,485 for 4383 acres at a rate of £23 per acre. As Figure 5.2 shows, the purchase of large estates continued throughout the period. Furthermore, in comparison with the Norton, Trist and Gilbert series of land prices, which include the period 1850–70, there is no clear evidence of a simple relationship between movements in year's purchase and the amount of money spent on land – the 1850s suggest a direct relationship whereas the 1860s hint at an inverse one. Although the amount spent on purchasing landed estates increased over the 1860s, the main reason for the differences between individual years was the activity of individual buyers: for example, Lord Overstone's spending of over £1.4 million on landed estates in 1860 accounts for that year's disproportionate size. While it is certainly true that new men like Overstone usually considered carefully the price of estates, the fact remains that they rarely cashed in these assets when prices began to fall in the 1870s. All this again suggests that it was the desire of new men of wealth to acquire land permanently rather than the speculative opportunities presented by low land prices which lay behind their purchases.[26]

Turning now to the occupational background of the 423 purchasers (Figure 5.3), there was a wide variety of sources of wealth. Merchants (including shipowners) were the largest single group, providing 22 per cent of all purchasers. However, finance and trade together only furnished 38 per cent, whereas industry supplied over 45 per cent. Of the largest group of industrialists, the manufacturers, one-half were textile manufacturers, of whom three-quarters were cottonmasters. In the

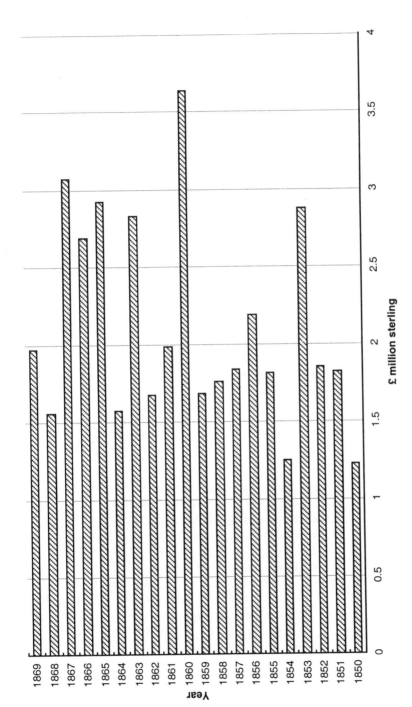

5.2   Land purchase by new men of wealth in the United Kingdom, 1850–69

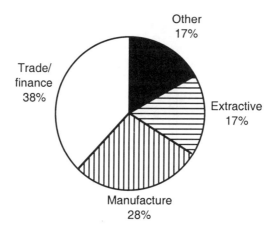

5.3 Source of wealth of *nouveau riche* land purchasers, 1850–69

extractive industries, ironmasters outnumbered those involved mainly in mining by nearly two to one. The fourth group, 'others', included a wide variety of occupations, the most significant ones being the law and civil engineering. There were only two changes in the profile of purchasers in this period. One was the growing number of those who made their money from railways largely as engineers but also as company promoters and solicitors. The other was the virtual absence of those who made their wealth through successful farming, although such men had been few in number since 1780 and only managed to penetrate the lower end of landed society. The only two exceptions in the equipoise decades, Matthew Marsh and Thomas Chirnside, had made their money from sheep farming but had been obliged to go to Australia to do so. A third man, James Caird, had also made his money out of farming, but largely by writing about it rather than actually doing it.

Turning to the wider issues of the relative significance of trade and finance and industry in economic growth and social change, caution must be exercised. For example, many of the wealthy industrialists moved into trade and finance to augment their wealth. However, while this breakdown does not disprove the view of Cain and Hopkins that the City had closer links with the aristocracy than industry, it does support the opinion that there was no hard-and-fast line between 'gentlemanly capitalists' and industrialists.[27] At the very least, while these figures do reflect the importance of trade and banking as sources of wealth, wealth generation from industry should not be underestimated. This view is supported by the fact that the occupational background of purchasers made little difference to the amount of money spent on landed estates. For example, the top ten buyers in terms of money spent consisted of three ironmasters, three bankers, two merchants and a textile manufacturer.[28]

Moving from the topmost to the middle ranks of the 423 purchasers, the typical buyer (based on the median) was spending £53,760 on acquiring an estate of 1285 acres and so joining the squirearchy. The considerable differences between the median and mean figures shown in Table 5.1 reflect an important trend among buyers. Many of the larger buyers were acquiring huge sporting estates of relatively low value; on the other hand, many of the buyers were acquiring some high-value land upon which a mansion and grounds were already situated. Thus when comparing the median figures with the means, the activities of these larger buyers serve to more than treble the acreage bought but only double the price paid and roughly halve the price paid per acre.

Table 5.1   Comparison of median and mean figures for new-wealth purchasers, 1850–69

	Median	Mean
Acreage bought	1,285	4,383
Purchase price (£)	53,760	102,485
Price per acre (£)	42	23

A breakdown of these 423 purchasers based on Beckett's model is also instructive. In total, 105 bought aristocratic estates, 179 gained estates of over 1000 acres and £1000 and 111 acquired gentry properties; the remaining 28 bought mansions in smaller estates but in one way or another lived as country gentlemen or were building estates which would become so after 1870. Those who bought smaller estates tended to do so in the vicinity of their place of work or in the Home Counties. Indeed, these figures do not fully reflect the probable growing number of smaller estates because examples of them are harder to discover and it is likely that short-range upward mobility would be greater than entry into the higher reaches of the landed élite. This impression is confirmed by contemporaries. In 1858, Lord Hatherton commented that in the vicinity of Staffordshire manufactures, 'where one of the old squirearchy has disappeared, many Gentry have sprung up – who have their villas and country residences neatly established over the country'. Nevertheless, the reduction in the average acreage bought if such small properties could be included would be offset by the fact that the figures also under-represent the acquisition of large Scottish and Irish estates for reasons discussed below.[29]

Only nine of these new purchasers were birds of passage who resold their estates before 1870, and their reasons for so doing are revealing. Although during the wider period from 1780 to 1880 there were a few who copied Josiah Bounderby in *Hard Times* in reselling their estates because they found that they preferred urban to landed society, only one of the 423 buyers in the equipoise decades, John Orr Ewing, might have done so (although the lack of a son and heir may have been as important).[30] The main reasons for resales were death or business failure. Although Rubinstein's study of wealthy probate estates since 1800 found 'there were no real life Charles Augustus Milvertons or even Augustus Melmottes in Britain', such a view of the universal virtue of Victorian businessmen is not sustained by this study. Taking Melmotte for a moment, Trollope based his character upon Albert Grant, the shady company promoter who seems to have flitted briefly into the squirearchy by the purchase of the Horstead estate in Suffolk in 1872. Within the equipoise decades one purchaser, John Sadleir, served as a model for yet another fictional fraudster, Merdle in Dickens's *Little Dorrit*. Sadleir committed suicide when his frauds were discovered and his estates had to be sold to satisfy creditors. Moreover, three sellers of estates in this period were obliged to do so to a greater or lesser extent by their business malpractice – George Hudson, Sir Morton Peto and John Attwood – all of whom had only acquired their estates in the 1840s.[31] Equally, buyers of estates could use sharp practice to secure them, as an example just outside the equipoise decades indicates. In the opinion of a judge in 1872, Richard Berridge was morally guilty of fraud in the way in which he had acquired the largest single estate in Ireland, although technically he had to be found innocent.[32]

Although few of the estates had to be resold, many were subsequently divided between heirs, as in the cases of James Morrison, William Hanbury Sparrow, Charles Cammell and Edward Sugden. The growing frequency of partible inheritance serves to reduce the size of individual estates during the period. Nevertheless, the fact that the subdivided estates were still sufficient to gain entry into the squirearchy does show that the desire to enter landed society remained the same – only that increasing numbers of businessmen did not consider that the order in which their offspring were born should determine which one was going to enter the landed élite.

The list of 423 purchasers is not comprehensive. For example, it includes only 37 men whose purchases were largely in Scotland and only 12 in Ireland.[33] This must under-represent the level of estate acquisition in such areas, considering both the activities of the encumbered estates court and Tom Devine's observation that 60 per cent of the large estates in the highlands and islands of Scotland had changed hands between 1820 and 1883. Unfortunately, these omissions are difficult to remedy in the apparent absence of any detailed national study of the purchasers in Ireland or Scotland. As a result, it is impossible to give an accurate geographical distribution of estates acquired.[34]

This is only one of the reasons why the survey understates the level of investment by the bourgeoisie in pursuing their landed ambitions. Apart from the under-recording of estate purchases in Scotland, Ireland and of smaller estates in general, other purchases could not be included simply because it proved impossible to date them accurately. For example, between 1845 and 1873, the trustees of James Brown, the Leeds wool manufacturer, added the 5500-acre Copgrove estate to the Rossington estate he had bought in 1838. Although Thompson states that his heir, James Brown junior, only withdrew from business to his estates after twelve years, this did not constitute sufficient evidence that the date of the second purchase was within the equipoise period, and so he was excluded.[35] Furthermore, it must be remembered that many buyers invested considerable sums in their estates. Mansion-building could be one such expense; Gathorne Hardy spent £32,988 to build Hemsted in Kent in 1859; New Lodge in Berkshire cost the family of Joshua Bates £35,000 and J.P. Heywood was charged £60,000 exclusive of decoration to construct Cloverley Hall in Shropshire.[36] In addition, new owners often indulged their whims about model farming. At the ultimate extreme Robert Campbell spent perhaps £250,000 on his industrial farm at Buscot in Berkshire, which obliged his trustees to sell the estate after his death.[37] Others spent more conservatively and wisely, but none the less they spent. Charles Mark Palmer spent £3600 on constructing a half-acre covered cattle stall at Grinkle Park in the North Riding, the largest of its kind. Estate improvement could be particularly costly to purchasers, particularly of highland estates. For example, Eric Richards calculates that Sir James Matheson spent over £500,000 on his Scottish estates after his purchase and reputedly drew no revenue during his lifetime from them. This was not an atypical example.[38] Another cost, both in time as well as money, was the variety of landed pursuits available to new purchasers – many engaged in foxhunting and nearly all of them became county magistrates. A few of the 423, such as Brooks the Manchester banker and property speculator, entered the higher ranks of the squirearchy by their landed purchases but then spent heavily in renting a country house and huge grouse moors like Glen Tana in

Aberdeenshire to complete the picture of a landed aristocrat.[39] Indeed, the expenditure of those who rented rather than bought landed estates, like David Bromilow, should not be overlooked. Bromilow rented the large Battlesden estate in Bedfordshire from 1863 but only fully entered the landed élite by the purchase of Bitteswell in Leicestershire during the 1880s. Nevertheless, he was already making a substantial annual investment in living as an aristocrat, even if only as a tenant.[40] Moreover, new money passed into the hands of the aristocracy by marriage, which prevented the dispersal of existing estates or allowed the acquisition of new ones. This of course is difficult to establish without very detailed records of estate debts and the wealth of the individuals, and almost impossible to quantify; but none the less it did happen. Certainly, shortly after the equipoise decades, the Earl of Rosebery's marriage to Mayer Rothschild's heiress in 1878 not only brought him the Mentmore estates but four years later allowed the purchase of the 2972-acre Malleny estate in Scotland for £125,000.[41]

To a certain extent, these landed ambitions must have caused a haemorrhaging of wealth and attention from their buyers' commercial interests, although on what scale, especially in comparison with Britain's industrial rivals, is hard to determine. The latest research suggests that this harmful effect was of a limited extent and commensurate with that experienced in Germany.[42] To look at one region, South Staffordshire, three of the four families (Hanbury Sparrow, George Jones, Foster and Walker) who bought aristocratic estates in the equipoise decades either withdrew from or ruined their businesses and lost their wealth. Most notoriously, the Walkers, the leading lights of the Patent Tree and Axle Company, allowed a cashier to defraud the firm of at least £75,000 which necessitated a reduction of share capital of £90,000.[43] In contrast to such neglect, historians have made much of those businessmen who sought status not in landed society but simply from the quality of their wares or their dominance of the business – like William Crawshay senior in South Wales or Herbert Minton in the Potteries. Nevertheless, this ambition might not apply to their heirs. William Crawshay told his eponymous son that 'a great House and Expensive Establishment will not fight our battle in trade', but as soon as the older man died, his offspring sold the house and estate at Hensol which had upset his father so much, only to buy a more expensive estate at Caversham in 1838 for some £100,000. Over the century two aristocrats (Lord Llanover and J.D. Berrington) and one squire (Henry Crawshay) bought their estates in part with Crawshay money.[44] Herbert Minton tried to turn down the chance of becoming a deputy lieutenant by saying, 'The fact is that I am not ambitious of worldly honours, but … am desirous of obtaining celebrity in the manufacture in which I am engaged.' However, Minton's nephew and heir, Colin Minton Campbell, while remaining an active businessman, had bought within three years of his succession a 500-acre landed estate at Woodseats and the right of shooting over 7000 acres.[45] Although there were some Walkers, there were many buyers like Campbell who did remain very successful businessmen, able to use railways to keep in close contact with work while enjoying their landed estate. Indeed, ownership of a landed estate, shooting and so on could be an important business acquisition. Certainly several purchasers, such as Hanbury Sparrow and William Orme Foster (like many of Thompson's sample of half millionaires who died between 1809 and 1860), enjoyed an 'aristocratic bourgeois' lifestyle, remaining successful businessmen after their landed acquisitions. Further, there were those like Lord Armstrong at Cragside in Northumberland who used their estates in part as business adjuncts to entertain potential customers.[46]

The case of Armstrong, ennobled in 1887, raises the issue of honours. Although several of the 423 acquired baronetcies, only three of them entered the peerage during the equipoise period – Denison, Loyd and Strutt. Although this may seem to confirm Burn's view of the closed nature of the landed élite, it does show that those who bought sizeable estates could enter the peerage. Strutt's peerage in 1856 was a particular breakthrough as he was the first industrialist to achieve that distinction. Already in 1847 Lord Hatherton had argued the case of James Watt junior in 1847, who had acquired 11,000 acres in Wales, saying that it would 'publish to the world that the Door of the House of Lords was open to distinction in arts as well as arms'. Although Hatherton did not persuade Lord Russell, Strutt's barony did announce to the world that industrialists as well as bankers could enter the nobility.[47]

To summarize: the increased activity in the land market between 1850 and 1869 noted by Thompson was largely the result of an acceleration in the purchasing activity of new men of wealth. Although these purchasers tended only to enter the squirearchy or the gentry by the purchase of a mansion, home farm and some labourers' dwellings, some of the largest accumulations of land of the century occurred during the period. Individuals like Morrison and Loyd, families like the Hardys and the Bairds and trusts like those of Denison and Thompson all bought large aristocratic estates during the twenty years between 1850 and 1869. These new men dominated the land market. Their only rivals were those few aristocrats whose sales elsewhere or non-agricultural incomes allowed them to compete, the occasional speculator or consortia of tenants. Far from being 'significantly more closed', British landed society was significantly more open.

Trying to assess the level of social mobility represented by this level of estate purchase is not easy. Altogether at the time of writing (December 1999), 1700 new men of wealth have been identified who bought estates of over 300 acres in the United Kingdom between 1780 and 1879. However, the most accurate figures for the total constituency of each social group (produced by Bateman in 1881)[48] only refer to England and Wales. Therefore Table 5.2 measures the purchasing activity of those new men who bought their estates in England and Wales between 1780 and 1879 against the total membership of each social group. This reveals a level of penetration into the aristocracy and squirearchy of over 21 per cent. This is significantly higher than the rate discovered by the Stones in their study of the purchase of large country houses in three English counties. The difficulty of detecting purchases of small mansion house estates again results in an increasing underestimate of the purchase of smaller estates; this accounts for the surprisingly low figure for new men among the gentry.

The gentrification of these leading members of the bourgeoisie over the century revealed in Table 5.2 was not a one-way process; it was mirrored by the long-term embourgeoisement of the aristocracy. Certainly the original hostility of conservative thinkers to these parvenus not only in their purchase of estates but also in their intermarriage with the aristocracy resounds through their diaries and published works even into the equipoise decades. In Shropshire, Sir Baldwin Leighton recorded with concern in his private diary every example of how his heavily indebted neighbours were forced to sell their estates to new men of wealth after 1840.[49] In literature, William Cobbett, R.S. Surtees and Anthony Trollope all satirized these new buyers, saving particular venom for the Jewish bankers and money-lenders. However, this hostility was already declining before the 'age of equipoise'. Many authors, like Dickens in *Hard Times*, recognized that old landed families like the Harthouses had to mix with the objectionable new rich like the Gradgrinds because of their economic difficulties.[50] The historians Cain and Hopkins have observed that there was already a growing alliance from the late seventeenth century between the City and the landed élite, forged by the events of the 1688 Revolution.[51] Moreover, as Boyd Hilton and Peter Mandler noted, by the 1820s a majority of the aristocracy had accepted a form of capitalist individualism. The 1832 Reform Act was consciously seen by Earl Grey and the Whigs as a means of forging an alliance with the middle classes and of maintaining a hierarchical social structure. Betty Kemp has portrayed the repeal of the Corn Laws as an attempt to preserve the landed interest by obliging them to adopt more modern farming methods and so be able to retain their

Table 5.2   Penetration of the landed élite in England and Wales, 1780–1879

Size of estate acres/rental	Social category	Total population	% of England and Wales owned	New rich entrants	New owners as % of total
3000+	Aristocracy	1,688	43.0	339 (355)	20 (21)
1000–2999	Squirearchy	2,529	13.0	452 (545)	18 (22)
300–999	Gentry	9,589	14.5	401 (492)	4 (5)
Total (300+)	Landed élite	13,806	70.5	1192 (1392)	9 (10)

Note: Figures in parentheses include 'dispersals'.

wealth in a free-trade economy. Already members of the landed élite were prepared to invest in estate development along capitalist lines and invest in transport enterprises and stocks and shares. Others, particularly the smaller ones, were prepared to become bankers, lawyers or civil servants. In 1864, the future Earl of Derby commented about Lord Claud Hamilton's chairmanship of a steam navigation company that 'the difficulty now is to find a peer or titled person not engaged in this kind of business'.[52] By the late nineteenth century many of them were company directors and not always token figureheads. To return to the squire of Statfold, F.S. Pipe Wolferstan, not only did he keep his estate intact but he was also able to build a model farm from his earnings as a lawyer and director of the LNWR. It is also worth considering that aristocrats had long gained some of their income as rentiers, just like many of the heirs of businessmen who were more shareholders than active entrepreneurs. As Ellis Wasson remarked, 'what preserved their power and their acres was ... an adjustment to the spirit of the new age'.[53] This narrowing of the distance between the two élites, together with the landed élite's increasing readiness to accept the new rich, was a major factor in the 'seamless' transition of leadership of the British élite from landowners to businessmen, particularly those of the City. As Cassis wrote, the merging of these two élites in the late nineteenth century 'was the formation of a renewed élite which added the financial power of the City to the privilege of the old aristocracy'.[54] In short, the impression Burn gives of a closed élite seems to be mistaken – the evidence suggests that there was a narrowing rather than a widening of the social divisions between the two social groups in the equipoise decades.

There will remain a few who are not wholly convinced by a case largely based upon estate purchases by the new rich. This level of penetration, 21 per cent of the aristocracy and squirearchy in England and Wales over one hundred years, could still be considered by some doubters too small to constitute an open élite. After all, in terms of honours, few of these new men actually gained much more than a baronetcy or reached the topmost level of landed society. Moreover, putting the figures another way, this level of upward social mobility only represents an average turnover of just over 5 per cent of the landed élite in each generation. Even during the equipoise decades, the 86 entrants into the aristocracy who can be absolutely pinpointed to this period only represent 3 per cent of this class's 2500 members in the United Kingdom in 1873.[55] Again, if this land purchase is expressed not as inflow to the landed élite but as outflow (by a proportion of the whole population of leading businessmen), the numbers may seem rather small. Anthony Howe reckoned that only 11.1 per cent of 351 leading cotton masters of Lancashire bought landed estates of over 1000 acres. Rubinstein calculated a very similar figure (11.8 per cent) from a study of 337 new men who left over £100,000 between 1873 and 1875.[56]

To deal with the latter problem first. Usually outflow figures are presented alongside inflow figures to give a better sense of the volume of mobility; until the current research, this has proved impossible. The only previous attempt, a sample of owners of 5000 acres and £5000 by Rubinstein, produced the result that only 12 per cent earned their family fortune between 1780 and 1883. There is good reason to think that this understates the purchasing activities of the new wealthy; apart from the high 5000-acre limit, 12 per cent of his sample were unknown, and new wealth could take time to translate into land. Moreover, wide 'outflow' studies give a misleading picture in part because only the wealthiest members of the middle class could hope to amass the considerable wealth required for entry into the landed élite. Therefore Thompson's studies of the purchasing activities of the super-rich for probate purposes gives a much fairer picture of the proportion of new wealthy who did enter the aristocracy. His research has shown that of 86 men who left over £500,000 for probate purposes between 1809 and 1879, 57 per cent bought landed estates in their lifetime and 19 per cent of their descendants did so too, often under trusts established by the wealth creator for the purpose. Those super-wealthy that did not buy land often had no legitimate children. Indeed, the equipoise research has shown that Thompson's research underestimated the purchase of landed estates by descendants – at least two, Seth Smith and Stephen Brunskill (heir to Henry Hewetson), were equipoise buyers of over 1000 acres, which would take the figure to 81 per cent. Further, it can take no account of men like George Philips, who expended nearly £700,000 on founding a landed family, and therefore appeared as 'insolvent' in the probate returns.[57]

Moreover, even if the open élite was a myth, it was a potent myth; its potency derived from the considerable numbers of new men of wealth who did enter the aristocracy and served as role models to their former peers. Certainly it was a myth which permeated the literature of the time. Take for example the archetypal fictional utilitarian Thomas Gradgrind, the former wholesale hardware merchant of Coketown. He became MP for the newly enfranchised town and promulgated his political economy. Yet despite his beliefs, he retired to a country mansion, Stone Lodge, on the moors a couple of miles from the town. He mixed with members of the landed élite like James Harthouse. Indeed, the entire Gradgrind School 'liked fine gentlemen. They pretended that they did not, but they did. They became exhausted in imitation of them; and they yaw-yawed their speech like them.' The myth enjoyed such currency in contemporary society that a foreign commentator, Hippolyte Taine, was convinced that 'almost every self-made man's ambition is to own an estate, establish his family in it, and enter the ranks of the local gentry'.[58]

Political historians have long accepted the role of myth in legitimizing political activity in general.[59] Indeed, leading politicians of the equipoise decades acknowledged the myth's role in legitimizing the entire political system. Lord Palmerston publicly extolled the social benefits of the fact that, unlike other countries, no 'impassable barriers ... exist in this country' to separate aristocracies of wealth or rank from the rest of society. Benjamin Disraeli argued that a succession of men with new wealth – Turkish merchants, West Indian planters, nabobs, loan-mongers and industrialists – emerged every half-century or so and at their zenith moved into land. All of them aspire 'to be "large-acred" and always will, as long as we have a territorial constitution; [this aspiration] was a better security for the preponderance of the landed interest than any corn-law'.[60] Society certainly recognized the continuing value of a landed estate as a means of acquiring status. It enabled one to become a magistrate and thus a member of the clique which essentially controlled local government until 1888.[61] Further, although the electoral influence of land was declining, even *The Economist*, the journal of free-market economics, famously remarked in 1870,

> Social consideration is a great and legitimate object of desire, and so great is the effect of this visibility of wealth upon social consideration that it would 'pay' a millionaire in England to sink half his fortune in buying 10,000 acres of land to return a shilling per cent and live upon the remainder, rather than live upon the whole without the land.[62]

Any myth, to be effective, must be sustained by a grain of truth; the weight of evidence produced here suggests that there was not a grain but a bushel to support it. Certainly someone with professional experience of the land market, Joshua Williams, the leading conveyancer, was persuaded by the number of middle-class men who bought their way into the landed élite to be able to write with sincerity in 1862 of 'a country like ours, possessing a powerful aristocracy, where every man who accumulates a fortune immediately lays it out in the purchase of land'.[63]

This trend continued after the equipoise decades. In 1875, Brodrick could still write of the middle class that although some of its members were increasingly content with civic dignities,

> The richest capitalists in manufacturing towns are deterred ... from aspiring to civic dignities. Their sense of self-importance and their sense of responsibility find a far more complete gratification in the colossal operations of trade, and in the management of country estates far removed from their place of business than is offered by a career of municipal statesmanship crowned with knighthood, or baronetcy itself.[64]

The perception that upward social mobility was available to all classes, supported by more than a sufficiency of examples, encouraged social cohesion and the acceptance of a hierarchical social system. Although there was often public dislike of the privilege and dominance of aristocracy, there was often private admiration. As Simon Gunn has shown, this was true even among those who never bought a landed estate, like the wealthy radical nonconformist James Watts who always displayed great pride in the fact that he had entertained Prince Albert at Abney Hall and secured a knighthood as a result. As Thackeray wrote in 1848, 'What a Peerage worship there is all through this free country.'[65] The belief in an open élite was perhaps an even more potent factor than the actual penetration of new men of wealth into landed society in preserving the hegemony of the aristocracy. As Habakkuk appositely pointed out, although a minority of new men of wealth purchased estates, this does not mean that the example of those who joined the landed élite did not have a 'powerful influence on all men of property'.[66]

This influence was part of a whole raft of closely related mechanisms which served to preserve the authority of the landed élite. The most obvious was the endorsement of the notion of 'self-help' and the publicity given to role models in books like Samuel Smiles's, *The Lives of the Engineers*, which emphasized the greater life chances available to those who used the opportunities furnished by mechanics' institutes and schools. Less directly, there were the attempts of evangelicals to indoctrinate the masses, not only by the growth of an Anglican-controlled education system, but also by church extension and renewed clerical enthusiasm. The growth of paternalism under the guise of philanthropy was subtly used by aristocrats to convert 'economic capital' to 'symbolic capital'.[67] They also helped to create an ethos in which the middle classes like Ebenezer Scrooge were encouraged to accept the duty of paternalism in part to maintain social cohesion. Nevertheless, the receptiveness of the bourgeoisie to aristocratic values, upon which all these mechanisms relied for their influence, suggests that the most crucial part of this intellectual system was the idea of an open élite, whether myth or not. As Thomas Escott, the Victorian literary journalist, perceptively wrote, the strength of English society was its blending of the three rival elements – the aristocratic, the plutocratic and the democratic ... the aristocratic principle is still paramount, it forms the foundation of our social structure, and has been strengthened and extended in its operation by the plutocratic.[68]

To return to Burn and the starting-point of this study: to the extent that equipoise did exist, it was not an acceptance of a rigid class system which helped to sustain it; rather the opposite. The evidence here drawn from the purchase of landed estates suggests that upward social mobility actually increased during the period. Moreover, if the open élite was a myth, there were more than sufficient role models to sustain it. Perhaps it is more useful to conclude this discussion by looking beyond Burn's narrow limits. The major characteristic of Britain for much of the whole century was its relative social calm despite strong forces for dislocation such as industrialization and urbanization. The perception of the openness of the British class system, sustained by a sufficiency of examples, seems to have been one of the crucial factors for this surprising level of social cohesion.

Notes

1. W.L. Burn, *The Age of Equipoise* (London: George Allen and Unwin, 1964), pp. 8, 253, 303–7, 314, 317–8 and 322–3. I must acknowledge the assistance of Sir John Habakkuk, Michael Thompson, Alan Metters, Valerie Purton, Janet Blacknell and the delegates at three seminars in the writing of this essay.
2. Asa Briggs, *The Age of Improvement* (London: Longmans Green & Co., 1959), p. 408; H.J. Habakkuk, *American and British Technology in the Nineteenth Century* (Cambridge: Cambridge University Press, 1967), pp. 177–8; M.J. Wiener, *English Culture and the Decline of the Industrial Spirit 1850–1980* (Cambridge: Cambridge University Press, 1981).
3. Donald McCloskey, *Enterprise and Trade in Victorian Britain* (London: Allen & Unwin, 1981), pp. 94–135.
4. W.D. Rubinstein, 'New Men of Wealth and the Purchase of Land in Nineteenth-Century Britain', *Past and Present*, XCII (1981), pp. 125–47.
5. L. and J.C.F. Stone, *An Open Elite 1540–1880* (Oxford: Clarendon Press, 1984).
6. F.M.L. Thompson, 'Life after death: how successful nineteenth-century businessmen disposed of their fortunes', *Economic History Review*, 2nd series, XLIII (1990), pp. 40–61; W.D. Rubinstein, 'Cutting up rich; a reply to F.M.L. Thompson', *EcHR*, XLV (1992), pp. 350–61 and Thompson, 'Stitching it together again', *EcHR*, XLV (1992), pp. 362–75; M.J. Daunton, 'Gentlemanly Capitalism and British Industry, 1820–1914', *Past and Present* CXXII (1989), pp. 119–58; H.J. Habakkuk, *Marriage, Debt and the Estates System: English Landownership 1650–1950* (Oxford: Clarendon Press, 1994), pp. 617 and 620.

7. W.D. Rubinstein, *Capitalism, Culture and Decline in Britain 1750–1990* (London: Routledge, 1993), pp. 147–8 and 140; see also Linda Colley, *Britons: Forging the Nation 1707–1837* (Yale: Yale University Press, 1992), pp. 147–94; P.J. Cain and A.G. Hopkins, *British Imperialism: Innovation and Expansion 1688–1914* (London: Longman, 1993).

8. J.V. Beckett, *The English Aristocracy 1660–1914* (Oxford: Blackwell, 1986), p. 50.

9. The others were J. Floyer of Hints Hall (1534 acres), Colonel R. Dyott of Freeford (1297 acres) and C.W. Swinfen Broun of Swinfen Hall (917 acres).

10. R. Trainor, 'The Gentrification of Victorian and Edwardian Industrialists', in A.L. Beier, D. Cannadine and James M. Rosenheim, *The First Modern Society: essays in English history in honour of Lawrence Stone* (Cambridge: Cambridge University Press 1989), pp. 167–97.

11. Bass owned only 2283 acres in 1883 but behaved aristocratically in terms of paternalism and building a mansion, like many leading Burton brewers: C. Owen, *The Development of Burton-upon-Trent* (Chichester: Phillimore, 1978), pp. 99–102.

12. For example Hamer Bass – *Tamworth Herald*, 20 December 1890 and 13 June 1895, and Brooks of Manchester – Leopold Hartley Grindon, *Manchester Banks and Bankers: historical, biographical and anecdotal* (Manchester, 1877), pp. 202–6.

13. D. Jeremy, ed., *Dictionary of Business Biography*, III (London: Butterworths, 1985), p. 178. Hermon is not counted among the 423 'equipoise' purchasers below as his purchase cannot be absolutely dated to the equipoise period; see also text above note 34.

14. Mary B. Rose, 'Diversification of Investment by the Greg Family, 1800–1914', *Business History*, 20/1 (1979), pp. 79–88.

15. Jeremy, *Dictionary of Business Biography*, IV (1985), p. 524.

16. R.O. Knapp, 'The making of a landed élite: Social mobility in Lancashire society', Ph.D., Lancaster University (1970).

17. F.M.L. Thompson, 'Business and landed élites in the nineteenth century' in F.M.L. Thompson, ed., *Landowners, capitalists and entrepreneurs: essays for Sir John Habakkuk* (Oxford: Clarendon Press, 1994), pp. 144–5.

18. Henry Perkins of Thriplow bought the 1355-acre Fowlmere estate in Cambridgeshire for £45,100 in 1867, but resold most of it almost immediately to John Mortlock of Melbourn and William Nash Woodham of Shepreth. *Estates Gazette* (1867), p. 235; *VCH Cambridgeshire*, VIII (1978) p.157; see Appendix for more detail about the methodology used.

19. However, he attributed this decline not to a reduced desire to enter the élite but to the forces of a reducing supply of estates and an increasing demand for them by the very rich. Geoffrey Best, *Mid-Victorian Britain 1851–1875* (London: Weidenfeld and Nicolson, 1971), pp. 252–4.

20. F.M.L. Thompson, 'The Land Market in the Nineteenth Century' *Oxford Economic Papers*, n.s. IX (1957), pp. 285–308; Shropshire Record Office, Loton Mss. Sir Baldwin Leighton's Diary December 1866; Black Country Museum, Sparrow Family Records, p.159.

21. Both non-agricultural rents and the desire to extend his Weston Park estate in Staffordshire and Shropshire led the Earl of Bradford to purchase the 3000-acre Tong Castle estate in 1855 for £180,000, despite severe

competition from the ironmaster George Jones: William Salt Library, R.M.C. Jeffery, 'The Durants of Tong Castle', undated pamphlet; Staffordshire Record Office D260/M/F/5/26/68, 20 November 1855.

22. G. Rogers, 'Social and Economic Change on Lancashire Landed Estates during the Nineteenth Century with special reference to the Clifton Estate 1832–1916', Ph.D., Lancaster University (1981), p. 70; Lancashire Record Office DDC1 1966 deposit Thomas Fair to Lady Clifton, 4 June 1864.

23. *Estates Gazette* (1879), p. 535.

24. Perhaps the best example of this was John Johnson who bought the St Osyth estate in Essex – his son was described as a grain merchant, foreign banker and steamship and coal owner in Debrett's *Baronetage and Knightage* (1881), p. 578.

25. Norton, Trist and Gilbert, 'A century of land values: England and Wales', *The Times*, 20 April 1889.

26. R. Michie, 'Income, Expenditure and Investment of a Victorian millionaire: Lord Overstone 1823–83', *Bulletin of the Institute of Historical Research*, LVIII (1985), pp. 59–77. See also Norman Mutton, 'The Foster family: a study of a midlands industrial dynasty 1786–1899', University of London Ph.D. (1974), pp. 213–16 – the capital value of Apley, bought by Foster in 1869, fell but the estate was retained although more would have been earned by selling and reinvesting in stocks and shares.

27. M.J. Daunton, "Gentlemanly capitalism' and British industry 1820–1914', *Past and Present*, CXXII (1989), pp. 119–58.

28. This contrasts with Rubinstein's research that commerce and finance were far more important sources of wealth than manufacturing or industry: W.D. Rubinstein, *Men of Property* (London: Croom Helm, 1981), p. 61.

29. Staffordshire Record Office D260/M/F/5/26/78, 2 August 1858.

30. Charles Dickens, *Hard Times* (1854; Penguin, 1969), pp. 196, 262–3 and 265; Anthony Slaven et al., eds, *Dictionary of Scottish Business Biography 1860–1960*, I (1986), pp. 356–8 under John Orr Ewing.

31. Rubinstein, *Men of Property*, p. 73. *Dictionary of Business Biography*, II, pp. 623–8; Anthony Trollope, *The Way We Live Now* (1875; Oxford, 1982) I, pp. 47–9, 311 and 422; II, pp. 43 and 311; Charles Dickens, *Little Dorrit* (1856/57); R.S. Lambert, *The Railway King* (London: George Allen and Unwin, 1934), pp. 158–9, 276 and 287; H. Peto, *Sir Morton Peto* (London: private collection, 1893), pp. 40–44 and 96; Stephen Forman, *Hylands* (Romford, 1990), pp. 51–9.

32. *Estates Gazette* (1872), p. 583, 'Jervis v Berridge'.

33. These figures of course overlook some of those 423 buyers who bought subsidiary estates in Ireland and Scotland.

34. T.M. Devine, *Clanship to Crofters' Clanship to crofters' war: the social transformation of the Scottish Highlands* (Manchester: Manchester University Press, 1994), p. 64; the only study known to the author of an estate sold by the encumbered estates court is W.A. Maguire, 'Lord Donegall and the Sale of Belfast', *Economic History Review*, XXIX (1976), pp. 570–84.

35. Thompson, 'Life after death', p. 55; cf. Kelly, *West Riding Directory* (1893) under Rossington.

36. Jill Franklin, *The Gentleman's Country House and its Plan 1835–1914* (London: Routledge, 1981), pp. 258–65.

37. J.R. Gray, 'An Industrial Farm Estate in Berkshire', *Industrial Archaeology*, VIII (1971), pp. 171–83.

38. E. Richards, *The Highland Clearances*, II (London: Croom Helm, 1985), pp. 456–7. Without this spending, he would certainly have died a millionaire.

39. Grindon, *Manchester Banks and Bankers*, pp. 202–6.

40. Walford, *County Families* (London: 1873) (London: 1878) and (London: 1881), under Bromilow; Kelly, *Leicestershire Directory* (1881) and (1891).

41. Richard Davis, *The English Rothschilds* (London: Collins, 1983), p. 174, *Estates Gazette* (1882), p. 152.

42. Hertmut Berghoff and Roland Möller, 'Tired Pioneers and dynamic newcomers? A comparative essay in German and English entrepreneurial history 1870–1914', *Economic History Review*, XLVII (1994), pp. 262–87.

43. *Tamworth Herald*, 29 January 1879.

44. J.P. Addis, *The Crawshay Dynasty. A study in industrial organisation and development, 1765–1867* (University of Wales Press: Cardiff, 1957) and Margaret Taylor, *The Crawshays of Cyfarthfa* (London: Robert Hale, 1967).

45. Staffordshire Record Office D260/M/F/5/5/2 H. Minton to Hatherton, 6 September 1854. *Estates Gazette* (1862) pp. 65 and 153.

46. Thompson, 'Life after death', p. 58.

47. Staffordshire Record Office D260/M/F/5/26/43, 16 September 1847.

48. J. Bateman, *The Great Landowners* (London: Harrison, 1883), pp. 501–15 reproduces his own tables from G.C. Brodrick, *English Land and English Landlords* (London: Cassell & Co., 1881), pp. 173–87. See also Appendix Note.

49. Shropshire Record Office. Loton Hall Mss. Sir Baldwin Leighton's diary (on microfilm).

50. An instructive example of these changing attitudes and the conversion of the myth of an open élite to reality from contemporary literature is provided by the Duke of Omnium. While publicly boasting of the openness of British society, the Duke privately opposed his son's marriage with the granddaughter of an American labourer as destroying the sanctity of his class; nevertheless, he eventually agreed to the match. Anthony Trollope, *The Duke's Children* (1880; Oxford, 1963), pp. 390–91.

51. Cain and Hopkins, *British Imperialism*.

52. Peter Mandler, *Aristocratic Government in the Age of Reform: Whigs and Liberals 1830–1852* (Oxford: Clarendon Press, 1990) and Boyd Hilton, *The Age of Atonement: the influence of evangelicalism on social and economic thought, 1795–1865* (Oxford: Clarendon Press, 1988). J.D. Vincent, ed., *Disraeli, Derby and the Conservative Party: The Political Journals of Edward Henry, Lord Stanley, 1849–69* (Hassocks: Harvester Press, 1978), 23 April 1864.

53. E.A. Wasson, 'A Progressive Landlord: the third Earl Spencer, 1782–1845', in C.W. Chalklin and J.R. Wordie, eds, *Town and Countryside: the English landowner in the national economy, 1660–1860* (London: Unwin Hyman, 1989), pp. 83–101.

54. Y. Cassis, 'Bankers in English Society in the Late Nineteenth Century', *Economic History Review*, XXXVIII (1985), p. 229. Interchange between

land holding and the legal profession, banking, and industries related to land, such as mining and brewing, was frequent and accepted. Sir G.N. Noel Bart. was a banker until he inherited his uncle's estates, *Gentleman's Magazine*, CVIII (1838), p. 657.

55. This proportion may seem low at first sight but it must be remembered that it excludes estates which were assembled over a wider period than the years 1850–69 and those estates whose date of purchase was probably between 1850 and 1869 but which cannot be precisely identified. Moreover, the inclusion of Scotland and Ireland which were greatly under-represented in my figures also has a depressive effect.

56. A. Howe, *The Cotton Masters 1830–1860* (Oxford: Clarendon Press, 1984), pp. 29–32; W.D. Rubinstein, 'Businessmen into Landowners', pp. 101–5.

57. W.D. Rubinstein, 'Wealth and Land in Britain', *Past and Present*, XCII (1981) pp. 135–6; Thompson, 'Life after death', pp. 59–60. Re Seth Smith, Edward Walford, *County Families* (London: 1873), p. 908 and (1880) p. 952 – total acreage 1399a, £2435; re Stephen Brunskill, Walford, *County Families* (1873), p. 143; White, *Devonshire* (1850), pp. 73 and 88; Patricia Cove, *Buckland Tout Saints: A Parish History* (Buckland Tout Saints, 1995), p. 79; total acreage 2926a, £5043. Another wealth creator whose heir's land purchases could have been omitted by Thompson was John Burcham, who died in 1841 with a reputed £600,000, whose grandson John Rogers bought the Holt estate, Norfolk, in *c.* 1864 of 2148 acres with a rental of £3043 – *Gentleman's Magazine*, CXI (1841), p. 668; D. Brown, 'From "Cotton Lord" to Landed Aristocrat: the Rise of Sir George Philips Bart., 1766–1847', *Historical Research*, LXIX (1996), pp. 62–82.

58. Charles Dickens, *Hard Times* (1854; London: Penguin, 1969), p. 54; other examples include John Jorrocks and Marmaduke Muleygrubs of Cockolorum Hall in Robert Smith Surtees, *Handley Cross* (1843), ch. 39 and Sir Roger Scatcherd of Boxall Hill, Sir Joseph Mason of Groby Park and Augustus Melmotte of Pickering Park in Anthony Trollope, *Doctor Thorne* (1858), *Orley Farm* (1862) and *The Way We Live Now* (1875); H. Taine, *Notes on England, 1860–1870* (1871; London: Thames and Hudson, 1957), p. 138.

59. Henry Tudor, *Political Myth* (London: Pall Mall, 1972), pp. 137–40.

60. 'Report of the Prize Giving at the South London Industrial Exhibition', *Illustrated London News*, 8 April 1865; Benjamin Disraeli, *Sybil* (1845), ch. VII. See also his speech in *Hansard*, 3rd series, LXXXVI, pp. 86–7, quoted in H.J. Habakkuk, *Technology*, p. 177. See also Benjamin Disraeli, *Lord George Bentinck: A Political Biography* (London: Colburn & Co., 1852), ch. 27: 'The aristocracy of England absorbs all other aristocracies, and receives every man in every order and every class who defers to the principle of our society, which is to aspire and to excel.'

61. Francis Cross, *Landed Property: its Sale, Purchase, Improvement and General Management* (London: Simpkin, Marshall & Co., 1857), p. 10.

62. *The Economist*, 16 July 1870, pp. 880–81.

63. Joshua Williams, *On the true Remedies for the evils which affect the Transfer of Land* (London: 1862), p. 599.

64. Asa Briggs, *Victorian Cities* (London: Pelican, 1968), p. 234.

65. S. Gunn, 'The failure of the Victorian middle class: a critique', in J. Wolff and J. Seed, eds, *The Culture of Capital* (Manchester: Manchester University Press, 1988), p. 39; William Makepeace Thackeray, *Book of Snobs* (London, 1848).

66. Habakkuk, *Marriage, Debt and the Estates System*, p. 617.

67. Pierre Bourdieu, *Outline of a Theory of Practice* (Cambridge: Cambridge University Press, 1977), p. 195.

68. T.H.S. Escott, *England: its People, Polity and Pursuits* (London: Cassells, 1891), p. 314.

Appendix   Entrants into the landed élite, 1780–1879

	1780s	1790s	1800s	1810s	1820s
1	Anthony Addington	John Bennett	R. Arkwright junior	Loftus Arkwright	Edward H. Adams
2	Claud Alexander	John Boileau	Francis Baring	James Balfour	Edward Barnard
3	Richard Barwell	Jacob Bosanquet	James Bateman	Thomas Bateman	William Draper Best
4	John Beckett	John Boughey	Moses Benson	Charles R. Blunt	Thomas Broadwood
5	Sylvanus Bevan	John Caldecott	Thomas Erskine	Sigismund Boehm	Joseph Cowper
6	John Blackburn	Thomas Clarke	James Farquhar	Matthew Boulton	Richard Gillow
7	John Blayds	John Cockerell	J. Farquharson	Charles C. Snell	Thomas Greene
8	William Cook	Samuel Crompton	Thomas Fowler	Michael Daintry	W. Williams Hope
9	George Dempster	Nathaniel Dance	R. Gosling	Kirkman Finlay	David Jones
10	Henry Drummond	James Duberley	Charles Grant	Henry Goulburn	William Laslett
11	Thomas Everett	Samuel Farmer	Benjamin Hall	Joseph Henley	William Leigh
12	William Forbes	William Fillingham	John Jackson	Edward J. Hollond	Robert Hart Logan
13	S. R. Gaussen	John Hanson	Roger Kerrison	Robert Jaques	Hugh Mackintosh
14	Samuel Gist	Charles Hoare	John William Lubbock	Mathias Kerrison	John F. Mills
15	Mr Glover	James Hordern	J. S. Muskett	Edward Knight	Robert W. Newman
16	Robert Grant	John Kennaway	John Pedley	Earl Nelson	Richard W. Prosser
17	Henry Grattan	John Langston	Samuel Salte (heir of)	William Newton	Francis Robertson
18	Robert Hanbury	Mannaseh Lopes	Samuel Smith	Edward Pellew	Phillip Rundell
19	James Hatch	Richard Meyler	Thomas Smith	George Philips	Purney Sillitoe
20	Charles Higgins	Thomas Mills	William Tennant	Robert Philips	Charles Baring Wall
21	John Motteux	William Mills	Joshua Walker	William Phillipps	20
22	William Paxton	Rene Payne	John Way	Thomas Poynder	
23	David Pugh	Robert Peel	J. Wedgwood II	David Ricardo	

1830s	1840s	1850s	1860s	1870s
W. Alston	Charles Austin	Charles Ansell	J. D. Allcroft	Lloyd Baxendale
Edward Applewhaite	Carlo Bainconi	Archibald Baird	Henry Alsop	Thomas Berridge
John Attwood	Francis Barchard	Daniel Baird	W. G. Armstrong	Henry Birkbeck
James Evan Baillie	James Campbell	George Baird	William Baker	Thomas Blackwell
Hugh D. Baillie	John Campbell	James Baird	Thomas Barnes	C. B. Borthwick
John Brocklehurst	James Conway	Robert Barbour	Henry James Bath	Frederick Bower
James Brown	Benjamin Disraeli	Arthur Berrington	John Boustead	Albert Brassey
John Dent	Charles Dixon	James Blyth	Henry A. Brassey	T. Broadwood
Charles Smith Foster	John Dobede	William B. Buddicom	Thomas Brassey	Edward Brook
Rowland Fothergill	John Dugdale	James Burke	Emanuel Briggs	James Chadwick
William Garnett	Edward Ellice	Benjamin B. Cabbell	Charles Brook	Nathaniel Clayton
John Garratt	Robert Garnett	Charles Cammell	William R. Brown	Richard Cory
John Gladstone	Josiah Garnett	Robert Campbell	James Caird	John Henry Deakin
Thomas Hudson	John Hall	John Chapman	Charles Cammell	William H. Forman
George Jacson	William H. Sparrow	Henry Clay	Thomas Chirnside	Abraham B. Foster
George Jones	John Hardy	Samuel Courtauld	Charles M. Clarke	Edward Green
James Kay	John Hargreaves	Richard Crossman	Francis Crossley	Robert Heath
William Lawrence	Francis Homfray	James Dalgleish	James Dugdale	John Henderson
Anthony Mactier	George Hudson	John Dugdale	Edward B. Evans	Edward Hill
James N. Matheson	John Shaw Leigh	Thomas Joseph Eyre	John Foster	James Holcroft
Henry Meux	Arthur Marshall	Vincent A. Eyre	John Fowler	S. M. Hussey
James Morrison	Thomas Marsland	Joshua Fielden	William Gilstrap	William Jackson
John Munro	Alexander Matheson	James Foster	W. E. Gladstone	William Keates

	1780s	1790s	1800s	1810s	1820s
24	Thomas	John	Joseph	Samuel	
	Quintin	Perry	Wilson	Romilly	
25	Drummond	John	William	Henry	
	Smith	Petrie	Yates	Russell	
26	John	Roger	25	J. Watts-	
	Smith	Pettiward		Russell	
27	Peter	Thomas		James	
	Thelluson	Phillipps		Scott	
28	Richard	Claude		Walter	
	Watt	Scott		Scott	
29	Thomas	Philip		William	
	Williams	Skipworth		Scott	
30	George	Robert		Simon	
	Wombwell	Smith		Taylor	
31	30	G. K.		William	
		Strutt		Turner	
32		John		Abbot	
		Tharp		Upcher	
33		Richard		Arthur	
		Watt		Wellesley	
34		Ive		Thomas	
		Whitbread		Wilder	
35		Luke		34	
		White			
36		James			
		Wildman			
37		Robert			
		Williams			
38		Mark			
		Wood			
39		38			
40					
41					
42					
43					
44					
45					
46					
47					
48					
49					
50					
51					
52					
53					
54					
55					

1830s	1840s	1850s	1860s	1870s
Mr Murray	George F. Miles	Henry L. Gaskell	Charles F. Hancock	Edward A. Leatham
Robert Peel	John Naylor	William Gibson	Charles Hardy	Thomas Lucas
Thomas Peel	Richard C. Naylor	George Glen	John Hawkshaw	William Morris
Charles C. Pepys	Francis Pearson	Thomas Greig	Henry Hood	Henry D. Pochin
Francis A. Phillips	Morton Peto	William Hall	James Hunter	Edward Smith
George Pritchard	John Grubb Richardson	Carl J. Hambro	John Johnson	William H. Verdin
Samuel Ryland	Richard Saunders	Gathorne Hardy	John Joicey	Joseph Whitaker
Samuel Sandbach	Robert Scott	John Hodgson	Hugh Jones	James Young
Bowyer E. Sparke	John Shakespeare	William E. Hubbard	John Ketton	William Younger
Richard Vernon	William Thompson	John T. Leather	J. Francis Mason	32
John Wood	George Wood	John D. Lewis	James Musgrave	
34	George Wright	John Lomax	J. L. Newall	
	35	Edward Mackenzie	William Nicholson	
		Dudley C. Marjoribanks	Roundell Palmer	
		James Merry	C. M. Palmer	
		T. Miller	W. M. Praed	
		John Morse	J. Rankin	
		G. F. Muntz	J. Rogers	
		P. Ormrod	W. H. Smith	
		H. Padwick	J. W. Spicer	
		A. Pryor	W. H. Stone	
		M. A. Saurin	F. J. Sumner	
		T. Smith	H. Taylor	
		W. F. Splatt	H. Ward	
		J. J. Stephens	H. Woods	
		T. Taylor	G. Wythes	
		C. Tennant	49	
		W. Tucker		
		E. Warner		
		G. Whalley		
		E. Wood		
		William Woodhouse		
		55		

Appendix notes

More details about the methodology and criteria employed, first in identifying the 682 new men of wealth (including descendants) who bought mansion house estates of £1000/1000 acres between 1780 and 1880 and then in subsequent 'equipoise' research, may prove of interest to some readers. The research began with using existing secondary studies of the subject, mainly the works of Sir John Habakkuk, Michael Thompson and Bill Rubinstein, to compile a database of 'already known purchasers'. This database included (among other things) details of source of wealth, name of estate(s) acquired, maximum acreage, rental (where possible in 1873 terms, partly to avoid excluding purchasers in the 1780s on the grounds of low rental) and date of acquisition. It was refined and augmented by details from many of the *Victoria County Histories*, other modern county histories, Burke and Savill's *Guide to Country Houses* and the other sources cited above. Where purchasers were named but their source of wealth was not identified, names were checked against Burke's *Landed Gentry*, Walford's *County Families* and other standard reference books. The sizes and rentals of the estates acquired were established by the details for the estate given in the *Return of Owners of Land*, compiled in 1873. If the estate had been sold on before 1873, details of its size and rental were assessed from various sources – often the entry for the estate under the 1873 owner (after due care had been exercised about any purchases or sales by subsequent owners of the estate). All the sources used to establish potential new wealth purchasers were studied over the whole period of study and therefore should not have resulted in any bias towards any particular period. For example, it may be argued that as the research used the 1873 *Return of Landowners* to a great extent, the database will tend to favour the later part of the period by overlooking those purchasers who bought estates but later lost them. As evidence that this is not the case, seven of the thirty in the 1780s list (well over one-fifth) are 'dispersals', that is, Barwell, Blackburn, Glover, Motteux, Quintin, Paxton and John Smith. Therefore if there is any bias towards any particular period, it is a bias within the secondary sources themselves which may overlook 'dispersals' for whatever reason. Any possible imbalance should be overcome by further research.

Of the 682 new men of wealth identified by May 1996 who bought landed estates of over 1000 acres and £1000 in the United Kingdom between 1780 and 1880, it proved only possible to date precisely the purchases of 352 – roughly half. The reasons for this are twofold: first, many new men acquired land piecemeal over a succession of years and so their purchases cannot be precisely dated; second, the sources employed do not allow an exact date to be established.

After May 1996, the research has focused on the 'equipoise' era using the sources indicated in the text. Nevertheless, research on other periods continued; for example, the *Gentleman's Magazine* has been read from 1780 to 1801, and a full study of the *Victoria County Histories* for Worcestershire, Warwickshire, Staffordshire, Oxfordshire and Durham has been completed. By these means over 1900 new wealth purchasers in England and Wales have been identified; it is upon this research that Table 5.1 is based. No attempt has been made to break down these purchasers by decade as the data were now obviously skewed towards the latter period. Equally, no attempt to make a geographic analysis of the location of purchases was attempted due to the obvious regional bias from only having worked through some of the *Victoria County Histories*. The small figures for penetration of the gentry by new men are only in part because of the difficulty of discovering purchases of 300+ acre estates. There are strong reasons to think that Bateman's breakdown of the landed élite by size of estate may well underestimate the number of 1000+ acre estates and overestimate the numbers of 300+ acre estates; but this problem will be discussed in a subsequent study.

Appendix sources

VCH Bedfordshire III (1912) and IV (1914); *VCH Cambridgeshire* V (1973); *VCH East Riding* IV (1979); *VCH Essex* IV (1956), V (1966), VIII (1983) and IX (1994); *VCH Gloucestershire* IV (1988) and XI (1976); *VCH Hampshire* III (1908) and IV (1911); *VCH Hertfordshire* II (1905); *VCH North Riding* I (1914) and II (1923); *VCH Oxfordshire* XII (1990); *VCH Staffordshire* VII (1996); *VCH Surrey* III (1911); *VCH Sussex* IV (1953), VI (1) (1980) and VI (3) (1987); *VCH Warwickshire* III (1945), VI (1951); *VCH Wiltshire* VII (1953), VIII (1965) and IX (1970); *VCH Worcestershire* IV (1924); W.G. Hoskins, *Devon* (1954); George Ormerod, *History of Cheshire* (1819; 1882) II; W.A. Copinger, *Manorial History of Suffolk* (1905); June Badeni, *Past and People in Wiltshire and Gloucestershire* (Norton Manor, Malmesbury, Wiltshire, 1992); R.O. Knapp, 'The making of a landed élite: Social mobility in Lancashire society', Ph.D., Lancaster University (1970); C.E. Searle, '"The Odd Corner of England": a study of rural social formation in transition Cumbria c1700–c1914', Ph.D., Essex (1984); James Barron, *The Northern Highlands in the Nineteenth Century* (1903); R.J. Colyer, 'The Land Agent in Nineteenth Century Wales', *Welsh*

History Review VIII (1976–7), 414–6; G. Mingay, *The Gentry* (1976); F.M.L. Thompson, *English Landed Society in the Nineteenth Century* (1963); H.J. Habakkuk, *Marriage, Debt and the Estates System: English Landownership 1650–1950* (1994); John Beckett, *The Aristocracy* (1986); J.M. Robinson, *Guide to the Country Houses of the North West* (1991); P. Reid, ed., *Burke's and Savill's Guide to Country houses Vol II: Herefordshire, Shropshire, Worcestershire and Staffordshire* (1980); J. Kenworthy Burne et al., *Burke's and Savill's Guide to Country Houses Vol. III: East Anglia* (1981); Francis Jones, *Historic Carmarthenshire Houses and their Families* (Carmarthen, 1987). *Gentleman's Magazine* (1780–1865); *Burke's Landed Gentry* (various editions); *Dictionary of National Biography*; F. Boase, *Modern English Biography* (1892–1901; reprinted 1965); R.G. Thorne, ed., *History of Parliament: The Commons 1790–1820* (1986) III–V; M. Stenton, ed., *Who's Who of British Members of Parliament I 1832–1885* (1976).

CHAPTER SIX

Domesticity:
a legal discipline for men?

Martin J. Wiener

Mid-Victorian Britain has long been known as a period peculiarly dominated by the ideal of domesticity. This ideal has in recent years usually
been portrayed as a powerful instrument for the disciplining of women.
Both the ideal and its applications in practice have been examined for
the particular ways in which they restricted, confined and subordinated
women. Yet there is a second face to Victorian 'disciplinary domesticity', which by no means negates the first but has nevertheless received
much less notice. This was the aspect of domesticity that promoted the
disciplining of *men* and a broader 'feminization' of social standards.
For at the same time that women were being increasingly pressed to
remain within the boundaries of the home, men were more and more
pressed to take on hitherto 'feminine' characteristics. If the conduct of
women was more subject to criticism by the standards of domesticity,
so too was the conduct of men, both within and outside the family. This
paradox has been too little explored.[1] This essay, therefore, aims not to
present a rounded picture, but to redress an imbalance. Its subject is one
particular 'benefit' of the domestic ideal to women, one almost lost
sight of in the general attention to its 'costs'.

The benefit to be examined here can be found within the realm of
legal regulation of the family. W.L. Burn's brilliant insights into the
expanding role of legal disciplines in the nineteenth century were for
some years largely ignored, but in recent years this situation has changed.
Much of the credit for the revival of interest in questions that much
concerned Burn must go to a movement – feminism – that only emerged,
or re-emerged, after his chief work had been done. Feminism's dictum
that 'the personal is political' brought the history of the family and
relations between men and women from the margins to the centre of
historical enquiry. Feminist-inspired scholars have begun to explore
often-obscured legal and social disciplines regulating personal life, even
if these scholars rarely refer to Burn's work.

In particular, recent historians of the family and of gender relations
have begun to chart just how, inspired in part by ideals of companionate

marriage and 'domesticity', nineteenth-century law increasingly regulated and sanctioned marital behaviour – male as well as female – deemed inappropriate by new Victorian standards. Legislation gradually provided wives a wide range of rights over their property, person and children, and a range of courts were established or empowered to grant mistreated wives divorces, separations and maintenance.[2] At the same time, courtship as well as marital behaviour was coming under greater legal regulation, with the increasing use of such forms of litigation as breach of promise of marriage suits. All these civil legal procedures not only provided new remedies for women – from whose angle such procedures are usually viewed – but enunciated and enforced new demands upon husbands and suitors for better treatment of their women.[3] These developments in the civil law were paralleled by little-appreciated changes in the *criminal* law, which was in a similar fashion increasingly penalizing disapproved male behaviour toward women, especially violent behaviour. Indeed, it is not too much to say that the violence of husbands against wives was virtually 'discovered' in this era and increasingly denounced and punished as a direct challenge to the new ideal of domesticity.

During the 1840s the national agenda of pressing social problems greatly expanded. Among the social problems discovered was domestic violence. Leading voices of 'progressive' opinion from Edwin Chadwick to Charles Dickens, from *Punch* to *The Times*, began to denounce the violence of husbands toward wives. Chadwick's *Report on the Sanitary Condition of the Labouring Population* paid great attention, as Mary Poovey recently noted, to the importance of encouraging domesticity as a way of 'civilizing' the labouring class, in particular working-class *men*, dangerously prone to drink, vagrancy, riot and violence generally. Chadwick saw as the hitherto-unappreciated agents of civilization working-class women, who were through their domestic virtues to tame and elevate their menfolk.[4] Similarly, in his fiction and journalism, Dickens not only forged some of the most powerful images of domestic felicity, but some of the sharpest critiques of male violence against women. Sikes's murder of Nancy resonated through the Victorian imagination. More prosaically, Dickens's periodical, *Household Words*, published several attacks upon lenient treatment of male murderers. In 1851, for example, Dickens co-authored and published in that journal an attack upon rural juries in particular for excessive tenderness to men who killed their wives. 'The fact', the article complained, 'of a woman being the lawful wife of a man, appears to impress certain preposterous juries with some notion of a kind of right in the man to maltreat her brutally, even when this causes her death; but, if she be not yet married, the case assumes a different aspect in their minds – a man has then no right to murder a woman – and a verdict of murder is found accordingly.'[5]

The 1840s also saw the metropolitan press take up the issue. In 1846, there was a Liverpool case in which a wife-killer whose prolonged attack covered his rooms in blood was convicted only of manslaughter. This set off a firestorm of criticism from middle-class papers like the *Daily News*, the *Examiner* and *The Times*; they denounced the general evil of domestic violence and the forbearance of the legal system toward it. The *Daily News* wanted to know, although 'we are advocates for the abolition of death punishments ... while death continues the legislative lot of the murderer, why is [this wife-killer] to escape from it?' It called for 'taking murder, even of wives, out of the class of manslaughter', while admitting that this was only a partial solution. More fundamentally, the paper saw a deeper cause of this lamentable indulgence of male violence in the false ideas of marital relations prevalent among the popular classes:

> The relation of husband and wife in uneducated or unrefined ap-
> prehensions, is not one of mutual dependence and intercourse of
> protection and comfort, but of absolute control on the one hand,
> and abject submission on the other. Too easy a justification of
> tyranny and violence is permitted, when the inflictor is a husband
> and the victim a wife. This can only be corrected by the parallel
> improvement of male and female education. Legislative reform will
> do little. A more perfect development of the woman will be fol-
> lowed by greater respect and tenderness from the man. There is no
> duty of employers more paramount than to impress purer and
> higher views of the relation of husband and wife on their work-
> men, supposing the employer to trouble himself at all about their
> improvement.[6]

The same week *The Times* reprinted in full a leader from the *Examiner* noting that 'there have been many similar verdicts lately; and it seems to be considered one of the marital rights to kick and beat a wife to death, or to break her neck by flinging her down stairs, without incurring the capital penalty. ... certain juries have done their best and their worst to give this unmanly class of offences the encouragement of impunity, positive or comparative'. It concluded, melodramatically (and incor-rectly), that 'the crime of murder is rapidly disappearing. What used to be called murder is now manslaughter, and what used to be called manslaughter is now a common assault.'[7]

This agitation in the press, however inaccurate in its history, reflected a wider unease in the growing middle-class public about both violence within the home specifically and about the state of English 'manliness' generally. During these same years parallel agitations were proceeding in the press and on the public platform, decrying a range of formerly quite 'manly' activities – among them duelling (among the aristocracy) and prizefighting (among the populace), public flogging of insubordinate seamen and soldiers, and a range of blood sports.[8] All these decried activities had a common link in their violence, whose relation to manliness was in the process of losing its traditional commonsensical quality. All of these newly problematic practices, however, were at least 'between men', and perhaps for this reason none drew the intensity of disapproval that now became attached to domestic violence. Despite the widespread reluctance to 'intrude' into the home, a parliamentary statute specifically aimed at protecting wives – the first such in British history – was passed in 1853.[9] This Act created a special offence of violence against women and children, with higher penalties than those attached to similar violence against men. Such legislation was not merely protective; it was part of an effort to vindicate a newer notion of manliness. As one MP observed in introducing a bill in 1856 to make violence against women and children punishable by flogging, the issue was at root not a woman's but 'a man's question ... It concerned the character of our own sex, that we should repress these unmanly assaults; and he believed that upon the men who committed them they had a worse and more injurious effect than they had upon the women who endured them.'[10] In 1857 the Associate Institute for Improving the Laws for the Protection of Women, a prostitute rescue organization created in 1843, changed its name to the Society (or Association) for the Protection of Women and Children. It began to send observers into police courts and to encourage prosecutions of brutal husbands and fathers.

By the 1860s, this new sensitivity to domestic violence had clearly penetrated the criminal justice system. The professional men who increasingly made up the judicial bench and the higher reaches of the Home Office (men who had certainly read their Chadwick, Dickens and newspaper leaders) began to press juries to crack down on violent husbands. However, juries did not always respond, and many wife-murder cases became struggles between state agents – High Court judges and Home Secretaries – and 'the people', in the form of juries and petitioners. In the courtroom contests over whether a murder or manslaughter verdict would be returned, and in the post-trial struggles over whether or not to carry out a death sentence, we can see the lineaments of a cultural struggle – all of whose actors were male – between older and newer notions of married life, and between older and newer notions of the limits of husbandly behaviour. Judges were placing violence against wives – regardless of circumstances – beyond the pale of

acceptability; the employment of physical force was in a sense beginning to be removed from the traditional arsenal of the husband in the
perennial contest of wills within the home. New 'ground rules' for
popular marital relations were being laid down by the courts in an *ad
hoc* manner. Not, however, without much foot-dragging by the representatives of 'the people', the juries, who were a good deal likelier than
judges or higher civil servants to extend understanding to a working-
class husband with 'wife trouble'. As a Glasgow bank clerk had written
to the Home Secretary some years before, pleading for a reprieve for the
killer of a quarrelsome, insubordinate wife:

> when a husband has to earn his bread, by the sweat of his brow,
> and feels that toil and torment are his earthly lot, and that torment
> too, springs from her who of all others should be his comfort,
> becoming moderation is more perhaps than can reasonably be
> expected. But after all, how is it possible that moderation can be
> used in all cases of this kind? I know an individual who is com-
> pelled to use violence for the purpose of keeping peace – or rather
> making quiet, in his own house – who has done it often – who has
> often intended to inflict bodily harm for no other purpose than to
> repress insolence and keep down noise – and he has no alternative
> but do this or leave his own house. What, my Lord, can a person
> so situated do?[11]

What indeed? This legal contest was not only a cultural one but a class
one (though this aspect was only occasionally mentioned openly in
court). As our corresponding clerk went on to complain, 'I am aware
that Lord Cockburn [the presiding judge] seemed to lay less stress on
the provocation than the jury. This rather grieves than surprises me,
because from his very circumstances he cannot be supposed to know the
provocation spoken of.'[12] In such cases 'gentlemanly' judges and civil
servants confronted overwhelmingly lower-class husbands, a struggle in
which jurymen, typically small tradesmen and farmers, were caught in
the middle, with sympathies on both sides. At the same time, this
struggle was also one of gender, in which the long-established boundaries of husbandly power over wives were being redrawn, and these
powers sharply restricted. Women may not have been direct players in
this contest, but they were very much concerned and played active parts
as witnesses before coroner's juries and trial juries: more often than not,
it was female neighbours and relatives who supplied most of the prosecution witnesses. This gender contest crossed the lines of class, often
placing upper-middle-class judges and working-class women on the
same side, against working-class men.

The legal issue over which much of this struggle took place was that
of 'provocation', which could reduce the offence to manslaughter,

which carried no fixed penalty, unlike murder, for which the only sentence was death. Even if a murder verdict was returned, provocation could serve as the basis for a commutation of the sentence to one of penal servitude for 'life' (in practice, twenty years). Wifely provocation most commonly took one of two forms – drunkenness or infidelity.[13] In March 1860, Edwin Salt, an Edinburgh excise officer, brutally killed his 'dissipated' wife by thrusting a fireplace poker into her vagina. None the less he was reprieved after a strong jury recommendation followed by a vigorous petition campaign that focused on her 'desperate' addiction to drink and her consequent neglect of her children and her husband's 'domestic peace and comfort'. The leading local paper, The Scotsman, supported reprieve, calling the victim a 'depraved' woman. The foreman of the jury assured the Home Secretary that they had only brought in a 'guilty' verdict in the expectation that Salt's life would be spared. The trial judge disagreed with the jury's recommendation, stressing the clear evidence of premeditation and questioning 'whether it would be safe to admit that the irritation produced by the drunken habits of a wife can be accepted as a palliation of such a [brutal] crime'. George Cornewall Lewis agreed with the judge but, under heavy pressure, eventually provided a reprieve, for which he was thanked by no less than the Lord Provost of Edinburgh, noting that it would be 'a great relief to the authorities in Edinburgh', fearful of popular disturbance.[14]

In 1863, Joseph Howes, a Sussex labourer, came home drunk and, as he later claimed, found his wife also drunk. So he beat her. He kept on, even after neighbours complained and urged him to stop, and she died that night. Howes's counsel made all the usual arguments, except insanity; he questioned whether the woman would have died if she had not already had a weak constitution due to her drinking, emphasized that Howes had used no weapon but his fists, strongly indicating the lack of any intent to kill, and provided witnesses testifying to his character as 'a peaceful and well-conducted man'. None the less, Baron Channell, in his summation, virtually urged the jury to convict of murder (a verdict which tended by tradition to be reserved for those who demonstrated their premeditation by using weapons such as knives, razors or guns). 'If a man used such brutal violence towards a woman', he concluded, 'and continued to do so, after having been warned and cautioned not to kill her, it was difficult to see that he could have meant anything else than to cause her death.' The judge went on to stress a point of law, the 'felony murder rule', that had up to then been largely confined to killings in the course of robberies, and rarely applied in domestic killings:

he was bound to tell them that, in point of law, it was not essential
that the prisoner should have intended to deprive her of life. If
death was caused by acts of violence, which amounted to a felony,
it was murder; to wound with intent to do grievous bodily harm
was a felony: so that if the prisoner had inflicted blows with intent
only to do his wife serious injury, or knowing that they would have
that effect, and they in the result caused her death, he would be
guilty of murder.

However, the jury (like every English jury before the twentieth century,
all-male) rejected the murder charge and convicted him only of manslaughter, an offence for which he could be sentenced to anything from
three months to life in prison. The judge gave him ten years.[15]

A similar compromise emerged from the trial of John Vickery, a
Surrey 'navvy', four years later. Vickery had killed his wife in compara-
ble circumstances. Provoked by her spending his money on drink, he
had beaten her to death with much brutality. Probably because of the
absence of a weapon, the grand jury had thrown out the coroner's jury's
finding of murder, and charged Vickery only with manslaughter. But
again the judge, Baron Bramwell, served as a back-up prosecutor, telling the jury that 'if they believed her death was the result [of the
beating], then they must find him guilty [of the manslaughter charge].
Could they really doubt that it was so?' Bramwell went on to note that
the prisoner's 'having been in a passion at the time was no defence; if it
were, we should all be at the mercy of passionate men'. The jury
convicted of manslaughter, but even for this reduced charge added a
recommendation to mercy. Bramwell rebuffed them: 'Gentlemen', he
observed, 'I have never yet disregarded such a recommendation from a
jury, but this time I really must.' In sentencing Vickery to five years'
penal servitude, he noted that 'I am really sorry for you, because it
appears that you have been an honest, hardworking man. But it is
necessary that people in your class should be taught – what I fear they
don't understand – that they have no right to beat their wives.' Observing that the woman had been repeatedly beaten and kicked, Bramwell
exclaimed, 'how any man could thus treat a woman and that woman
his wife, and the mother of his children, I cannot imagine'.[16]

In 1872, angered when his wife came home late and drunk, a Preston
bricklayer, William Bradley, pushed her into the kitchen fire and held
her there. Both were known to be drunkards, and lived together unhap-
pily. Despite the deliberation presumably involved in holding her over
the fire, he was charged only with manslaughter. Moreover, a dying
deposition from the wife, blaming her own drunkenness, was introduced as evidence. The jury followed this, and though it found him
guilty of manslaughter (as it could hardly avoid doing), it recommended

him to mercy on the ground that 'the wife's state of drunkenness might have provoked him'. However, Mr Justice Willes denounced the prisoner's act as especially heinous because it had been directed against his wife, 'whom he was bound to cherish and protect'. 'He would never', Willes was reported as going on, 'permit the idea to prevail that men had a right to maltreat their wives as they liked.' He sentenced Bradley to ten years' penal servitude, unusually heavy for a manslaughter verdict, with mercy recommendation. He noted that he would have passed a still heavier sentence but for the recommendation of the jury. The *Pall Mall Gazette* seized upon the case to denounce such husbands and such juries: 'From more than one trial which has been held lately', the paper observed,

> it would seem that a new mode of correcting wives – by placing them on the fire – is growing into favour among husbands. Nay, it would even appear from a verdict recently given by a Lancaster jury that the punishment in question is felt to have so peculiar an appropriateness under certain circumstances that a husband must not be too severely judged for resorting to it on such occasions.

The paper particularly attacked the jury recommendation to mercy on the ground that his wife's drunkenness may have provoked him – actually a quite common and traditional ground for mercy recommendations. 'No grosser provocation', the paper complained with heavy irony,

> can present itself to an intoxicated man than the discovery that his wife is intoxicated also; and when once his passions are fully aroused by this discovery the idea of putting her on the fire would suggest itself so naturally and with such irresistible force that to refrain from this act would demand a larger measure of self-control than can be reasonably expected from our weak and erring humanity.[17]

In another murder of a drunkard wife in Newcastle three years later, after lecturing a jury to obtain a conviction, Lord Denman urged a like-minded Home Secretary Cross not to interfere, complaining of what he saw as a 'growing disposition, especially in these Northern Counties, [to believe that the slightest] provocation however feeble in the nature of a defensive blow given even by a woman to a man is enough to reduce the crime to manslaughter'. The *Newcastle Daily Journal* said in its leader much the same as the judge said in confidence, declaring that

> it is necessary that helpless women should be preserved, as far as the law can preserve them, from the sudden fury of passionate husbands; and the provocation involved in the administration of a 'smack', in retaliation for being forcibly dragged from the street into the house, is no excuse or even palliation for so ruthless an assault.[18]

One form of husbandly violence had long had a special sanction – immediate retaliation for a wife's adultery. It too became a target in the judicial 'civilizing offensive' of the mid-Victorian period. During 1864 several trials placed 'the unwritten law' at the centre of public debate, and began its retreat to the margins of English criminal justice. On the same day at the Winchester Assizes, Baron Bramwell heard two cases of men taking revenge upon unfaithful wives. The wife of Robert Hallett, a farm labourer, had been found dead, her throat cut. In the words of *The Times*'s reporter, 'she appeared to be a very abandoned woman, and was in the habit of going about with other men'. Hallett confessed that 'on the night this occurred she told me she had been along with different men. She excited me, so I don't know what I did.' The prosecution offered much evidence of his anger in recent weeks, even of his saying that he'd cut her throat. However, his counsel urged that 'for all that appeared, the woman had inflicted the wounds, or one of her paramours might have come in and inflicted them'. The jury retired for about an hour, an unusually long time, and then came back into court and asked the judge whether they could return a verdict of manslaughter if they thought the man did it in a moment of passion arising from jealousy. 'Certainly not', replied Bramwell.

> If a man takes the life of another it is murder, unless he can satisfy the jury of something which shall reduce it to manslaughter. The only scrap of evidence to that effect was that some days after the transaction he said she had cut his throat first; but he did not make that excuse until he had had time to think about his defence.

The jury went back out for another hour and a half and came back to acquit him altogether.[19]

Bramwell, no doubt displeased by this outcome, was to get his own back in the very next case. The wife of William Bartlett, a Devonshire labourer, had left him and taken up with another man. Bartlett went to her, asking her to come home. When she rebuffed him, he cut her throat. It was not a moment's impulse; he had spoken to a friend beforehand of his intention to kill her if she refused to return, to prevent her from going to India with her new man. Although her wounds were serious, she pulled through. At his trial, evidence showed that, in the words of *The Times*, 'she was a most abandoned character', and witnesses testified to his previous kindness to her. None the less (probably because there were witnesses to the act, and also because his life was not at stake), he was convicted of attempted murder. Despite local sympathy for Bartlett, Bramwell sentenced him to the maximum possible penalty, life imprisonment. 'Any application for mercy', he sternly announced, 'must be made to another quarter.'[20]

An even more dramatic clash between popular and judicial views of marriage was displayed in the trial of George Hall, a young jeweller's stamper in Birmingham, just three days after Bramwell's struggles at Winchester. Hall's wife had also left him, but on their wedding night. He had courted her for seven years, but she had kept company with another man up to the day of their marriage. Although she went back to her parents' house to live, she apparently began again to see her former lover. Her parents returned her to her husband, but she only remained for some days before departing for good. She refused his repeated pleas to return. When he threatened her, she brought charges against him. Goaded beyond his endurance ('my shopmates used me cruelly', he complained), he bought a pair of pistols, went to her father's house, where she was then living, asked her to come walk with him, and on this walk shot her to death. His attorney made great efforts to summon up the 'unwritten law', despite lacking any relevant evidence, by declaring: 'Who knows what had happened on the fatal evening? Perhaps he might have seen something that so enraged him that he executed instant vengeance upon his wife.' Despite this effort Hall was found guilty, but the jury strongly recommended him to mercy on account of the great provocation he had received. Hall then made a most affecting speech of his love for her, her cruel treatment of him, and his abiding religious faith. 'She came to me again', he cried, 'after being in bed with that man. Is there the heart of a man in a Christian land who will condemn or sanction the condemnation of a poor man under those circumstances?' Upon concluding, 'the poor wretch', *The Times* observed, 'then fell, in a fainting condition, into the arms of the warders ... The scene in court during the delivery of this address was indescribable. Everyone present was visibly affected, and the women who thronged the gallery sobbed aloud.' Even the judge, Mr Justice Byles, appeared 'much moved'. A leading Birmingham paper went further and claimed that 'Judge, Jury, Court, bar and spectators looked on and listened awestruck. Murmurs of sympathy greeted each reference to [his wife's lover], and tears and sobs accompanied the speech during its whole delivery.'[21]

The battle for Hall's life began thereafter: while Byles passed along the jury's recommendation to mercy without further comment (suggesting his lack of support), the Home Office was deluged with letters and petitions from persons humble and great. In Birmingham, 'a little army of zealous workers' was observed 'employ[ing] themselves, unorganized and unsolicited, in this cause',[22] while 'the great and good' of the city also joined in: the main petition (which finally tallied 62,763 signatures) was headed by John Skirrow Wright, a leading manufacturer and political associate of Joseph Chamberlain, and supporting representations were made to the Home Office by the Mayor of Birmingham, both of the city's MPs and the Lord-Lieutenant for Warwickshire, who cited 'the very strong feeling among all classes in the county'. However, the Home Secretary, Sir George Grey, resisted all of this, asking his officials,

> is it to be held that a man may deliberately take away a woman's life under these circumstances without incurring the penalty which the law attaches to wilful murder? It is not sympathy with the man under the circumstances, but the effect which a reprieve must have in other cases under similar circumstances which ought to govern the decision.

He took the unusual step of consulting the Lord Chancellor, Lord Selbourne, who stiffened his back. 'Cases of adultery', Selbourne observed, 'occur constantly and often under circumstances of the greatest provocation to the injured husband and it would be of the most dangerous consequences to society if such provocation were accepted as a reason for not capitally punishing the husband when he commits a coolly premeditated murder.' Indeed, 'a more deliberate and coolly premeditated murder can hardly be imagined'.[23] But public pressure was too much, and Hall was nevertheless reprieved, just hours before he was to hang.[24]

To conclude: mid-Victorian criminal cases like the foregoing place the advancing ideology of 'domesticity' in another light from that most commonly trained on it in recent years – one accentuating its effects on men. These cases suggest that one aspect of Victorianism was a prolonged struggle, waged chiefly not by public movements or parliamentary legislation but in the daily work of the criminal courts (a field of whose importance Burn was unable to convince his fellow historians), to impose new, 'bourgeois' standards of physical restraint upon men beneath the middle class, particularly in their relations with their wives and girlfriends. As was true of the meaning of womanliness, the meaning of manliness was in process, and at least in the criminal courts this powerful concept was moving away from older models in which the readiness to employ violence was integral. In this struggle and consequent movement, to which little attention has been paid by modern historians, we may see a beneficent face of the often-decried rise of the 'policeman-state' in nineteenth-century Britain. If it was in part a class struggle, it was also a gender struggle. It was as well, perhaps, a genuine stage (if we dare say such a 'Whiggish' thing) in modern moral development.

Notes

1. Some ways in which the domestic ideal empowered middle-class wives have recently been brought out by Elizabeth Langland, *Nobody's Angels: Middle-Class Women and Domestic Ideology in Victorian Culture* (Ithaca: Cornell University Press, 1995) and Claudia Nelson, *Invisible Men: Fatherhood in Victorian Periodicals, 1850–1910* (Athens, GA: University of Georgia Press, 1995).

2. See M.A. Shanley, *Feminism, Marriage, and the Law in Victorian England, 1850–1895* (Princeton: Princeton University Press, 1989).

3. For recognition of how they regulated men, see A.J. Hammerton, *Cruelty and Companionship: Conflict in Nineteenth-Century Married Life* (London: Routledge, 1992); Ginger S. Frost, *Promises Broken: Courtship, Class and Gender in Victorian England* (Charlottesville: University Press of Virginia, 1995).

4. Mary Poovey, *Making a Social Body* (Chicago: University of Chicago Press, 1995), ch. 6.

5. [Horne, Richard J., and Charles Dickens], 'Cain in the Fields', *Household Words*, 10 May 1851.

6. *Daily News*, 28 August 1846.

7. *The Times*, 31 August 1846.

8. On some of these agitations, see Donna T. Andrew, 'The Code of Honour and Its Critics: The Opposition to Duelling in England, 1700–1850', *Social History* 5 (1980), pp. 409–34; Antony Simpson, 'Dandelions on the Field of Honor: Dueling, the Middle Classes, and the Law in Nineteenth-Century England', *Criminal Justice History* 9 (1988), pp. 99–155; Peter Gay, *The Cultivation of Hatred* (New York: Knopf, 1993); Eugene Rasor, *Reform in the Royal Navy: A Social History of the Lower Deck 1850 to 1880* (New York: Archon Books, 1976). On similar developments across the Atlantic, see Myra C. Glenn, *Campaigns against Corporal Punishment: Prisoners, Sailors, Women, and Children in Antebellum America* (Albany, NY: SUNY Press, 1984); Elizabeth Clark, "The Sacred Rights of the Weak': Pain, Sympathy, and the Culture of Individual Rights in Antebellum America', *Journal of American History* 82 (1995), pp. 463–93.

9. Burn was one of the very few writers to draw attention to this measure. See *The Age of Equipoise*, pp. 155–6.

10. Lewis Dilwyn, MP: *Hansard's Parliamentary Debates*, 3rd series, House of Commons, 7 May 1856, 142, col. 169. However, the very revulsion against flogging that was part of the unhappiness with traditional 'manliness' prevented this bill from passing.

11. R. *v.* Templeton (1840), PRO, HO18/22/25.

12. Ibid.

13. An example of the former is noted in *The Age of Equipoise*, p. 35n.

14. PRO HO12/125/39772. See *The Times*, 1 and 6 March 1860, for an account of his trial.

15. *The Times*, 6 August 1863.

16. *The Times*, 28 March 1867.

17. *The Times*, 29 July 1872; *Pall Mall Gazette*'s remarks reprinted (approvingly) in the *The Times*, 1 August 1872.

18. R. *v.* Anderson (1875), PRO HO45/9395/49945.
19. *The Times*, 4 March 1864.
20. Ibid.
21. *The Times*, 7 March 1864; *Birmingham Daily Post*, 4 March 1864.
22. *Birmingham Daily Post*, 8 March 1864.
23. PRO HO144/9400/52638.
24. For a fuller account of Hall's case see my 'The Sad Story of George Hall: Adultery, Murder and the Politics of Mercy in Mid-Victorian England', *Social History*, 24:2 (May 1999).

CHAPTER SEVEN

Helps and Ruskin
in the age of equipoise

Stephen L. Keck

Possibly no one embodied the 'age of equipoise' as well as Sir Arthur Helps (1813–75). While subsequent generations soon overlooked Helps, he was a significant figure in mid-Victorian Britain, one who certainly promoted the balance which W.L. Burn had in mind when he characterized the generation between 1852 and 1867 as one which was content to achieve 'equipoise' among the many and varied changing social and cultural elements which defined the middle of the nineteenth century. As we shall see, in the face of many potentially divisive issues Helps counselled his readers to accept principled disagreement and resist plans for massive social transformation. Unlike most historians of nineteenth century Britain, Burn did regard Helps as significant. Burn held that, along with Martin Tupper and Samuel Smiles, the now forgotten Helps was representative of writers who successfully addressed the public's need for large graspable truths.[1] In a footnote Burn asserted that Helps 'proved very popular with readers who, with no wish for major changes in the purposes and organization of society, were not averse from considering a few modest improvements'.[2]

If Helps's desire to facilitate gradual improvements make him an archetypical exemplar of equipoise, then John Ruskin, whose very utterances of complaint and promises of profound transformation have often stood as signposts for various features associated with 'Victorianism', embodies the disruptive energy which made the balance of cultural forces attractive to so many. Although Burn cited Ruskin for his critique of private luxury, he conceded that 'John Ruskin is perhaps too exotic a figure, too much of the professional prophet, to be the best of witnesses'.[3] The relationship between these two figures – who were friends – has never been fully explored, though John R. Debruyn has made a significant contribution to the study of both by tracing their correspondence.[4] However, Debruyn's meticulous research rarely actually engages their ideas directly, and the intellectual significance of the relationship between these two Victorians remains to be explored.[5]

For our purposes, examining Helps and Ruskin through two representative and related texts – 'War: A Conversation with the Friends in Council' and *The Crown of Wild Olive* – will hint at some of the facets of their complicated relationship and, more important, will make it clear that while much set these men apart, their significant differences reveal some common assumptions. These areas of contact buttress Burn's argument for a balanced generation. To be brief, these writings will suggest that Helps fitted comfortably into the mental culture of the mid-Victorian world; Ruskin felt the need to challenge and act against it.

Helps's development and career

Helps had entered Eton in 1829 and then went up to Cambridge where he received his BA in 1835. At Cambridge his abilities were obvious to his contemporaries and he was made an early Apostle.[6] In the same year (1833) Henry Lushington and Stephen Spring Rice became Apostles[7] and it was Spring Rice (later Lord Monteagle) who assisted Helps to gain access to significant administrative positions. As an Apostle Helps became acquainted with many key intellectuals such as Tennyson, F.D. Maurice, Monckton-Milnes, Richard Chenevix Trench, Charles Buller, Arthur Hallam, Robert Phelps (who would become the Master of Sidney Sussex) and Charles Kingsley,[8] who would continue to exchange ideas with Helps after he left the university. In 1835 he published *Thoughts on the Cloister and the Crowd*; with its basic division between purely intellectual issues and calls for improvements in public governance, it at once demonstrated the impact of both Cambridge and the Apostles on his development.

Helps's early years read as an effort to achieve harmony between purely academic pursuits and administrative service; both his intellectual achievements and governmental experience could be understood to oscillate between two poles: the one as a public moralist, writing 'from the cloister' to persuade his contemporaries on various public questions; the other as a policy-maker, trying to bring about what would be best for the 'crowd'. Soon after publishing this first work, Helps took a position in government. After serving as private secretary to Lord Monteagle (Chancellor of the Exchequer in Lord Melbourne's government), in 1840 Helps moved to a position under Lord Morpeth, the chief secretary for Ireland, where he stayed until the fall of the Melbourne government in 1841. Next, he served as one of the commissioners of French, Spanish and Danish claims regarding the bombardment of Copenhagen (during the Napoleonic Wars).[9]

Upon the completion of the Commission, Helps moved away from government by devoting himself to literary pursuits, first in London and then at Vernon Hill, a house in Hampshire which he bought in 1843. During the 1840s Helps abandoned his early attempt to write historical dramas and instead devoted his energies to many of the most poignant issues of the decade.[10] Given these agendas, it was only appropriate that Thomas Hughes later recalled that Helps played a major role in the 'condition of England question'. Helps, Hughes continued, was at the very least 'one of the earliest advocates of every considerable social reform for a full generation' and furthermore, his *Claims of Labour* (1844) was a 'new departure' in literature.[11] *The Claims of Labour*, which received critical attention on both sides of the Atlantic, also revealed early hints at what might be called an 'equipoisal' mind.[12] While the book has been remembered for its incisive treatment of urban poverty and labour conditions, it also sought to trace the mutual relationship between owners and workers. Rather than make radical demands, Helps was concerned to show that the solutions to industrial problems had to be well considered, broad-based, and probably gradual. In addition, Helps joined his friend and fellow Apostle Charles Kingsley in writing a series of papers called 'Politics for the People'. However, it was *Friends in Council*, first issued in two volumes in 1847 and followed by issues in *Fraser's Magazine* (1855–56) and by additional publications during the next two decades which established Helps's reputation in the minds of his contemporaries.[13] Typical of many mid-Victorian readers was William Whewell who claimed 'I would rather read the Councils for averting moral than physical evil'.[14] The American transcendentalist lecturer and preacher, Ralph Waldo Emerson, came to understand Helps as 'omniscient',[15] and in *English Traits* complained that British newspapers, principally *The Times*, did not contain pieces by well-informed men such as 'Milnes, Carlyle, Helps, Gregg, [and] Forster'.[16]

In the first volume of *Friends in Council* (1847), Helps explored the connections between individual character, moral questions, the pursuit of knowledge and public issues. The text is divided into sections in which three figures, Ellesmere, Dunsford and Milverton (joined in later stages by Midhurst), conduct fictitious dialogues on essays regarding 'conformity', 'recreation', 'living with others', 'history', 'slavery' and other subjects. However, the real basis for these dialogues were conversations at Vernon Hill between Helps, Kingsley, the painter and caricaturist John Doyle (1797–1868), his son (also a painter and caricaturist) Richard Doyle (1824–83), Dr Richard Phelps, George Lewes, W.G. Clark (Cambridge Public Orator), Ralph Waldo Emerson, Theodore Martin, Thomas Woolner and later John Ruskin. The use of the Friends became Helps's favourite way to approach subjects, and the device ensured his success as a writer. George Smith, the publisher of Smith Elder, believed that Helps's books did well because the author of *Friends in Council* wrote 'the kind of book which a seriously-minded young man makes a point of reading'. More important, the publisher understood that Helps's works commanded a 'wide constituency'.[17] The 'fictional Friends', then, became familiar to the Victorian reading public.

The importance of the *Friends* series went beyond wit, caricature and entertainment. Upon the publication of Helps's *Social Pressure* (1875), Hughes addressed the complaint that 'we have had these "friends in council," it has been said, *ad nauseam*', arguing that he wanted the series to continue until 'the conditions of life of all English citizens have been made as satisfactory as they can be'.[18] Like Hughes, Leslie Stephen regarded Helps's writings and ideas as important. Stephen recalled how these works affected his generation, arguing that Helps amounted to a secular preacher, who appealed to the public as Joseph Addison had in the eighteenth century. Stephen maintained that Helps was 'the most popular of the lay preachers' and that he was successful because he fused 'genuine thought' with 'real literary skill'. Stephen held that Helps's skill stemmed from his ability to address the widest segments of public opinion by appealing to topics which were not inherently or obviously political, but which were 'dear to the intelligent reader'.[19] Stephen's memory had not been faulty; the reviewer for *Fraser's Magazine* spoke for many when he praised Helps, who published *Oulita the Serf* (1858) anonymously, for his ability to make personal connections with his readers:

> there are few books which are so calculated as *Friends in Council* to make the reader wish to know who is the author whom he has learned to revere and love ... Yet it is not for us to add the author's name to a title page which the author has chosen to send nameless into the world: though we may be permitted to say, that whoever may be the writer of the works to which we have been alluding, though we never exchanged words with him, and never saw him, still, in common with an increasing host of readers, we cannot think of him as other than a kindly and sympathetic friend.[20]

If contemporaries such as Stephen saw Helps as a champion lay preacher, other Victorians could look back on his writing for its wisdom, a wisdom consistent with many equipoisal themes.[21] For instance, in the review of *Oulita the Serf* Helps received praise for writing with 'gentle playfulness', 'intense honesty', 'comprehensive sympathy' and, most important, 'the desire to do justice for all'.[22] Elizabeth Gaskell spoke for

many when she wrote to her sister that: 'Those in Friends in Council &
[sic] are admirable examples of how much may be said on both sides of
any question, without any (dogma) decision being finally arrived at, &
certainly without any dogmatism'.[23] In short, during the 1840s and
1850s Arthur Helps succeeded in developing an impressive literary
reputation.[24]

Despite these successes, in 1860 Helps moved away from a purely
intellectual career 'in the cloister' by accepting Palmerston's offer of the
Clerkship of the Privy Council. It was in this position that Helps played
a key role in drafting orders of Council which dealt with the cattle
plague (see Matthew Cragoe's essay in this collection, Chapter 8). More
generally, as Clerk of the Privy Council, Helps witnessed and assisted
the move towards the centralization of state power.[25] This position
brought him close to the Queen and the Prince Consort; it was the
anonymous author of *Friends in Council* who suggested (and rigorously
edited) what proved to be one of the most successful books of the
Victorian era – Queen Victoria's *Leaves From the Journal of Our Life
In the Highlands* (1868). It might be argued that Helps's contribution
towards the public presentation of the monarchy meant that he had
played a significant role in the creation of 'Victorianism'.

From 'War' to equipoise

Helps's 'War: An Essay and Conversation By Friends in Council' (1859),
written in response to both the experience of the Crimean War and the
diplomatic problems which surfaced before the end of the decade (the
possibility of war between France and Austria over northern Italy and
fears of a French invasion of Britain), illustrates some of the equipoisal
tendencies in his writing. Despite the fragility of the international situation, Great Power obligations towards colonies, and the maintenance of
large standing armies, Helps argued that the means existed to counter-
balance the possibility of war. Through the voice of Milverton, Helps
made the case that it was some of the very improvements of the age
which would make possible the preservation of peace.

Helps opened the satire with his Friends already across the Channel,
holidaying amidst the ruins of the French fortress of Namur. Against
this picturesque setting, Milverton read an essay on war which ana-
lysed the nature of large-scale conflict and made a case for peace on
the grounds that modern civilization had too much at stake in its
preservation. Not only, argued Milverton, had the Crimean War demonstrated that international conflict was costly, but the complexity of

modern society was such that its well-being depended upon the interplay of many factors – public opinion, industrial production and other
economic forces – the realities which served to discourage large-scale
wars.

Despite the fact that militarization had increased the prospects for
war in Europe, Milverton accepted the reality of progress. He read to
his friends a passage from his essay which articulated the commonplace
mid-Victorian argument that war slowed the pace and even prospect of
human improvement:

> we are just beginning to understand something about the most
> potent elements in the universe, such as heat, light and electricity;
> just beginning to investigate the laws of disease among town
> populations, and the modes of mitigating it; just beginning to
> endeavour that the poor should live in a state of less abject squalid-
> ity than that in which they have heretofore lived: and all our
> attention is to be diverted from these great objects to modes of
> attack and defence, and our minds to be confused by the noise of
> drums and trumpets. Surely this is a great evil, and never greater
> than at the present time of hope and promise.[26]

If Milverton's essay reflected a typical mid-Victorian assumption about
the reality of progress, it also illustrated some contemporary fears.
Milverton addressed not only the immediate diplomatic situation (the
looming war between France and Austria), but he explored more subtle
questions such as the origins of conflict, the nature and costs of aggression and the economic pain produced by major wars. Milverton wove
into his analytical treatment of war a discussion of medieval conflict
which may well have struck readers of the *Friends in Council* (and later
volumes) as satire. Milverton virtually adopts a 'medievalist' approach
of using the Middle Ages as a yardstick with which to measure the
meaning of modern improvements. With hints of Carlyle's *Past and
Present*, Milverton explained that the chronicle of Monstrelet (Helps
could be confident that his readers could recognize Carlyle's Latin
Chronicle of Jocelin of Brakelond in *Past and Present*) provided a useful
example of an alternative to war because it cited duelling as a way of
settling disputes. Clearly, Milverton was not really interested in advocating duelling; his purpose was satirical – to illustrate the difference
between medieval and modern outlooks.

Instead, Milverton agreed that the resources to meet this problem lay
in the present, locating the cultivation of public opinion as a possible
barrier to the outbreak of war. While he did not have faith in public
debate as inherently wise or informed, Milverton noted that improved
communications meant that the larger public could be easily persuaded
to recognize and oppose bad policy. In addition, Helps believed that the

potential power of public opinion also opened up the possibility for creating groups which might argue for peace:

> Public opinion also is more potent, and reaches even to thrones with singular facility. Again, there is a much greater power of combination that there ever was before, not only amongst people of the same race and country, but throughout the whole civilized world. It is not impossible that great leagues and associations may yet be formed amongst the principal peoples in the world, having for their object to put a restraint upon the intolerable burdens and miseries of needless wars.[27]

In essence, Milverton reminded his readers that civic duty could play a significant part in the preservation of peace. Unlike Mill, who published *On Liberty* in the same year, Helps saw in the growing public the possibility of useful 'leagues and associations'. Mill, of course, famously made a spirited argument for individual liberty, but wrote rather darkly about the dangers associated with the 'tyranny of the majority'. Mill worried that the growing salience of public opinion meant that social conformity might restrict individual genius; Helps was more optimistic: he looked to the constructive force of public debate to limit bad policies. However, characteristically Helps also explored public indifference. Milverton's assessment of unavoidable wars – conflicts in which the defence of a nation or society was at stake – revealed his fascination with the mobilization of human resources. During 'unavoidable wars' the needs for self-preservation generated a much more significant employment of normally unrealized civic potential:

> We all know that there are occasions when, as on the threat of foreign invasion, a nation gathers itself up in all its strength, when selfish aims are thrown aside, when ordinary life is felt to be tame, and buying and selling are not much thought of, when even great griefs, that are but private, fall lightly on us, and when the bonds of society are knit together so closely, that the whole nation produces and presents its full power of resistance. Then it is that the ambitious man forgets his ambition, the covetous man, if possible, his money; the civic crown with its glorious motto, '*ob cives servatos*', becomes the chief desire of all brave men, and tender mothers feel like the Spartan matron of old, who, as she adjusted the buckle on her group of warriors' arms could exclaim, 'Come back, either with it, or upon it'.[28]

Milverton recognized that the sacrifices made for the public good during 'unavoidable wars' were unlikely to occur under 'ordinary' conditions. However, the relationship between war and civic duty prompted Milverton to note that the national leaders ought not to wait for conflict to 'think of their own poor people at home'[29] who have already suffered because of previous wars. That is, it should not require war to produce prudent and compassionate social policy; these same symbols – the image of the civic crown, Spartan self-sacrifice, the relationship between man and woman in the cause of national defence – might also be mobilized for a 'still nobler occasion':

> when, without one thought of self-aggrandisement, or aspiration after mere glory, or any of the pride of strength, a nation quietly resolves that it is its duty for the interests of the world, or for the defence of the oppressed, to come out to battle; and it does come out sternly and sadly.[30]

In addition to arguing that war should not be necessary for the faithful exercise of public duty, Milverton championed the possibility of intervention. Milverton's essay represents a moderately liberal message: the militarization of Europe threatened to undermine genuine improvements, but within the complexity of nineteenth century civilization there existed the resources which could be used to both maintain existing social arrangements and preserve peace.

Having used Milverton's ideas to tackle the larger issue of militarism, Helps employed the other Friends to pour further scorn on contemporary fears. 'An odd idea has often struck me', remarked Ellesmere, 'about an invasion of the French':

> Of course by some accident or other they might some day land a large body of troops in England. They would proceed perhaps to occupy some large town. Sunday would come. Imagine fifty thousand of the lower class of Frenchmen contemplating an English Sunday. They are pleasant, handy, little fellows those French common soldiers. They would commune with one another, and would say: – 'If we were to conquer this country our rulers would make us occupy it. This English Sunday would then decimate our ranks by *ennui.*' The next morning would see them in full retreat to the coast. Meanwhile the English of the great town would discover what handy little dogs the Frenchmen were, what cooks, what pleasant cheery fellows, and they would run after them, imploring them to stay. The worst blows would be exchanged while the French were endeavouring to get away from their hospitable entertainers. Ever after, when rattling their dominoes in their sunny *cafes*, these invading Frenchmen would tell their companions of the awful Sunday they had spent in England. 'A good people, a kind people, those English', they would say, 'but so dull, and such bad cooks, and no sun there. We will march with our Emperor anywhere but to England.'[31]

The satire might be crude and the ridicule heavy-handed, but the Friends' readers were encouraged to first enjoy the dialogue and then conclude that the prospects of a French invasion were not as great as feared.

Helps encouraged his readers to relax, laugh and take some emotional distance from a situation which had produced tension.

Yet, if Helps's writing was marked by levity, it could also be earnest. His response to the Sayers–Heenan fight (described by Burn as 'almost an anachronism'[32]) serves as a postscript to 'War'. The contest between a Briton and an American in April 1860, which drew several thousand spectators, fascinated many Victorians in spite of themselves. Palmerston, as Burn noted, acknowledged that the fight itself was illegal, and, yet, he contended, 'it was an exhibition of manly courage, characteristic of the people of this country'.[33] Helps regarded the fight in a similar light to the satirical arguments made in 'War', hoping that it 'might be a thing productive of much good, if it only led people into a deeper aversion to the great prize-fights which are looming in the distance all over the civilized world'.[34] There is certainly an element of deliberate naïvety here, but it also suggests that at a time when Mill and Acton were worried about the rising power associated with nation-states, Helps had little sensitivity to the emotive power and disruptive force of nationalism.

However, Helps, as his championing of the publication of Victoria's diaries shows, was hardly opposed to the establishment or maintenance of English values, and in his writings he could be considered an advocate of an Englishness based upon individual freedom, the sanctity of private life, and the importance of social responsibility. Certainly, one of the messages which readers of the Friends would have recognized was the essential goodness of English society – even if it was in need of reform. Between 'War' and his response to Sayers–Heenan, then, lay a view of his time as one that contained the seeds of larger conflict, but was still somehow manageable.

Seeking to manage or alter public opinion meant that Helps had left the Cloister to help the Crowd, making him an advocate of a balanced, nuanced and relaxed approach to both international issues and domestic questions. Helps, who as Clerk of the Privy Council played a direct role in much of the administrative debates of the 1860s, then, represented the forces of equipoise. In fact, for nearly thirty years he exercised influence on both the making of public policy and the intellectual culture which was often at odds with it. Helps's life and development seem to be marked by attempts at personal equipoise: he sought a balance between positions which gave him significant governmental and administrative responsibility and, separately, a development of ideas which were meant to inform his contemporaries. More important, Helps's strategies for meeting the rapidly changing mid-century world – pluralism, accommodation, satire, adaptation, and so on – meant that he lifted his pen to show his contemporaries that they might eschew extreme measures so that they might live wisely and modestly.

In many respects, *Friends in Council* reflects some of the equipoisal tendencies which Burn identified as characteristic of the mid-century. Burn could have easily employed the Friends (either particular characters or specific series) to show that the attempts to describe or characterize Victorian debate as either 'individualistic' or 'collectivist' were not particularly useful. Helps's vision of British society was not one which was 'atomized': *Friends in Council* worked because it effectively satirized a familiar range of ideas, figures, proposals, schemes and ploys. To try to read *Friends in Council* as a document of mid-century writing is to witness a complex set of social relationships.

Ruskin and the challenge of equipoise

One careful reader of Helps's 'War' was John Ruskin. Indeed, when in the early 1860s Ruskin lectured on 'War' at the Royal Military Academy, he urged his audience to read Helps's tract. Ruskin had always read Helps with some care, and while Ruskin scholars have been slow to pick up the connection between the two men, it seems clear that *Stones of Venice*, particularly parts of *Modern Painters* and, above all, *The Ethics of the Dust* reveal the influence of Helps.[35] In this case Ruskin had not only studied Helps's 'War' carefully – perhaps using it as the inspiration for his own lecture on the subject – but, in addition, he absorbed much from Helps's discussion of unavoidable wars, and the economic and social costs of modern war. Apart from these larger issues, Ruskin may also have been inspired by Milverton's discussion of the Spartan idiom and the motif of the 'civic crown', as he gave the title *The Crown of Wild Olive* to the collection of lectures which included 'War'. It is clear, though, that Ruskin had learned more than Helps had intended, for the lessons he proceeded to draw were quite different.

Helps regarded the subject of war as the opportunity to make a plea for detachment and balance; in contrast, Ruskin saw the subject as the occasion to make an argument about the possibility of massive social transformation. While it is not necessary to trace Ruskin's intellectual development, it is useful to mention that during the 1850s and 1860s he was in various ways attempting to outflank political, social and economic orthodoxies. From the 1840s Ruskin had pushed his ideas in many directions. The final volume of *Modern Painters* (1860) was followed by works of a more radical cast: *Unto this Last* (1860), *Essays on Political Economy* (1863) (which was famously republished as *Munera Pulveris* in 1872), *Sesame and Lilies* (1865) and *The Ethics of the Dust* (1866), all of which sought to subvert contemporary assumptions about either social policy or the organization of intellectual life. *The Crown of Wild Olive* (1866)[36] fitted into this trajectory by giving Ruskin one more way to explore the possibility for significant social change.

The Crown of Wild Olive was based on three lectures which Ruskin had delivered in the previous years – at Woolwich, Bradford and Camberwell. Unlike Helps's piece on war and government, these lectures as edited reflected Ruskin's wider, multiple and, at times, confused agenda. They combined the call for social reform with cultural criticism, Christian doctrine and Greek mythology, mixing ideas derived from the detailed study of art and architecture with a selective reading of history to embrace a wide, organic vision of what might become Britain's future.

Despite such an ambitious agenda, Ruskin did not dwell on the specific issues – such as the administrative minutiae in which Helps was immersed as Clerk of the Privy Council and which occasionally provided topics for the Friends to discuss – but looked forward to the possibility of a society which would be shaped by the higher motivations which he identified with the *wild* olive. Adopting this phrase from Aristophanes, Ruskin asked his readers:

> if this life be *no* dream, and the world no hospital, but your palace-inheritance; if all the peace and power and joy you can ever win, must be won now, and all fruit of victory gathered here, or never; – will you still, throughout the puny totality of your life, weary yourselves in the fire for vanity? If there is no rest which remaineth for you, is there none you might presently take? was this grass of the earth made green for your shroud only, not for your bed? and can you never lie down *upon* it, but only *under* it? The heathen ... knew that life brought its contest, but they expected from it also the crown of all contest.[37]

Ruskin pointed out that the crown of wild olive was not indicative of material prosperity, but represented 'kindly peace'. He offered his readers the same prospect: 'you may win' this type of 'grey honour, and sweet rest'.[38] This last phrase was borrowed from the Hellenic poet Pindar (518–438 BC), who claimed that 'he that overcometh hath throughout the remainder of his life *honeyed* sunshine, on *account of the games*'.[39] Ruskin's translation of the '*honeyed* sunshine' involved much more than Helps's hope that statesmen remember the disadvantages, as he offered his readers the vision of change which involved not only compassionate social policy, but also the prospect of cultural renewal. The honeyed sunshine, in other words, meant nothing less than a move away from the ordinary concerns of the 1860s; instead, it would mean a much better life because it would be characterized by:

> Free-heartedness, and graciousness, and undisturbed trust, and requited love, and the sight of the peace of others, and the ministry to their pain; these, – and the blue sky above you, and the sweet waters and flowers of the earth beneath; and mysteries and presences, innumerable, of living things, – may yet be here your riches; untormenting and divine: serviceable for the life that now is; nor, it may be, without promise of that which is to come.[40]

Helps's 'civic crown' had involved sacrifices made during a national struggle; in contrast, Ruskin's 'wild olive' suggested what Milverton and the other Friends had sought to avoid: the possibility of social and cultural change on a vast scale.

While the scope of potential change was especially daring in the most famous lecture of the three, 'Traffic', it also held true for the last lecture 'War', which Ruskin delivered at the Royal Military Academy in Woolwich in 1865. Just as Ruskin exploited his Bradford setting in 'Traffic' – by linking the building of the new Exchange to a criticism of commercial value – in 'War' he challenged an audience made up largely of military personnel by asserting that the subjects of art and war could be connected; in fact, this lecture was also vintage Ruskin: he tied together two seemingly unrelated subjects in order to pursue a much broader agenda, which included not only cultural criticism but also the promise of substantial change. Like Helps, Ruskin did not welcome war (though unlike Milverton he did champion British intervention in Italy),[41] but he was much bolder in claiming that war could be the stimulus for vital human achievements. Indeed, Ruskin found a correlation between the creation of significant art and a nation's capacity to wage war: 'it is not every lecturer who would tell you', he commented dryly, 'that ... war was the foundation of all great art'.[42]

> The common notion that peace and the virtues of civil life flourish together, I found to be wholly untenable. Peace and the *vices* of civil life only flourish together. We talk of peace and learning, and of peace and plenty, and of peace and civilization; but I found that those were not the words which the Muse of History coupled together: that, on her lips, the words were – peace, and sensuality – peace, and selfishness – peace, and death. I found, in brief, that all great nations learned their truth of word, and strength of thought, in war; that they were nourished in war, and wasted by peace; taught by war, and deceived by peace; trained by war, and betrayed by peace; – in a word, that they were born in war, and expired in peace.[43]

Ruskin was not advocating war for the sake of art; instead, he wanted his readers to see that the self-discipline needed to fight wars was a precondition of good art. While this was consistent with Milverton's argument about the ways in which the threat to a nation brought out its civic virtue, it also had roots in *Stones of Venice*. Ruskin had argued that Venice had produced its best art and architecture when it was threatened; the decline of the city came with peace and prosperity. With respect to the nineteenth century, Ruskin moved in a different direction to Helps. Milverton's essay had stressed that this civic energy might be directed to realizing compassionate social policies. Ruskin took Milverton's hope and carried it much further, arguing that it could be harnessed to alter and even reshape British society and culture. The 'game of War', Ruskin continued, is only that in which the *'full personal power of the human creature* is brought out in the management of its weapons'.[44] Therefore, both the relationship between civilian and military power and the actual vocation of the soldier had to be understood broadly:

> the ideal of soldiership is not mere passive obedience and bravery; that, so far from this, no country is in a healthy state which has separated, even in a small degree, her civil from her military power ... it is the error especially of modern time, of which we cannot yet know all the calamitous consequences, – to take away the best blood and strength of a nation, all the soul-substance of it that is brave, and careless of reward, and scornful of pain, and faithful in trust; and to cast that into steel, and make a mere sword of it; taking away its voice and will; but to keep the worst part of the nation – whatever is cowardly, avaricious, sensual, and faithless – and to give to this the voice, to this the authority, to this the chief privilege, where there is least capacity of thought ... your vow of the defence of England will by no means consist in carrying out such a system. You are not true soldiers, if you only mean to stand at a shop-door, to protect shop-boys who are cheating inside. A soldier's vow to his country is that he will die for the guardianship of her domestic virtue, of her righteous laws, and of her any-way challenged or endangered honour. A state without virtue, without laws, and without honour, he is bound *not* to defend; nay, bound to redress by his own right hand that which he sees to be base in her.[45]

Ruskin, then, used the issue of war to challenge social inequalities. While it is too much to claim that Ruskin was calling for the militarization of civilian life, his reconceptualization of the domestic or social significance of war urged his audience to be open to the large-scale transformation of society. Ruskin had clearly moved beyond Helps; the latter had conceived of militarization as a major problem for Europe, while the former invoked it as a departure point for social change.

However, Ruskin understood that modern wars might pose new challenges for both civilian and military authorities. The events of the American Civil War led him to conclude that the use of industry, science and technology made modern war qualitatively different from earlier conflicts. Anticipating twentieth-century discussions of 'total war', Ruskin asserted that future conflict would involve all of society:

> If you have to take away masses of men from all industrial employment, – to feed them by the labour of others, – to provide them with destructive machines, varied daily in national rivalship of inventive cost; if you have to ravage the country which you attack, – to destroy, for a score of future years, its roads, its woods, its cities and its harbours; – and if, finally, having brought masses of men, counted by hundreds of thousands, face to face, you tear those masses to pieces with jagged shot, and leave the living creatures, countlessly beyond all help of surgery, to starve and parch, through days of torture, down into clots of clay – what book of accounts shall record the cost of your work; – What book of judgment sentence the guilt of it?[46]

Instead, Ruskin admired the virtues of ancient warriors, particularly the Spartan warriors, for their composure and strength. Anticipating the valorization of Hellenic culture which would become vivid in *The Queen of the Air* (1869), Ruskin wanted his readers to be impressed with the fact that the Spartans '*sacrificed to the Muses* before an action; ... they *sacrificed on the same occasion in Crete to the God of love*, as the confirmer of mutual esteem and shame'.[47] The nobility of Spartan motivation stood in contrast to 'Christian war', which was preached by 'Christian ministers' and 'was inspired and sanctified by the divinely-measured and musical language, of any North American regiment preparing for its charge'.[48]

Despite the dangers of modern conflict, Ruskin saw in war and militarization the hope for national transformation. Milverton had argued that on some relatively rare occasions war could produce civic virtue, but Ruskin aimed higher: he was interested not only in participation in national life, but also in the transformation of character:

> you must fulfil your vow to your country; but all industry and earnestness will be useless unless they are consecrated by your resolution to be in all things men of honour; not honour in the common sense only, but in the highest ... You have vowed your life to England; give it her wholly; – a bright, stainless, perfect life – a knightly life. Because you have to fight with machines instead of lances, there may be a necessity for more ghastly danger, but there is none for less worthiness of character, than in olden time. You may be knights yet, though perhaps not *equites*; you may have to call yourselves 'canonry' instead of 'chivalry', but that is no reason why you should not call yourselves true men.[49]

The appeal to chivalry meant that Ruskin's perspective was intention-
ally 'gendered'. However, since he was largely concerned about the
domestic implications of military power, he found the threat of war
could also be a stimulus. Preventing war could also be a catalyst for
improved behaviour, as the collective behaviour of women could stave
off unnecessary conflict.

> Let but every Christian lady who has conscience toward God, vow
> that she will mourn, at least outwardly, for His killed creatures.
> Your praying is useless, and your church-going mere mockery of
> God, if you have not plain obedience in you enough for this. Let
> every lady in the upper classes of civilized Europe simply vow that,
> while any cruel war proceeds, she will wear *black*; – a mute's
> black, – with no jewel, no ornament, no excuse for, or evasion
> into, prettiness – I tell you again, no war would last a week.[50]

Even if Ruskin is hard to take at face value, it should be clear that the
issue of war represented the chance for massive social change.

The issue of equipoise

What do Ruskin and Helps tell us about their time? As Burn conceded,
it is probably impossible to judge an age, generation, decade, or even
shorter period of time by the lives and ideas of a couple of figures, but
the careers of Sir Arthur Helps and John Ruskin further illuminate
some of the broader realities of the mid-Victorian generation. After all,
both authors were well positioned to understand their society; the
success of each suggests that their writings were popular with the
public.

Helps portrayed and symbolizes a sober, balanced and dispassionate
approach to the problems with which the world had become familiar.
His career – at various points between the relatively cloistered academic
life and the creation and implementation of public policy to manage the
crowd – flourished between 1852 and 1867. He wrote the *Friends* series
to show that often-divisive issues could be understood and encountered
in many different ways – through satire, humour, analytical argument –
and that in this way they might be safely domesticated. John Hullah,
who wrote Helps's obituary in *Macmillan's Magazine*, summed up his
career and commitment to the dispassionate approach to public questions:

> Few writers of any class – fiction of course excepted – have been
> more largely read; few of this particular class so largely. For his
> subjects though always important, were not always 'interesting'.

They were not of a kind respecting which a cry or crusade could be got up. His thoughts seemed always to be turned on those evils which escape notice of, or at least are avoided by, those whose objects in life are influence, money or notoriety ... For he habitually checked in himself and others sweeping conclusions respecting anything or anybody. He had something to say for the worst cause, which is less common, because far more difficult, for the worst man. His considerations for the 'other side' seemed sometimes excessive.[51]

Helps, then, tried to nudge public opinion towards social reform. However, his method of dialogue – with its multiple viewpoints, humour, irony, sarcasm and, above all, playfulness – emphasized that these were issues which need not polarize. To put it another way, it was Helps's mission to humanize the process of reform by domesticating some of the threatening social issues of his day.

Helps was also emblematic of 'equipoise' because he played a direct role in some of the era's administrative developments. During the cattle plague he was instrumental in establishing the guidelines for the transportation of cattle and other animals. Helps was connected to many of the centralizing tendencies of the mid-Victorian period; he was a proponent of the growth of central state power on the one hand, and enrichment of private, domestic life on the other.

The message for Victorians which comes from Helps's understated prose was that men and women already possessed the resources to make their lives pleasant and wise. Not only did Helps preach acceptance and reform, but also the wisdom derived from understanding that in virtually any human endeavour comes an inevitable mixture of folly and intelligence. *Friends in Council* did not try to capitalize on the visible changes of the nineteenth century to offer its readers the prospect of empowerment. Instead, Helps eschewed the possibility of social transformation or promises of utopia. Yet *Friends in Council* did portray characters – which many identified with – whose defects were as attractive as their ideas. In short, Helps allowed his readers to be content with the pace of their rapidly changing world.

To understand the neglect of Helps, it is useful to recall a truism that Clio smiles on and remembers those who are unbalanced, egocentric, arrogant, often mad, naïve, obsessed, beautiful and ugly. Helps was none of these things. Neither his fair-minded, humane treatment of social issues, nor his steadfast work as Clerk of the Privy Council made him colourful or interesting. The publication of the Greville memoirs brought the following responses from Helps: 'There will be no papers found after my death, no diaries ... I resolved from the first that there should be the instance of a man who saw and heard much what was deeply interesting, but private, and could hold his tongue and restrain his pen forever.'[52] Helps could write to D.D. Christie: 'Do not write a biography of me, if you can possibly avoid it. There is nothing to be told; and if there was anything you know how I detest notoriety.'[53] Perhaps Helps belonged so well to his era that his passing from the awareness of subsequent generations could be said to match the experience of more ordinary aspects of his time.

Ruskin, of course, was almost the mirror image. Just as Helps's career and ideas 'fitted' into the 'equipoisal' context, Ruskin's prominent achievements challenged many of the assumptions which mid-Victorians found attractive. With his stress on totality, organic vision, appeals to 'infinitude', and his insistence that change not be confined to political or governmental issues, Ruskin stands out as an extreme example within an era defined by balance or equipoise. However, Ruskin was at once influenced by the more restrained figures such as Helps, and yet was also shaped by some of the powerful historical forces which flourished before and after the age of equipoise. And what had Ruskin thought about the 'great prizefight'? Unlike Helps, Ruskin had been excited by the event, seeing Tom Sayers as a great national hero. He had long admired boxing as 'the noble art' and the Sayers–Heenan event had confirmed his enthusiasm. Ruskin was so eager to meet Tom Sayers that he approved of a plan to bring the English prizefighter to the Working Men's College. George Allen, a carpenter who was later to become Ruskin's chief publisher, was instructed to bring the best wine from Denmark Hill 'to drink to Tom Sayer's health'. Unfortunately, as one of Ruskin's early biographers explained, Ruskin's assistant, Mr Butterworth, was unable to persuade Sayers to come, bringing instead only a portrait.[54] Ruskin, the most influential art critic of the age, was greatly disappointed to have only a portrait, when he could have met a prize-fighter and celebrated his courage.

Helps, of course, had been the one to connect the great prizefight to international relations, but it was Ruskin's attitude which would prove to be more forward-looking. If Helps proved insensitive to the coming of modern nationalism, Ruskin's emotional bonding with a national heroic figure presages all too vividly the identification which men and women in the latter half of the nineteenth century would have with their nation-states. The point here is not that Ruskin failed to make a symbolic connection or that his enthusiasm overwhelmed his judgement, but that his response to this event was representative of trends which would be played out in vivid displays of nationalism. That is, in contrast to Helps, Ruskin's attitude hints of what was to come through much of Europe: the strong emotional connections between national competition, athleticism and the celebration of the heroic. Given Ruskin's genius for positing organic connections between seemingly unrelated subjects, and given his instinct to make global or totalistic claims, his regard for Sayers shows further that his life and career were the opposite of the traits of equipoise. To put it a little differently, Ruskin aimed to unite many disparate things; Helps sought to get his readers to appreciate the essential and intrinsic differences between them.

Arguably one of the tests of a seminal mind is the degree of latitude with which its disciples and adherents interpret or even misinterpret its chief ideas. In the case of Ruskin, a plethora of interpretations have been generated, but it is worth noting that some of the most significant have involved nations and projects of massive transformation. To be sure, a thinker should never be held accountable for the way in which his or her work is interpreted, but it is worth recalling that figures ostensibly diverse as Mahatma Gandhi, Cecil Rhodes and Leo Tolstoy – all fascinated in one way or another with organic nationalism – claimed to be profoundly influenced by Ruskin. Moreover, 'the later Ruskin' could readily espouse nationalist, imperialist or even jingoist rhetoric. To cite only a few examples, Ruskin's defence of Governor Eyre, his celebration of Herbert Edwardes (one of the 'Princes of the Punjab'), his advocacy of colonization, his enthusiasm for missionary work, and celebration of medieval England as the basis for improving national character all suggest that his organic and totalistic vision would lend itself to nationalistic construals. Whereas Helps was plainly uncomfortable with the growth of sentiments which would support militarism, in Ruskin we find an anticipation of what would later be commonplace: a strong identification between an individual and his nation's perceived military power.

Therefore, Ruskin's *The Crown of Wild Olive*, for all of its Helpsian influence, points forward to the era beyond 1867. If Ruskin was 'too exotic', it certainly seems to be the case that he was profoundly affected by the age of equipoise; perhaps it is not too much to ask whether his conversion of modest Helpsian ideas into a larger metaphysical social challenge was in many ways indicative of his frustration with the balanced hues of mid-Victorian Britain. Ruskin's *Crown of Wild Olive*, then, must be remembered not as an embodiment of 'equipoise' but as a determined response to what Burn characterized as the 'generation in which the old and the new, the elements of growth, survival and decay, achieved a balance which most contemporaries regarded as satisfactory'.[55]

Notes

1. W.L. Burn, *The Age of Equipoise* (London: George Allen & Unwin, 1964), p. 49.
2. Ibid., p. 43.
3. Ibid., p. 97.
4. John R. Debruyn, 'John Ruskin and Sir Arthur Helps', *John Rylands Library Bulletin*. vol. 59 (Autumn, 1976), pp. 75–94 and 299–322. The surviving correspondence between Helps and Ruskin comprises letters dating from 1848–73. While this is not a substantial body of material, it is revealing about both men. For example, the early letters show that Ruskin was keen to impress and cultivate Helps. Later letters suggest that they remained relatively close. Since Helps had many of his private papers destroyed (lest they compromise people who had held his trust – the Queen, Palmerston, Carlyle, W.E. Forster, Stephen Spring-Rice, etc.), unfortunately we are left with only fragments of what was probably an interesting correspondence. It has not been collected into a single volume; instead parts of it have been published in two places: E.A. Helps, *The Correspondence of Sir Arthur Helps, K.C.B, D.C.L* (London, 1917), and *The Works of John Ruskin* (1903–1912); in addition a couple of significant manuscripts can be found in the Pierpont Morgan Library (New York).
5. For the most part, Ruskin's biographers have overlooked Helps. For a notable exception see Tim Hilton, *John Ruskin: The Early Years 1819–1859* (New Haven and London: Yale University Press, 1985), pp. 218–19 and 247. None the less, this remains an understudied relationship. After all, there are many places where Ruskin acknowledged intellectual and literary debts to Arthur Helps. Some of these admissions come from unexpected sources. To cite one example, Arthur Munby recorded spending an evening with Ruskin who spoke at great length:

> And then it all came out. He did not indeed say aught of a change of opinion of himself: but those who believed him still an artistic Calvinist(!) must have been astonished when he began. He spoke of the grave religious doubts and search of nowadays; and said that he for his part has been greatly enlightened therein by a recent suggestion from a friend (Helps, Vernon thought [Vernon Lushington] it was); which was, that the *attempt to combine religion & ethics* was foolish and fatal. On this text he preached for half an hour with intense earnestness; a mixture, as it were, of unitarianism and positivism: speaking, as he himself said, in an 'audacious and impudent' way of God: not that he was the least irreverent – far from it – but apostlewise, as if he were telling out a new revelation. God, says he, hates you to unhappy: hates self-denial therefore: will have men *not* pry into another world and sacrifice everything to that; but will have them look at this world, enjoy and fulfil their being here, be manly and brotherly, and take delight it, when they have comprehended it, the unique nobleness and splendour of Humanity.

(Munby, cited in Derek Hudson, *Munby: Man of Two Worlds* (London: John Murray, 1972), pp. 141–2.)

6. Like many other parts of Helps's life, his career as an Apostle remains

nearly invisible. For example, Richard Deacon quotes Helps on the procedure for picking subsequent Apostles, but does not provide a reference for the passage. For more on this topic see Richard Deacon, *The Cambridge Apostles* (London: Robert Royce Ltd, 1985), p. 2. However, for a more complete treatment of Helps's relationship with the Apostles see William Lubenow, *The Cambridge Apostles, 1820–1914* (Cambridge: Cambridge University Press, 1998), pp. xi, 42–3, 49, 64, 126 and 159–60.

7. Ibid., pp. 202–5.
8. Helps, *Correspondence*, p. 3.
9. Ibid.
10. Among Helps's early writings are historical dramas: *Catherine Douglas, A Tragedy* (1843) and *Henry II*.
11. Thomas Hughes, 'Social Pressure', *Macmillan's Magazine* (January 1875), p. 186.
12. The success of this book illustrates that Helps had readers on both sides of the Atlantic, as it is quite clear that *The Claims of Labour* was taken seriously in the American South. For example, Edward J. Pringle capitalized on the arguments of *The Claims of Labour* to assail Helps (and more generally anti-slavery) when reviewing *Uncle Tom's Cabin*. For more on Pringle and the debate with Helps see Stephen L. Keck, 'Slaves or Labourers: Revisting the 1852 Debate Between Sir Arthur Helps and a "Carolinian" (Edward J. Pringle)', in *The Proceedings of the South Carolina Historical Association 1997* (1997), pp. 12–23.
13. Helps also established his reputation as a significant historian. While he was developing and publishing his ideas as part of the Friends' writings, Helps also produced a four-volume history of the development of the Spanish Empire in the Americas, entitled *Conquerors of the New World and their Bondsmen*. The reputation of these volumes was such that Macaulay urged Palmerston to offer him the Regius Professorship at Cambridge. Macaulay felt that Helps had worked on 'some very interesting portions of modern history' and that he 'has treated those portions of history ably and popularly'. The appointment to the Regius Professorship 'will be applauded by the public'. Macaulay to Palmerston, 2 December 1859, Thomas Pinney, ed., *The Letters of Thomas Babington Macaulay*, vol. VI (Cambridge: Cambridge University Press, 1981), pp. 257–8.
14. Whewell to Helps (4 January 1854). Helps, *Correspondence*, p. 164.
15. Ralph Waldo Emerson to Lidian Emerson (28, 29 and 30 June 1848). *The Letters of Ralph Waldo Emerson*, ed. Ralph L. Rusk (New York: Columbia University Press, 1939), vol. IV, p. 93.
16. Ralph Waldo Emerson, *English Traits, The Complete Works of Ralph Waldo Emerson* (Boston, MA: Houghton Mifflin, 1903), p. 394.
17. George Smith, cited in Leonard Huxley, *The House of Smith Elder* (London: printed for private circulation, 1923), p. 148.
18. Thomas Hughes 'Social Pressure', *Macmillan's Magazine*, vol. 31 (January 1875), p. 186.
19. Leslie Stephen, *The Life of Sir James Fitzjames Stephen*, cited in J.W. Robertson Scott, *The Story of the Pall Mall Gazette* (Cambridge: Cambridge University Press, 1950), pp. 156–7.
20. 'Oulita the Serf', *Fraser's Magazine*, vol. 57 (May 1858), p. 528.
21. For example, Lucy Soulsby, author and headmistress of Oxford High

School, advocated *Friends in Council* along with works by Aurelius, Kant and Hegel as sources for practical wisdom. In addition, Soulsby also advocated the collection of 'story books'. These books were to be culled from the works of Mrs Oliphant, Pater, George Eliot, Charles Kingsley, Henry Kingsley, Dickens, Thackeray, Hawthorne and Helps. With respect to Helps she favoured *Realmah* and *Ivan de Biron*. For more on this topic see Lucy Soulsby, *Happiness* (London: Longmans, Green and Co., 1899) and *Record of a Year's Reading* (Oxford and London: A.R. Mowbray and Co., 1903). An interesting discussion about Soulsby can be found in Kate Flint, *The Woman Reader* (Oxford: Oxford University Press, 1993).

22.   'Oulita the Serf', p. 528.
23.   Elizabeth Gaskell to Marianne Gaskell. *The Letters of Mrs Gaskell*, J.A.V. Chapple and Arthur Pollard, eds (Manchester: Manchester University Press, 1966), p. 541.
24.   There are many more examples of Victorians who looked to Helps for style. To cite a few examples, the philosopher Alexander Bain (1818–1903) explained in his autobiography that he was 'greatly struck' with Helps's first major work, *Thoughts in the Cloister and the Crowd*. Bain acknowledged that he had the 'occasion to peruse Helps's maturer writings, and to utilize them as illustrations in rhetoric'. Alexander Bain, *Autobiography* (London: Longmans, Green and Co., 1904), pp. 133–4. In addition to Bain, F.J. Rowe and W.T. Webb, professors of English Literature at Presidency College, Calcutta, republished Helps's *Essays Written in the Intervals of Business* because his prose was 'useful reading for the Indian student'. Furthermore, they also regarded Helps's 'well-bred' style of expression as an asset because it illustrated a number of important values: 'among the marks of good-breeding are repose of manners and repression of excited feeling, joined to consideration for the views of others; and the reader can hardly fail to notice in Helps's style a quiet smoothness (rather than strength), an absence of dogmatic statement, and a desire to find favourable points even in those opposed to him'. Arthur Helps, *Essays Written in the Intervals of Business*, F.J. Rowe and W.T. Webb, eds (London and New York: Macmillan and Co., 1889), p. x.
25.   Helps's role in the practice of public medicine furnishes a clear example of his involvement with the growth of centralized administration. For more on this topic see Royston Lambert, *Sir John Simon 1816–1904* (London: Macgibbon & Kee, 1963), pp. 304–29.
26.   Arthur Helps, 'War: A Conversation with the Friends in Council', *Fraser's Magazine*, vol. 59 (March 1859), p. 260.
27.   Ibid., p. 268.
28.   Ibid., p. 272.
29.   Ibid., p. 274.
30.   Ibid., p. 272
31.   Ibid., p. 274.
32.   Burn, *The Age of Equipoise*, p. 284.
33.   Palmerston cited in Burn, *The Age of Equipoise*, p. 284.
34.   Arthur Helps, *Fraser's Magazine*, (1860), cited in Helps, *Correspondence*, p. 238.
35.   With respect to *Stones of Venice*, there is an interesting kinship between

his use of 'the incomplete picture' as a way of organizing historical discussion and Helps's analysis of rhetoric in the first volumes of *Friends in Council*. In addition, Tim Hilton (*John Ruskin: The Early Years*) is the only recent biographer of Ruskin to explore these connections. Lastly, Ruskin himself often acknowledged Helps. For more on this topic see E.T. Cook and Alexander Wedderburn, eds, *The Works of John Ruskin*, 39 vols (London: George Allen, 1903–12), vols V, p. 425–7, VII, p. 372 and XIX, p. xxv.

36. XVIII, pp. 398–9.
37. XVIII, pp. 397–8.
38. XVIII, pp. 398–9.
39. XVIII, p. 399.
40. Ibid.
41. For more on Ruskin's views of foreign affairs see XVIII, pp. 537–45.
42. XVIII, p. 460.
43. XVIII, p. 464.
44. XVIII, p. 470.
45. XVIII, pp. 483–4.
46. XVIII, p. 472.
47. XVIII, p. 473.
48. XVIII, p. 474. Ruskin revealed that his grasp on the American conflict was uneven at best when he claimed that the Spartans won the battle of Corinth with the loss of eight soldiers while the North at 'indecisive Gettysburg' lost 30,000.
49. XVIII, pp. 488–9.
50. XVIII, p. 492.
51. John Hullah, 'Sir Arthur Helps', *Macmillan's Magazine*, vol. 31 (April 1875), pp. 550–51.
52. Arthur Helps, cited in John Debruyn, 'Ruskin and Helps', p. 75.
53. Ibid., p. 75. The letter is dated 14 October 1864.
54. E.T. Cook, *The Life of John Ruskin* (1911; New York: Haskell House Publishers Ltd, 1968), pp. 26–7.
55. Burn, *The Age of Equipoise*, p. 17.

CHAPTER EIGHT

'The hand of the Lord is upon the cattle': religious reactions to the cattle plague, 1865–67

Matthew Cragoe

The outbreak of the deadly Rinderpest virus which swept through Britain between 1865 and 1867 was the largest challenge presented to British agriculture between the repeal of the Corn Laws and the general downturn of prices after 1873.[1] Apparently introduced on 16 June by an infected consignment of continental beasts sold at the Metropolitan Cattle Market in London, the disease spread quickly. By 14 October, the 'cattle plague' had broken out in twenty-nine English counties and had also crossed the borders into Scotland and Wales. Throughout November and December, and into the early months of 1866, the plague continued its ravages: only from the spring of 1866, after the government had introduced a policy of compulsory slaughter for infected beasts, did the disease show any signs of abating. In total, the plague claimed the lives of nearly 300,000 cattle,[2] counties such as Cheshire, the dairying capital of England, losing nearly three-quarters of their herds. Urban dairies, however, also suffered badly,[3] and total losses topped £5 million.[4]

In W.L. Burn's *The Age of Equipoise*, the cattle plague is discussed in the context of one of his four great 'disciplines', the law. For Burn, the confused administrative response to the plague underlined the ambivalence of all parties, the government included, to the role it was proper for the state to play in such circumstances, and reveals that the boundaries between those who were 'for' state intervention and those who were 'against' were not consistent. In 1866, it was the agricultural interest, long regarded as implacably hostile to the interference of central government in the affairs of the localities, which sought their intervention.[5]

The cattle plague was not simply an administrative conundrum, however, and in this essay it will be examined in relation to another of the great social disciplines identified by Burn, religion. For the appearance of the plague prompted a widespread campaign aimed at persuading the government that a day of fasting and humiliation should be appointed. Since many were familiar, as Burn notes, with a biblical God who expressed His anger through the infliction of punishments such as plague and famine, it is not surprising that they interpreted the cattle murrain in similar terms, as a sign of God's displeasure.[6] The godly urged that the proper response on the part of the nation was to hold a day of fasting and humiliation in which His forgiveness for their transgression could be sought. Only if such atonement were made, they argued, would the plague be removed. During the weeks leading up to Easter 1866, when medical cures had failed, and 'stamping out' had yet to demonstrate its efficacy, a considerable debate raged in the press on the subject. And although the government chose not to appoint a national day of fasting and humiliation, informal days were observed in many dioceses.

This sequence of events will provide the focus for this essay, and an attempt will be made, through an examination of the campaign to appoint days of humiliation, to locate the moral boundaries of Burn's England, that England of 'the rectory and the modest mansion house and the farmhouse' rather than of 'factories and co-operative stores'.[7] It begins with a general examination of days of humiliation, a topic which has received little scholarly attention. After exploring their function and incidence, and offering a brief case study of two other mid-Victorian examples, 1847 and 1854, we turn our attention to the campaign of 1866. The following section examines the debates surrounding the days of humiliation and then we explore the various ways in which the informal days were observed. The insight this provides into the state of religious feeling in mid-Victorian England is considered in the conclusion.

Days of fasting and humiliation[8]

The tradition of holding days of fasting and humiliation in order to propitiate the Deity belonged, as *The Times* remarked in 1854, to 'the ancient custom of England and all Christian States'.[9] Fast days were appointed by a proclamation of the Crown, and appear to have been called for one of two purposes: either to beseech a divine blessing on British arms, or to implore divine forgiveness of the national sins which had led to the sending of a plague. In order to emphasize their unique character, they were held on weekdays, and thus all normal labour ceased. The need for national recognition of other acts of divine origin, such as the preservation of the monarch from assassination, or the birth of a new child to the royal family, was met by the issuing of special prayers of thanksgiving, which were read out during the normal Sunday services.[10]

Occasional examples of fast days can be found in the period before the Civil War (such as that ordered 'during this tyme of mortalitie, and other afflictions' in 1563, or those in 1625, 1636 and 1640 in respect of plague) but they became far more frequent after the Restoration in 1660.[11] Fasts were appointed in 1661, 1665 (twice), 1666 (in respect of the Great Fire of London), 1673, 1678, 1679 and 1680. The accession of William III, regarded as it was, in David Cressy's words, as 'one of England's most fortunate providences',[12] did nothing to slow the frequency of such celebrations. In part this was due to England's constant involvement in various continental wars: fast days for the success of English arms were held in 1689, 1692 and each year between 1695 and 1697, 1699 and 1703, and 1705 and 1711. Under the Hanoverians there were fasts on account of the plague in 1720 and 1721, and fasts each year between 1739 and 1747, with the exception of 1743, on account of either the War of Jenkins's Ear or the Jacobite rebellion. Between 1756 and 1762 an annual day of fasting was observed, now formalized into part of the Lent programme, a tradition which was maintained during the services held in respect of the American Revolution in 1776, 1778–79, 1781 and 1782. The wars against revolutionary France and Napoleon were marked in like fashion: fast days were appointed each year between 1793 and 1801 and 1803 and 1813.

The long period of peace following the end of the war with France naturally limited the opportunities for the holding of fasts, but the tradition did not die out. Despite the fact that, as Boyd Hilton has remarked, liberal opinion was turning against the concept,[13] the appearance of cholera in 1832 was met with a day of humiliation, and the Irish famine was treated thus in 1847. The tradition retained sufficient life, as Olive Anderson has discussed, for days to be appointed on the return of war in the 1850s.[14] During Lent, 1854 and 1855, fasts were held to implore divine blessing on British arms in the Crimea, and the Indian Mutiny of 1857 was treated in the same manner.[15] The observation of days of humiliation was, therefore, a familiar duty to the mid-Victorian generation, and one that commanded considerable support, if contemporary reports are to be believed. An examination of the fast days held in 1847 and 1854 will help establish the context for the days of humiliation observed with respect to the cattle plague in 1866.

The seriousness with which contemporaries viewed the call to a day of national humiliation and fasting in both 1847 and 1854 can be gauged by the reaction of *The Times*. On both occasions, the newspaper which, as Tom Morley remarks, represented 'the sovereign opinion of

... the ruling classes',[16] was at great pains to justify the days of humiliation. 'It is a matter of usage to see the misfortunes of our country', it remarked in 1847, 'as Divine judgements on our sins. That it is no idle form, but the bounden recognition of an awful reality, we firmly believe.'[17] In this spirit, the editor invited all ministers in the metropolis to submit the texts from which they had preached on the fast days and published them, over two full pages, on the day after the fast.[18] Other provincial papers followed suit, reprinting the sermons preached in their vicinity, a strong indication of the interest which such services generated among the reading public.[19]

Days of fasting and humiliation, therefore, continued to be of interest to the mid-Victorian generation. Quite what form the 'fasting' took is not clear. In 1847, a Kentish clergyman published a pamphlet, for distribution among the poor, in which he acknowledged that since total abstinence might damage health, people should consider substituting 'dry bread or some coarse food in place of their ordinary meals'. He went on to warn against the 'too common expedient' of simply exchanging meat for fish: such, he cautioned, was not a sufficiently self-denying gesture, and was certainly not what had been understood as fasting by biblical figures such as David or Daniel.[20] His views were typical of those entertained by other writers on the subject who declared that total abstinence was not necessary.[21] In any case, fasting, as another author explained, need not mean only the 'refraining from necessary food', but could also be applied more broadly to imply a 'ceasing from our worldly engagements or pleasures, that we may make it a day of humiliation and reflection, of penitence and prayer'.[22]

Whatever decision people came to with regard to the question of food, it is quite clear that to a large extent the latter counsel was heeded: mid-Victorian fast days as a whole had a solemn air. *The Times* described that in 1854, for example, as 'a sort of Sunday, rather duller than Sunday itself; closed shops, comparatively silent streets, public walks full of quiet people, and, at certain hours, long lines of churchgoers'. The unique character of the day was further marked by most factories ceasing work for the day. In Manchester and the surrounding towns, in both 1847 and 1854, the vast majority of the mills closed down for the day, while in provincial towns all business was suspended.

The services themselves, meanwhile, seem to have been very popular: as Olive Anderson remarked, the response of the public 'was far greater than even the saints had hoped'.[23] The general experience of the 1847 fast day in London, according to *The Times*, was that 'the congregations were more numerous than is usually the case ... on the Sabbath days'.[24] St Paul's was described as being 'crowded to excess'; at St

George's, Bloomsbury, all available seating was quickly filled, 'and many were consequently obliged to continue standing', whilst at both St Pancras and St Martin-in-the-Fields, 'hundreds of persons who were desirous of being present were unable to obtain admittance'. Nor were the congregations solely composed of the well-to-do: at St Marylebone, it was remarked that 'the poorer classes formed a large proportion of the congregation'. A similar popularity was evident outside the capital: the Collegiate Church in Manchester was attended by 4000 people, 'one of the largest congregations ever remembered within its walls'. Similar reports were made from satellite towns such as Warrington, Oldham, Rochdale and Stockport.[25] In country areas, meanwhile, the pattern was once again repeated, with churches across counties such as Kent and Lincolnshire being reported very full: small towns like Barton witnessed 'an almost universal attendance at all the public places of worship in the town'.[26] Similar reports were made in 1854.[27]

The infrequency of fast days in the nineteenth century may well have been an important factor in their success in 1847 and 1854: the Revd Mr Fuller of St Peter's, Pimlico, for example, felt it was so, and argued that 'curiosity was excited as to the duties properly belonging to the day and the manner in which they ought to be discharged', and many attended whom it would otherwise be difficult to reach.[28] Those that did attend doubtless found the experience interesting as well as spiritually uplifting. *The Times* pointed out that, 'under a ritual that admits of so little choice or variety as ours, a few prayers that one does not know by heart, something rather *apropos*, and an allusive selection of lessons, gospels, and epistles, are a very great novelty'.[29]

Naturally, not everyone thus released from work attended a religious service. *The Times* in 1847 was all too aware that 'a general fast in the British metropolis in the middle of the nineteenth century on account of a remote provincial famine will supply abundant materials both to the witty and the dull'.[30] Indeed, there were many who chose not to spend this unexpected leisure-time inside church. The *Manchester Guardian* reported in 1847 that great numbers had made excursions to the countryside, to Alderley Edge and Bowden, and that the demand for horses was so great that none were available for hire but those booked two days earlier. The parks, meanwhile, were full from morning till evening with promenaders who had so little inclination to fast that, despite the caterers at Queen's Park and Philip's Park having laid in extra 'sandwiches, veal pies, confectionery, tea and coffee, lemonade, &c.', for the day, supplies were exhausted by four o'clock. 'Outdoor sports and exercises' were also much in vogue in Manchester, as they were in Lincoln, where a cricket match was held between eleven printers and eleven tailors and shoemakers.[31] Nevertheless, there were many reports that those who did not choose to go to the services behaved with great decorum, and that examples of intoxication were extremely rare.[32]

Thus the idea of holding days of fasting and humiliation under the patronage of the state seemed an appropriate response to the advent of natural calamities and wars well into the Victorian period. When the Rinderpest plague appeared among cattle in the autumn of 1865, and, in Burn's words, began to spread 'widely and hideously',[33] quickly reaching epidemic proportions, it was unsurprising that a section of public opinion should turn once again to the expediency of instigating some ceremony of national atonement.

Easter, 1866

It is perhaps tempting to depict the growing pressure for the appointment of a day of humiliation throughout January and February 1866 as being connected with the failure of either medical science or government regulation to quash the cattle plague. Despite the merits of several much-publicized 'cures' being canvassed in the pages of the press, the plague remained impervious to all treatments that the British veterinary establishment could throw at it. The powers of local authorities to isolate and slaughter infected cattle, meanwhile, were still in their early days, and the efficacy of such techniques was not yet proven. There certainly were some who began openly to despair of any secular cure being found: 'as the cattle plague baffles all human wisdom of science and experience', wrote one correspondent of the evangelical *Record*, 'should we not nationally, as well as individually, own that "this is the finger of God," and, as a nation, humble ourselves before Him?'[34]

Yet very few adopted so extreme a position, and it would not do to represent the pressure for a day of humiliation as the last refuge of a people whose confidence in the scientific 'spirit of the age' had been undermined. Indeed, it would suggest a firmer distinction between 'secular' and 'religious' attitudes than actually existed, for there had been a significant religious element in the cocktail of measures pitted against the plague from the outset. One of the first actions taken by the government was to ask the Archbishop of Canterbury to issue 'A Form of Prayer to Almighty God; for Relief from the Plague now existing amongst Cattle'.[35] This prayer was read in every parish church throughout the country for the duration of the crisis. Some parish clergymen also composed their own special prayers and hymns to supplement the official prayer, or held special services on account of the plague.[36] The

Bishop of Carlisle went so far as to hold a private day of humiliation in the cathedral on Friday, 12 January 1866, which, by all accounts, went off very well.[37]

Nevertheless, as Lent, the traditional season of atonement, approached, the idea began to gain ground that a national day of fasting and humiliation, similar to those held in 1847 and 1854, might be in due season. The proposal was widely debated, and marked by a strikingly larger degree of opposition than had been evident either in 1847 or 1854. Within the Church of England, enthusiasm was largely confined to the evangelical wing, associated with publications such as the *Record*. More striking, however, was the hostility of the newspaper press, and particularly *The Times*, which had been so supportive of earlier days of humiliation. It is to these debates that this section is devoted.

The strongest support for the day of humiliation could be found in the columns of the *Record*, though its editorial position was considerably more temperate than that of correspondents, such as the writer quoted earlier. Indeed, it was at pains not to disavow the utility of science, arguing that the elusiveness of a medicinal cure 'ought not to discourage perseverance in the attempt to trace the causes and discover a remedy'.[38] Nevertheless, it believed 'Our God is a God of Prayer' and urged the day of humiliation as a necessary complement to existing efforts. This moderate stance found many supporters. At a county meeting in Cumberland, for example, Mr T.H. Graham 'thought it right that as a nation they should humble themselves on a certain day in the presence of Almighty God, but that they should also adopt the most stringent measures to prevent the spreading of the plague'.[39] John Jones of Kingston, a farmer, similarly felt that, 'whilst the ... farmers generally approve of the measures which have been adopted by Government in reference to the cattle plague, they believe also in a superintending Providence', and wished for a day of humiliation.[40] The general tenor of the debate was well captured by Dean Close, during a meeting for farmers at Carlisle: 'He did not expect a miracle in answer to their prayers', he said. 'He and all rational believers admitted that the Rinderpest and every other plague was the result of natural causes; but they believed God controlled those natural causes, and natural causes might take it away.'[41]

If there was broad support for a day of humiliation amongst evangelical Anglicans, however, there were also important currents of hostility within the Church. The Broad Church *Clerical Journal* was only ever lukewarm in its support for the project,[42] whilst the ritualists seem only to have been interested in so far as the day promised to further their efforts to reintroduce regular 'vigils, days of fasting and abstinence' at

Easter.[43] The idea ran into particularly strong opposition at the Convocation of York in February 1866.[44] The Revd Canon Randolph objected that too many holy days, such as Good Friday, were simply used for leisure, and that they could not expect a day of humiliation to be observed any better: if it was 'perverted to riotous living', the day would do more harm than good.[45] The poor, argued others, could not afford the absence from work that such a day entailed. Finally, some expressed reservations about involving the state in such a proceeding since the dissenters, at least, would not respect it.

An even stronger tide of opposition surfaced in the newspaper press once it emerged that the Archbishop of Canterbury, encouraged by the success of the experiment in Carlisle, had asked the Home Secretary to appoint a national day of humiliation. Grey's answer had been a polite negative: the government did not, he said, consider the crisis a 'national' one, since it affected only the inhabitants of rural areas. Furthermore, he admitted that the argument concerning the loss of wages to the working classes had been important in persuading the government not to sanction a national fast. In any event, he continued, the religious element was already taken care of: 'The duty of imploring the Divine Blessing on the means of checking the progress of the disease' was 'fully recognised on the part of the Nation by the constant use in every church in England of the Form of Prayer ordered by Her Majesty in Council in September last.'[46]

The *Pall Mall Gazette*, which had all along mocked the idea that either prayers or days of humiliation could stay the plague, seized with delight on Grey's refusal: 'he clearly desired to cold water the scheme', it said, 'but did not quite see how to do it without shocking some estimable constituencies or committing himself to some awkward doctrinal position ... What he *feels* is evidently that to pray against the cattle plague is not the mode in which sensible Englishmen should meet it.'[47] Though this probably misstates Grey's position somewhat (he was, after all, a moderate evangelical, and the Home Secretary who granted the day of humiliation in 1847 on account of the cholera), his decision did fall into line with a great deal of sceptical opinion, the expression of which marked a real change from the situation in 1847 and 1854.

The keystone of this scepticism was a firm belief in the ability of secular means to combat the disease. Grey himself betrayed his confidence in the power of science to deal with the problem, as a draft of his letter to the Archbishop of Canterbury in the PRO demonstrates: 'by ... the judicious use of the means which increased knowledge and experience have suggested for checking the disease', he argued, 'there may ere long be cause for thankfulness for a general mitigation of the severity of this calamity'.[48] Others expressed similar opinions. *The Times*, which had been favourable to the fast days of 1847 and 1854, adopted a more hostile tone in 1866: it implied an 'extraordinary amount of faith', it said, 'to acquiesce in an observance which gives to a Church Service a special miraculous efficacy'; the 'great majority of men', it added, 'were they not kept in order by their own wives and children, not to speak of lady friends and the clergymen, would boldly avow that they think no good can come of it – to the poor cattle at least'.[49] The editor of the *Cheshire Observer* also opposed the idea, but noted that once the request for a day of humiliation had been made, it was very difficult for any individual to stand out against it without subjecting themselves to charges of impiety.[50] The social pressure to conform notwithstanding, however, he argued that if the government was to be memorialized at all, it should be for a larger supply of vaccine, or some system of compensation for those who had suffered from the plague. 'We believe', he added, 'in the proverb that "God helps those who help themselves", and have far more faith in the efficacy of vaccination than fasting.' Others simply felt the prayers were an irrelevance. Another correspondent of the same paper denied that the Rinderpest was the work of God and felt, besides, that the cattle plague was not the most severe crisis facing the nation: what of 'the winter plague, the poverty plague, the consumption plague, the large family plague, [or] the bad trade plague'? He signed himself, with heavy irony, 'John Bull'.[51]

The days of humiliation

Although Grey declined to give the state's sanction to the project, he did suggest that the bishops might organize their own, informal, days of humiliation: this the Archbishop of Canterbury duly invited his suffragans to do.[52] As a consequence, days were appointed at different times during February and March across the country.[53] In this section, the response to the informal days of fasting and humiliation will be examined, and, as will be demonstrated, vociferous though the ranks of those who opposed the plan undoubtedly were, there was still a large constituency in the country ready to answer such an appeal.

As in 1847 and 1854, the services were in many areas strikingly well observed. In country parishes, where people had first-hand knowledge of the plague, this was perhaps not surprising. In the diocese of Ely, for example, it was reported that not only were the churches full in the parishes of King's Cliffe and Littleport, but that the farmers had given their labourers paid leave so that they could attend the services. In many of the older, country towns, as at Ely itself, a similar situation prevailed. The cathedral was full for morning service at 11, and all shops were closed, business being entirely suspended. In the evening, other churches were well filled.[54] In country towns across England, a similar pattern was followed. At Ipswich, Canterbury, Chester, Norwich, Southampton, Stratford-upon-Avon, Plymouth, Malvern and Northampton, businesses closed and trade was suspended either during the hours of Divine Service, or for the whole day. Much the same was true of London.[55] As in 1847 and 1854, many shops and businesses closed and the services were very well attended, to the extent that crowds were locked out of St Paul's. And despite the fears expressed at the York Convocation, nonconformists joined the day of humiliation in many areas. The Wesleyans, for example, observed 9 March as a national day in all their congregations across the country,[56] while the dissenting ministers of all denominations joined with their Anglican brethren at Northampton in taking out an advertisement in the local newspaper to declare the fact that they had all agreed to observe 29 March as a day of humiliation.[57]

No special service was issued for the days of humiliation; the Archbishop merely sanctioned the use of the Commination service. The effect of this was to focus the attention of congregations even more firmly upon the sermons. These in turn, displayed that same unshakeable attachment to the reality of divine providence that was strikingly displayed in 1847 and 1854.[58] In many churches, preachers dwelt upon the dangers of disregarding the literal word of the Bible. Dr Miller, at Birmingham, for example, launched a rousing attack against those who increasingly disregarded the Old Testament and encouraged the concomitant decline of belief in the ability of prayer to remove such a plague. 'Were the old laws obsolete?' he asked. 'Was the Old Testament an old almanac? Did they argue that God would not now act as He had done in olden times?' No, he concluded, the 'instruction of the Old Testament lived ... was written for the warning of the people now'.[59] Prayer was the key to the removal of the plague. The Revd R.C. King of St Katherine's in Northampton struck a similar note when he argued:

> Man may not be able to trace how He works, or why, but to deny that He does so work is to depose Him from His throne, and land ourselves in atheism and hardness of heart. If, as some would tell us, the question is merely one of sanitary regulations and Orders in Council, and such instrumentalities, and nothing else, then must we seek a non-natural meaning of half the Old Testament history; and much of the history and precept of the New.[60]

To such men, the plague services offered a platform from which to defend a whole system of religious thought.

Although there was some unanimity in accounting for the divine origins of the plague, the particular sin or sins to which the Deity wished to draw attention were harder to pin down. The unsatisfactorily tolerant attitude of the state to Roman Catholics was a favoured theme. James Bateman, of Biddulph Grange, touched a familiar nerve when he noted that, as the Irish famine (of 1845) 'followed immediately on the passing of the Bill for the endowment of the Romish College at Maynooth, we can scarcely err in regarding the present judgement as a "sign of wrath awakened" at the contemplated endowment of the Romish priesthood'.[61] Dean Close at Carlisle singled out the vice of drunkenness as the one 'more especially calculated to provoke the divine displeasure'.[62] Dr Miller of Birmingham agreed that 'the frightful national sin of drunkenness' was undoubtedly a major cause, but added that the bankruptcy of the missionary societies, which testified to a want of proper zeal, and the 'indelicate' productions of the print shops, which were openly displayed, were also offensive.[63] The Revd R.C. King covered most of the available options when he suggested that the plague had been sent in recognition of their failure to send the Lord's word to the East, and added, as other causes, the desecration of the Sabbath, infanticide, drunkenness and indifference.[64]

In general, the days of humiliation were, therefore, a marked success. Many men similar to the Herefordshire churchwarden who attended his local church to discover 'whether in this AD 1866, the Almighty deals with His people as He did with the Israelites of old, under the Mosaic or Jewish dispensation' undoubtedly went home with the sure conviction that he did.[65] Despite the government's refusal to sanction a national day of humiliation, large numbers of people evinced an earnest desire to participate in this traditional ritual, and a willingness to have the plague interpreted for them in essentially Old Testament terms.

Such enthusiasm was not, however, universal. In stark contrast to the situation in 1847 and 1854, in 1866 the populations of the great northern cities appear to have remained indifferent to the call for a day of humiliation. In Lancashire, for example, the informal day was almost completely ignored both by the public and the local press. The only indication that there was anything unusual taking place in the Manchester suburb of Hulme, for example, was that a few of the omnibuses ceased to run during the divine service on the day of humiliation. At Rochdale, on 23 March, the services were only 'moderately attended';[66] at Salford a week later, 'there were special services in nearly all the churches of the borough but, with one or two exceptions, the congregations were not very numerous. There was a partial closing of shops in the vicinity of some of the churches.'[67] At Manchester, the service at the

Collegiate Church was well attended but there was no outward sign in the town of the day's significance. Similar reports were made of Oldham. In the north-east, meanwhile, an equal lack of enthusiasm was displayed.

The clear division between the newer industrial areas and the rest of the country was also manifested during an unusual division in the House of Commons. Although the government had refused to recommend a day of national humiliation, Gladstone, the Chancellor of the Exchequer, moved that on the morning of the day of humiliation in London, all House of Commons business be suspended for two hours until one o'clock, in order to allow MPs to attend the services.[68] To Gladstone's surprise, John Bright, MP for Rochdale, and normally a supporter of the government, opposed the measure, arguing that the Bishop of London had no authority to call a day of humiliation, and deprecating the value of prayer under the circumstances. After a heated debate the House divided, and though the government won the division comfortably, by 259 to 112, the minority was nevertheless considerable. An analysis of the division list confirms the impression given above. Many Conservatives voted with the government, with county MPs heavily represented in the majority. In the minority, however, were, among others, the MPs of Rochdale, Bury, Manchester, Birmingham, Huddersfield, Sheffield, Grimsby, Walsall, Sunderland, Stockport and Salford.

Why did these areas, where strong support had been evident for the days of humiliation in 1847 and 1854, decline to become involved in 1866? There appear to be two over-riding reasons. First, the whole crisis was coloured in the industrial areas by the hostility of the manufacturers towards the aristocracy. The attempt by the landed interest to secure legislation which would allow local authorities to raise a fund from the rates to compensate farmers whose beasts were compulsorily slaughtered, for example, evoked bitter protests. The editor of the *Nonconformist* accused the landowners of 'the most beggarly selfishness':

> There is not an interest in the Kingdom which is not liable to reverses ... and there is not an interest that would not have scorned to exhibit such an abject want of self-reliance in misfortune ... Might seizes from right the property it wants, and, by a hocus-pocus invented to blind the eyes of the people whom it robs, calls it 'compensation'.[69]

The landed interest was, argued the manufacturing interest, still clinging to protection and not facing its responsibility to look after itself.[70] If free trade provided one source of opposition, support for free trade in religion presented another. Any chance that a day of humiliation and fasting might be taken up enthusiastically in the industrial areas disappeared when the government declined to name a national day and passed control to the bishops of the Church of England. Almost all the MPs who voted against the suspension of select committee business in the House of Commons, whether they represented industrial areas or not, declared themselves in the pages of *Dod's Parliamentary Companion* to be wholly opposed to any connection between Church and state.[71] In the absence of a lead from the manufacturing and voting classes, the fact that the rest of the population failed to rally to the call is not surprising.

Conclusion

The debates surrounding the days of humiliation and fasting demonstrated starkly both the strength and the limits of Burn's England. In the world dominated by the rectory, the manor and the farmhouse, or in the old well-established towns of the south, many were prepared to acknowledge the call of the Established Church. People clearly believed that under a well-ordered providence, prayer was an essential weapon in the armoury of resources which could be mobilized against the disease. That not all believed in the efficacy of prayer, and attended the services from a feeling of social obligation, was doubtless true: nevertheless, the significant factor is that go to church they did. Religion, or at least the Anglican version of it, was, as Burn states, one of the great social disciplines. So well observed were the days of humiliation in the heartland of Burn's England that the remark of the *Record*'s editor, that the observance of the humiliation days 'constitutes a significant rebuke to the timidity exhibited by the Premier [Russell]',[72] was not unjustifiable.

In the newer industrial towns of the north, however, Burn's world of 'factories and co-operatives', this was manifestly not the case. Here, hostility to the aristocracy and antipathy to the state Church combined to negate the attraction of the days of humiliation once the government had refused to set them on a national footing. Here, perhaps, the 'age of equipoise' was already history.

Notes

1. The plague has received little attention from historians: S.A. Hall, 'The Cattle Plague of 1865', *Medical History*, 6 (1962); Arvil B. Erikson, 'The Cattle Plague in England, 1865–1867', *Agricultural History*, 35 (1961),

pp. 94–103; J.R. Fisher, 'The Economic Effects of Cattle Disease in Britain and its Containment, 1850–1900', *Agricultural History*, 54 (1980), pp. 278–93; P. Phoofolo, 'Epidemics and Revolutions: the Rinderpest in late Nineteenth-Century Southern Africa', *Past & Present*, 138 (1993), pp. 112–43. PRO, HO/45, 7689, 72, printed circular, 22 September 1865, described the symptoms as involving 'a great depression of the vital powers, frequent shivering, staggering gait, cold extremities, quick and short breathing, drooping head, reddened eyes with a discharge from them, and also from the nostrils, of a mucous nature, raw looking places on the inner side of the lips and roof of the mouth, diarrhoea or dysenteric purging'.

2. M. Pelling, *Cholera, Fever and English Medicine, 1825–65* (Oxford: Oxford University Press, 1978), p. 2.

3. PP 1866–67, XVIII, *Report on the Cattle Plague in Great Britain during the years 1865, 1866, 1867*, p. 229; for Cheshire, ibid., p. 536. *Northern Weekly Express*, 16 September 1865, 'The Cattle Plague-Hartlepool', 4 November 1865, 'The Cattle Plague in Newcastle', for the catastrophic impact of the plague on several old dairymen in Newcastle. Urban milksheds were notoriously unhealthy: R. Perren, *The Meat Trade in Britain, 1840–1914* (London: Croom Helm, 1978), p. 61. *Cheshire Observer*, 3 February 1866, letter of T.H.G. Puleston for the impact of the plague on one parish; cases were rumoured of farmers having committed suicide over their losses: Cheshire RO, DSA 94/9, Lady Alderley to her husband, 5 January 1866.

4. PP 1866–67, XVIII, p. 225.

5. W.L. Burn, *The Age of Equipoise* (London: George Allen & Unwin, 1964), pp. 212–16, 223.

6. Ibid., pp. 311–12. See also B. Hilton, *The Age of Atonement: The Influence of Evangelicalism on Social and Economic Thought 1785–1865* (Oxford: Oxford University Press, 1988).

7. Burn, *Equipoise*, p. 7.

8. This section is based upon a study of the collection of Special Forms of Prayer held at the Lambeth Palace Record Office (hereafter LP).

9. *The Times*, 24 March 1847, editorial.

10. The timing of these prayers was often staggered to take account of problems of communication. Thus, in 1762, the special prayer of thanks for the capture of Havana contained the rubric: 'to be used throughout the cities of London and Westminster ... on Sunday the third of October 1762, and in all churches and chapels throughout England and Wales on the Sunday after the Ministers thereof receive the same'. LP, G 199, 28.28.

11. The special forms of prayer referred to in the following paragraphs can be found at Lambeth Palace, arranged chronologically, between call marks LP, G 199, 6.1; and 47.10 (21 March 1855).

12. D. Cressy, *Bonfires and Bells: National Memory and the Protestant Calendar in Elizabethan and Stuart England* (London: Weidenfeld & Nicolson, 1989), p. 185.

13. Hilton, *Age of Atonement*, pp. 213–15.

14. O. Anderson, 'The Reactions of Church and Dissent towards the Crimean War', *Journal of Ecclesiastical History*, 16 (1965), pp. 209–20.

15. B. Stanley, 'Christian Responses to the Indian Mutiny of 1857', in W.J. Sheils, ed., *Society for Church History, vol. 20: The Church and War* (1983), pp. 277–89.

16. T. Morley, "The Arcana of that great machine': Politicians and *The Times* in the late 1840s', *History*, 73 (1988), p. 38.

17. *The Times*, 24 March 1847, editorial.

18. *The Times*, 26 April 1854, 'The Day of Humiliation', pp. 7–10.

19. *Manchester Courier*, 19 April 1854, 'The Day of Humiliation'; *Stockport Advertiser*, 28 April 1854.

20. *Kentish Observer*, 18 March 1847, letter of 'A Clergyman': 'How shall we spend fast day?'

21. *The Times*, 23 March 1847, letter of 'A Layman': 'How shall we keep the fast?'

22. *Manchester Courier*, 20 March 1847, letter of 'Vigil', 'The General Fast'.

23. Anderson, 'Reactions of Church and Dissent', p. 216. 'Saints', that is, evangelicals.

24. *The Times*, 25 March 1847, pp. 2–3, 'The Fast Day in the Metropolis'.

25. *Manchester Courier*, 27 April 1847, 'The General Fast'.

26. *Lincolnshire Chronicle*, 2 April 1847; *Kentish Observer*, 1 April 1847, 'The General Fast'.

27. *The Times*, 27 April 1854, pp. 7–10, 'The Day of Humiliation'; *Manchester Courier*, 29 April 1854, 'The Day of Humiliation'; *Boston Guardian*, 3 May 1854, 'The Day of Humiliation'.

28. *The Times*, 25 March, 1847, 'The Fast Day in the Metropolis: St Peter's, Pimlico'.

29. *The Times*, 27 April, 1854, editorial. Not all agreed: *Lincolnshire, Spalding and Boston Free Press*, 2 May 1854, letter of 'Justitia', 'The Form for the Recent Fast', felt the service was too complicated, and preferred the Jewish prayer.

30. *The Times*, 24 March 1847, editorial.

31. *Manchester Guardian*, 27 March 1847, 'The Fast Day in Manchester' and 'The Manchester Public Parks'; *Lincolnshire Chronicle*, 2 April 1847.

32. *Manchester Courier*, 27 March 1847, 'The General Fast'.

33. Burn, *The Age of Equipoise*, p. 212.

34. *Record*, 24 January 1866, letter of 'Z.Z.', 'The Cattle Plague'. See also *The Hereford Times*, 17 February 1866, letter of 'J.J.', 'The Cattle Plague and Radnorshire'; ibid., 17 March 1866, letter of John Jones, Kington, 'The Cattle Plague'.

35. LP 36.73; The prayer was modified in August 1866 (36.74), and replaced in November (36.75); LP, Longley Mss, 7, f. 305, Lord Derby to Longley, 2 November 1866; other unofficial prayers were also published: '*Old Jonathon', or The District and Parish Helper*, 1 February 1866, 'The Cattle Plague and the Cholera'. The *Cornhill Magazine* for March 1866 gave a mocking description of the essentially secular method by which such prayers were constructed, the Archbishop of Canterbury submitting his draft for approval and correction by the Privy Council before it was authorized for use in churches; *Nonconformist*, 7 March 1866, p. 182.

36. *Cheshire Observer*, 10 February 1866, editorial; *Oldham Standard*, 24 March 1866, 'Crompton', Revd J.M. Neale composed a hymn which was so well received by the congregation that it was decided that it should be

sung every Sunday for as long as the Special Prayer was read. It also had a wider popularity: letter of 'M.A.', 'The Cattle Plague', in *The Church Times*, 24 March 1866. For a hymn from 1747, sung in Osmotherly Church, Yorkshire, see *Herts Gazette*, 14 October 1865, 'A Cattle Plague Psalm'. *Record*, 26 January 1866, letter of C. Bourne, 'Prayer and the Cattle Plague'. The Bishop of St Asaph authorized his clergy to hold individual services, *Record*, 22 January 1866, and this was undoubtedly popular: *Baner Ac Amserau Cymru*, 20 Ionawr 1866, p. 7, letter of 'Y', 'Myfyrfod Uwch Ben Pla y Gwartheg'.

37. The sermon was reproduced at length in *Record*, 19 January 1866, 'The Cattle Plague'. The bishop chose as his text Jonah, c.3, v.5 and c.4, v.11.
38. *Record*, 5 February 1866, editorial.
39. *Record*, 14 February 1866.
40. *The Hereford Times*, 17 March 1866, letter of J. Jones, 'The Cattle Plague'; and see Archbishop of York's comments, *Christian Times*, 2 March 1866.
41. *Record*, 28 March 1866, 'The Cattle Plague'.
42. *Clerical Journal*, 8 March 1866, editorial.
43. *The Church Times*, 17 February 1866, letter of 'H.S.' 'Fasting Days and the State of the Times'; *Church Review*, 17 March 1866, 'English Church Union: York branch'.
44. *Clerical Journal*, 15 February 1866, 'Convocation of York'.
45. The phrase is the Bishop of Peterborough's: *Northampton Herald*, 24 February 1866, letter to Archdeacon Davys.
46. PP 1866, LV, p. 49, 'Correspondence concerning a day of Humiliation', for a copy of Grey's letter to Longley, 26 January 1866.
47. Quoted in *Record*, 21 February 1866, editorial.
48. PRO, HO/45, 7943, f.42, Sir George Grey to Archbishop Longley, draft, no date [26 January 1866].
49. *The Times*, 21 March 1866, editorial.
50. *Cheshire Observer*, 27 January 1866, editorial. *The Times* made a similar point, 21 March 1866, editorial.
51. *Hereford Times*, 10 March 1866, letter of 'John Bull', 'Prayers and Plague: Cattle and Crime'.
52. LP, Longley Mss., 7, ff. 228–9, letter to Bishops in Province of Canterbury, 15 February 1866.
53. *Manchester Daily Examiner*, 9 March 1866, 'An extraordinary sermon', by Revd C.H. Crauford, Oldwinsford.
54. *Northampton Herald*, 17 March 1866, 'Kettering: Day of Humiliation'. The day was Wednesday 14 March.
55. The London day had to be moved because it was found to clash with the Queen holding a court: LP, Tait Mss., 82, ff. 111–12, Tait to H.M. the Queen, 9 March 1866; f. 113, Lord Sydney to Tait, 9 March 1866; f. 123 Lord Sydney to Tait, 13 March 1866.
56. *Christian Times*, 2 March 1866, reproduces a circular sent by the President of the Wesleyan Conference to the Superintendent of the circuits. They also did so in 1854, Anderson, 'Church Reactions', p. 217.
57. *Northampton Herald*, 10 March 1866.
58. Anderson, 'Reactions of Church and Dissent'; Stanley, 'Christian responses'.

59. *Birmingham Daily Post*, 15 March 1866, 'The Day of Humiliation: Sermon by Dr Miller'. *Northampton Herald*, 31 March 1866, 'Wellingborough'.
60. *Northampton Herald*, 24 March 1866, 'The Day of Humiliation'; and see sermon of Revd T. Browne at St Edmunds.
61. *Record*, 5 February 1866, letter of J. Bateman.
62. *Record*, 9 March 1866.
63. *Birmingham Daily Post*, 15 March 1866, 'The Day of Humiliation: Sermon by Dr Miller'.
64. *Northampton Herald*, 24 March 1866, 'The Day of Humiliation: St Katherine's'.
65. *The Hereford Times*, 1 March 1866.
66. *Manchester Courier*, 26 March 1866, 'The Cattle Plague'.
67. *Manchester Courier*, 29 March 1866.
68. *Hansard*, 3rd series, 182, cc. 498–507, 'Day of Humiliation: Committees', for the debate.
69. *Nonconformist*, 28 February 1866, editorial, 'The Landlord Stampedo'.
70. *Carlisle Examiner*, 2 October 1865, editorial, 'False Hopes'; *Oldham Chronicle*, 17 February 1866, editorial.
71. *Dod's Parliamentary Companion, 1866* (London, 1866), *passim*.
72. *Record*, 19 March 1866, editorial.

CHAPTER NINE

Sensational imbalance: the child acrobat and the mid-Victorians

Brenda Assael

In *The Age of Equipoise*, children, who constituted 30–40 per cent of the population in mid-Victorian Britain, are neither seen nor heard except on matters concerning education.[1] Yet their role in this period calls into question the 'enviable stability' which characterized the age for Burn.[2] The codifying of laws relating to employment, education and the age of consent, among others, did not come without a fight either inside or outside Parliament, especially among those who viewed state interference as inherently intrusive and therefore undesirable in democratic society. This essay concerns one segment of the population of children, namely performers, who in contrast to their peers in the textile and mining industries affected by the Factory Acts of the 1830s and 1840s, remained untouched by legal controls. This gulf widened when the statutes were further extended in the next generation to include children in other industrial occupations, such as bleaching and dyeing, paper staining and cartridge making.[3] While the employment of children in the entertainment world was, relative to these other occupations, not extensive, it was highly visible given the fact that these 'prodigies' were displayed spectacularly in theatres, music halls and circuses.[4] Since Burn was concerned with the role of public opinion in the shaping of mid-Victorian morality and law, he would have been interested in these workers; to be sure, they sparked much controversy during this period. Furthermore, given his interest in 'disruptive forces', he might have found in their potentially destabilizing influences a challenge to his notion of mid-Victorian equipoise.[5] With the benefit of a sophisticated historiography of childhood, a literature which developed concurrently with the publication of Burn's book, it is possible to use the controversy over child performers, particularly acrobats, to explore the nuances of the 'age of equipoise'.[6]

The impact that performance had on the minds and bodies of young children was the kernel of the controversy surrounding them. As anxiety about their public role mounted, so too did that surrounding their training for specific performance 'trades' such as acrobatics which, by definition, were considered physically taxing. Despite their public role in the ring, the itinerant status of these children made them difficult to trace, a fact which heightened public anxiety about their work. Their invisibility obviously presents important (although not insurmountable) obstacles for the historian. Much of what we know about the child acrobat was written by spectators and those observers, preoccupied by issues of morality, who watched spectators watching the displays. In order to reveal and dissect these contrasting 'gazes', this essay first considers child acts in the ring and how spectators wrote about them within the context of periodicals and newspapers. This section asks, what were the *meanings* of the acts? As the second section shows, moral opinion, outraged by this interest, was hotly articulated in the 'waif novel', a term used by Anna Davin to describe a strand of writing within 'Sunday school literature'; it is also a sub-category of what Margaret Nancy Cutt called 'tract fiction'.[7] As Davin has shown, these books, published largely (although not exclusively) by evangelical presses, appeared mainly from the mid-1860s and were influenced by discourses on ragged children, nineteenth-century didactic writing for children, sentimental fiction and reports by social reformers.[8] They centred on poor boys and girls who, due to adult cruelty and neglect, become waifs.[9] Morally lost and spiritually deprived, these children ultimately find salvation in Christ after travelling along a long road marred by brutality and sadness. Child acrobats provided a perfect subject for such literary treatment not only because of the physicality of their work but also because the reading audience, composed mainly of children, recognized them from the street, circus and theatre.

While it is impossible to draw a direct causal link between waif novels and political opinion except in cases such as Ellen Barlee's *Pantomime Waifs; or a Plea for Our City Children* (1884), whose introduction was written by Lord Shaftesbury, it is clear that the two sets of discourses were synchronous during the mid-nineteenth century.[10] To be sure, some parliamentarians were willing to face the challenge of saving the real-life counterparts of those fictional 'prodigies'. The third section of this essay thus examines how a growing combination of social pressures provoked debate in Parliament over the legitimacy of controlling the acrobatic trade, leading to a heated response from the performance community. W.L. Burn considered that the age of equipoise drew to a close with the advent of the second Reform Act in 1867. At this point, child acrobats still remained unprotected. Yet within another decade, Parliament's long arm had extended to them something of that protection which children in other areas of British life had long felt. In 1879, Parliament passed a statute that fined any parent or guardian who exposed any child under fourteen years of age to 'dangerous performances', including acrobatics.[11] It is argued in this essay that the mid-Victorian period (if taken up to the early 1870s) was crucial for the escalation of moral panic surrounding child acrobats, which led eventually to legal discipline over them. The speed with which the state came to the rescue of performing children in 1879 would not have been possible without the head of steam generated by journalists, novelists, concerned politicians and other social observers in the mid-Victorian period. Yet the presence of this reforming zeal is something that implicitly challenges Burn's notion of an 'age of equipoise'.

Physical dangers

In a story first printed in *All the Year Round* in 1865 and republished in 1870 under the title, 'The Unkind Word and Other Stories', the didactic authoress Dinah Mulock (Mrs Craik) wrote of a Scottish doctor called Adam Black, who, with his small nieces, visited a circus and witnessed a trapeze display involving 'a mere boy' called Signor Uberto. In anticipation of the boy's appearance in the ring, his nieces asked if they might leave the ring since they expected that the performance would shock them and be dangerous to the performer. However, the doctor responded that 'it was too late', and continued:

> Besides, for myself, I did not wish to leave. That strange excitement which impels us often to stop and see the end of a thing, dreadful though it may be, or else some feeling for which I was utterly unable to account, kept me firm in my place.[12]

Quite apart from the attitudes expressed by his nieces, which might bear further consideration if we were to examine the interesting question of children watching other children, Mulock's account of Black's observation is significant for its pathos: 'I could not help putting myself into the place of the young man, and wondering whether he really did recognise any danger ... '. The 'pleasing anguish' that he experienced as a result of entering into the same mental world as the performer kept him firmly in his seat for a reason for which, as he said, he was unable to account. In the performance, the boy 'mounted, agile as a deer, the high platform at the end of the circus, and swung himself off by the elastic ropes, clinging only with his hands, his feet extended, like one of the floating figures in pictures of saints or fairies'. When the other trapeze reached him, the 'young man dropped lightly into it, hanging a moment in air between whiles, apparently as easily as if he had been born to fly'. He does this 'turn' four times successfully. On the fifth, however, the boy suddenly falls and Black's 'pleasing anguish' turns to horror. He observed that 'it was so sudden ... a crash on a mattressed platform ... from which rolled off a helpless something'. As the surprised audience emits screams, the doctor goes to the scene to help the 'poor young man'. In a moment of silent reflection, he blames himself for patronizing the display. 'I felt somehow as if I had murdered him, or helped to do it.'[13]

Real-life spectators also showed that they were never fully prepared for the worst. And in situations that produced fatal or near-fatal results the spectator's 'gaze' turned into the spectator's 'gasp', as in the case of a display called the 'Leap for Life' by *Les Frères Trevannion* in 1869 at the Wellington Circus and Music Hall in Cheltenham. In it, one of the boys 'slipped from the grasp [of his brother and fell] ... a distance of 35–40 feet, amidst the shrieks of men, women and children'.[14] Such scenes became even more alarming when they involved not only young boys but also small children. Writing to the *Royal Leamington Spa Courier* in 1869, one contemporary doctor admitted to having taken his children to see a circus at Leamington where they saw

> a child advertised as only four years old [who] ... suspended his frail body at a height of 60 feet from the trapeze. At this elevation, the child was straining his self in a pitiable manner, in going through the 'fearfully dangerous' tricks.

The doctor went on to say that if the boy continued these performances he would be met with 'one of those terrible fatalities which are now becoming so common'. He recommended that Henry Austin Bruce of the Home Office 'take ... steps as will prevent a repetition of scenes like this "which no government but an English one would ever dream of permitting for a single night"'.[15]

That 'these children' were engaged in a trade that was not legally protected by law and that was mortally dangerous prompted state interference, particularly after officials such as Henry Austin Bruce received alarmist letters such as that of the Leamington doctor citing examples of these displays. Likewise, the Chief Commissioner of Police alerted Bruce about an article that appeared in the *Daily News*, reporting that 'a female performer ... carried a child of tender years strapped [across] her back' along a tightrope at the Holborn Amphitheatre in 1870.[16] Bruce then contacted the proprietors of the establishment where the performance took place and, as a consequence, the child was removed from the exhibition, although the female performer continued her display.[17] However, beyond the power of making these 'suggestions', Bruce had little authority in cases such as this. Recalling a similar enforcement difficulty when he was at the Lord Chamberlain's Office, Spencer Ponsonby Fane remarked before the 1866 Select Committee on Theatrical Licences and Regulations that 'if we had been actually forced to proceed by law [to control these dangerous exhibitions at the metropolitan theatres over which we had jurisdiction], I am afraid our powers would have been found rather ineffective'.[18]

Concern was not only linked to sensational stories that occasionally arose in the press and elsewhere, but also to the perception that the number of children involved in the acrobatic trade was rising. The question of scale is important since many of these children found encouragement for their work within the commercially expanding leisure market.[19] 'Nothing fills a house better', one contemporary observed, 'than juvenile acrobats.'[20] According to the *Era Almanac*, a yearly theatrical magazine whose figures provide only an imperfect outlook on the state of the trade, there were 66 acrobat troupes in Britain in 1867–68, rising to 90 in 1877 and 98 in 1878.[21] These numbers were slightly higher than those suggested by one acrobat called Jean Battier in 1872, when he estimated that 'there are about 20 troupes now in England, varying from four to seven in number, and from six to fourteen years of age'.[22] Considering the number of acrobats who advertised in the 'help wanted' pages of its weekly counterpart, the *Era*, it is clear that acrobat troupes numbered more than one hundred – an estimation that takes into account the fact that the troupes often assumed different names and thereby appear to have inflated numbers in the trade papers.[23]

Who were the performers? Some of them belonged to the working classes and had an interest in earning a 'quick shilling' and leading the glamorous life of the successful acrobat. Arthur Munby, the famous diarist, noted in a visit to the Cambridge Music Hall near Shoreditch Station in London in 1868 that

> the boxkeeper ... informed me that 'Zuleilah' [the acrobat performing] is a Miss Foster, a publican's daughter of the neighbourhood; that she only became an acrobat two or three months ago, stimulated like the rest of them by the success of *La Pereira* [another contemporary acrobat].[24]

Another performer called Little Azella, 'a Jewess', also came from a non-theatrical background. Standing behind her sister at one performance at the Temperance Music Hall on the same evening, Munby engaged her in conversation and found out that 'Little Azella [whose real name was Betsy Asher] is only nine years old ... and [has] only been at it three weeks, besides eight days [and] ... practiced [*sic*] at home'.[25] In many other cases, children were trained from a young age by their parents, many of whom belonged to the trade. Mdm Bertoldi, known as the

'Boneless Wonder', recalled that 'my father ... put both my sister ... and myself into strict training ... when I was but a little mite. [It was then that] I worked with my father and my sister in a triple gymnastic act.'[26] Fuelled by stories about performers and by the rise in the number of accidents to child performers, moral opinion became more vocal. While the directive for this voice came from no single body, it is notable that evangelical writers of juvenile fiction were particularly keen observers and wove forceful morality tales for children which gripped the Victorian imagination.

Moral dangers

Put simply, the major problem acrobat children posed for evangelicals was that they strayed both from respectable codes of behaviour and, more importantly, from religion. Evangelical writers found in them a ready-made subject for literary salvation and found presses such as the Religious Tract Society (RTS) and the Society for the Promotion of Christian Knowledge (SPCK) willing to spread their message.[27] These writers spun morality tales that combined evangelical concerns about children's religious education with high melodrama and mid-Victorian fantasy and anxiety.[28] Despite the influence that sentimental fiction writers had on waif novelists,[29] the latter's characterization of the child performer deviated from the former; for example, in Wilkie Collins's *Hide and Seek* and Charles Dickens's *Hard Times*, Madonna and Sissy Jupe (in both cases, circus girls) embody 'fancy', 'imagination', 'romance' and 'creativity', not moral impoverishment as found in the waif novel.[30] That a discrete body of waif novels featured the child acrobat as a subject for rescue[31] is significant not only because many believed that the performer's real-life counterpart was in need of saving but also because the street, stage or circus ring provided a provocative fictional venue where a nightmarish world underpinned by cruelty could be spectacularly witnessed by the reading public, which included middle-class and working-class children. To be sure, these books were distributed to Sunday school children as prizes in an effort to encourage and maintain good behaviour and reward attendance; they were also on the shelves of 'juvenile Theological libraries', libraries in elementary schools, and reading rooms in well-served parishes.[32] The contrast between the rational recreation of reading and the irrationality of performing, as it appeared in the waif novel, could not have been more stark.

Evangelical concern for these child prodigies is pointedly expressed in *The Little Acrobat and His Mother* (1872). Focused on an acrobat boy 'who is in the service of travelling gymnasts', it tells a story about 'his adventures, hardships, and subsequent deliverance from an evil course of life'.[33] The child, who suffers from physical neglect by his mother, is looked upon with pity and revulsion by a merchant and his friend, Mr Werner, the director of an asylum for 'orphans and forsaken children', both of whom have seen the boy perform:

> 'How old do you suppose that boy is?' said Mr Werner.
> 'I should say about ten years old', replied his friend.
> 'I think he is more than that; children who lead that sort of life seldom grow. I should like to get him into my asylum.'[34]

The imagined effect that institutionalization would have on the boy's body could only bring desirable ends from Mr Werner's point of view. In the minds of Mr Werner and his companion, the world to which the acrobat-boy belonged was deeply troubling. At the root of the boy's problem was his mother: 'she was so dirty and idle' and her heart 'was hardened by a long life of sin', the narrator affirmed.[35] It was not only her physical neglect of her son, but also her intellectual one that resulted in his early decline. Her son was illiterate, not even knowing his real name when Mr Werner asks him,

> 'What is your name?'
> 'Acrobat.'
> 'I know your profession is that of an acrobat, but what is your Christian name?'
> 'Acrobat.'[36]

Physical and intellectual neglect translated into moral degeneracy: 'how many sins this poor boy must have committed, and seen committed, without even knowing that they were sins', Mr Werner lamented.[37] Upon being 'rescued' by him and brought into the asylum, Acrobat is evangelized, a process which ultimately saves him, as literary convention would have it, from his strange ways. Acrobat eventually attempts to 'rescue' his mother from the darkness of her un-Christian existence, a resolution that clearly reflected the RTS's moral agenda.

Such waif novels were not only critical of the parents who neglected their children's early education; they were also critical of the audiences that patronized the exhibitions and thereby encouraged the performers' steady, devilish descent. *The Mountebank's Children* (1866), published by the SPCK, portrays a stereotyped image of this *demi-monde*. In it, the performances of the travelling circus are attended by 'many idle country people' whose 'roars of laughter were heard till late at night'.[38] They paid to see Master Frederick and his sister, Milly, a 'little girl' and contortionist, whose mother 'oils' her joints 'all over everyday, because

she is learning to turn her joints backwards'.[39] In the display, she
'throw[s] her head and arms backwards until she could hold her feet in
her hands, and putting her face between her arms, she formed a circle
with her body'.[40] The audience's interest in Milly awakens when Moss-
man, her manager, 'rolled her over and over ... with a stick in his hand'.
Whereas her display sparks awe in the audience, it is meant to provoke
pity in the reader. Like Acrobat, Milly is presented as a frail, poorly
child whose pitifulness is enhanced by a performance that renders her
'exhausted and panting' at the end of it.[41] Here and elsewhere, the use
of children in fiction served to arouse the sympathy of the reader. As
such, the representation of the child acrobat converged on Enlighten-
ment assumptions that children were fundamentally innocent and
Romantic sensibilities relating to the contemporary 'cult of childhood'
as well as revised ideas on the subject of child labour.[42] When children
strayed from their natural, virtuous paths, as acrobats did, the reason
for this was seen to be corrupt influences beyond their control.

Lord Buckhurst, who later agitated for legal change for these performers, said that the public's bad taste was to blame for the continuation
of their displays (and accidents), adding that 'the[y] must be demoraliz-
ing [not only to the children who performed them], but to the people
who witnessed them [as well]':[43] he believes the crassness of the exhibition in which the performer's body was twisted and turned necessarily
resulted in his or her degradation and, by extension, that of the audience. In *The Mountebank's Children*, Milly wears a tight bodice, and
bends into a hoop, as we have seen, showing the audience her frontal
anatomy which, according to the author, could only serve to demoralize
her.[44] The later novel, *An Acrobat's Girlhood* (1889), similarly presented an acrobat-child, Trixy, as 'bend[ing] herself backward in a half
circle in front of Mr La Fosse [her manager] on [a] bicycle with her face
upside down', an image which horrifies her sister who witnesses the
display.[45] 'Yes, the people were shouting and clapping their hands while
my poor little sister felt almost [like] dying', she added.[46] Seen from one
perspective, the image of Trixy's private rehearsal was worse than Milly's
public display if only because the former was beyond the public's moral
scrutiny. As in earlier evangelical writing for children, these stories were
meant to 'inflate the sordid' by sharply contrasting the grim realities
that industrial life produced, such as child labour and cruelty, on the
one hand, and 'an imaginary world where universal human values and
natural justice ordered existence' on the other.[47] In the context of the
waif novel, the circus ring and its world 'behind the scenes', signifying
danger and disorder, offered a 'system of meaning' that exposed the
larger insecurities and doubts which underpinned the mid-Victorian

age. Oddly, while the RTS and the SPCK struggled to gain public sympathy for the child acrobat (as well as other waifs and strays), the skill with which the authors depicted mental and physical abuse added a spectacular dimension to their already sensational stories.

What made their physicality more worrisome in both real life and the novel was that these children were seen to be bound to their managers like slaves, and made to rehearse and perform 'degrading' tricks that exposed their visibly misshapen bodies. For example, Acrobat's manager forces him 'to fast when he was ordered, to twist his body and limbs into all sorts of strange shapes, and sometimes to remain for a long time in the same position, mostly a very fatiguing one ... '.[48] For Shaftesbury, a noted advocate of children's welfare since the creation of the Factory Acts, such static confinement was dangerous, cruel and 'appalling'. He recollected 'the case of a child, about 14 or 15 years of age, who was in training for the acrobatic business ... and [stood] on his head for a considerable time, until from its continual practice it had become a second nature to him'.[49] As a consequence, it was said, the development of the acrobat's body became stunted by this training and a 'number must become diseased or crippled under the process'.[50] The act of investigating these stories, he said, simply involved 'going his nightly rounds' and playing 'eyewitness' to incidents of cruelty, as one of his friends did. On one occasion, 'he heard shrieking and piercing cries, and on going up into the room from whence the sounds proceeded he found seven or eight children, with two or three women standing over them with sticks, beating them ... '.[51] Like many other urban explorers interested in revealing the 'frank brutalities' of working-class life, Shaftesbury's unnamed friend moved within an 'unchecked' underworld, crafting sensational stories about urban dangers and obscenities which reinforced existing stereotypes about performing children.[52] These observations were well timed. They coincided with a view among some politicians in the House of Lords that legal action had to be taken for the sake of the child acrobat.

Pressure for legal regulation

Those peers who supported state intervention, however, faced formidable opposition. Initially, neither the growing number of circus troupes nor the public's increasing awareness of acrobatic training and performance seemed likely to motivate legal regulation. Indeed, the very lifeblood of the leisure market's expansion was the *laissez-faire* climate of mid-Victorian Britain.[53] For this reason, Lord Buckhurst, a Conservative peer and ally of Lord Shaftesbury, faced many dissenting voices in the House of Lords when he introduced a private bill in 1872 which was designed to protect the lives and limbs of acrobat children. Some politicians, such as the Earl of Morley, said that while they 'did not wish to defend the taste of those who took pleasure in witnessing dangerous exhibitions of this kind', they 'did not think bad taste was to be corrected by an Act of Parliament any more than drunkenness'.[54] Yet Buckhurst argued that the object of his legislation 'was not to interfere with the indulgence of that taste where it was legitimate [however bad], but ... merely to protect young children of tender years from being compelled to take part in acrobatic performances which were dangerous ... '.[55] His view emerged from a widening belief that state intervention could be justified where it helped those too weak to help themselves, as demonstrated by the new child-labour provisions introduced in the 1860s as well as by the compulsory vaccination of children by an Act of Parliament in 1867.[56] Buckhurst's argument was, however, met with derision. The Marquis of Salisbury, for example, suggested that the bill be applied to jockeys who also 'went through muscular performances for gain [laughter]'.[57] The Lords were clearly amused by this problem since, as one contemporary writer caustically noted, they 'have indulged in much laughter' which, he lamented, 'is not surprising'.[58] Other peers simply believed that the wording of the measure was not precise enough and therefore moved that it be withdrawn.[59]

Another stumbling-block was disagreement over the age group that the bill was meant to protect. Buckhurst's interest in the Children's Dangerous Performances Bill had extended beyond just helping children 'of tender years'. The bill, in its initial form, aimed to protect acrobats until sixteen years old, indicating that the terms 'young persons' and 'children' were, for the purposes of the statute, conflated. When the bill was reintroduced in 1873, Buckhurst's goals became more modest and the bill called for protection of children under twelve years. By 1879, when it received the Royal Assent, the age restriction had been raised to fourteen.[60] Significantly, in the naming of the statute in 1879, the term 'young persons', which had been adopted, was dropped and replaced by 'children'. This view was consistent with the one adopted by the Royal Commission following the passage of the Factory Acts in 1833. Its members said that at the beginning of the fourteenth year 'the period of childhood ... ceases and that of puberty is established, when the body becomes more capable of enduring protracted labour'.[61] That the bill aimed to regulate sixteen-, twelve- and then fourteen-year-olds arguably illustrated the extent to which those politicians supporting it viewed acrobats (at least initially) as different from other labouring children and were thus uncertain as to the age at which they no longer needed protection.[62]

When it was introduced in 1872, the bill provoked resistance not only among some politicians but also among members of the acrobatic trade, serving to unite them in a common struggle. Their very livelihoods were at stake: 'should this Bill pass it will throw out [of] employment some hundreds of professionals who have no other means of living', said J.H. Ricardo of the Ricardo Troupe.[63] Many in the trade agreed with his analysis of the subject. That is, because acrobat children often performed with their parents in troupes, the bill, it was argued, would adversely affect 'professional' families.[64] Implicit in these arguments was the idea that there was an important difference between legitimate acrobat families and those daredevils who gave the trade a bad name. It was common knowledge, said one gymnast called 'Raslus', that recent stories about children falling from ropes related to novices, not professionals like himself: 'I do not think it just that because a number of ambitious, untrained boys and girls', such as Zuleilah and Little Azella, 'are permitted to try their 'prentice [sic] hands and feet without the experience necessary for gymnastic performances, that we, who have devoted perhaps the better part of a lifetime, and overcome the difficulties, should have to suffer'.[65] As professionals, 'Raslus' and others did not believe that their trade was dangerous. On the contrary, said the DeCastro Brothers, 'we take every precaution against danger. On the stage, we have a thickly padded carpet and we are very careful of our boys during the performance'.[66] In fact, it was because of their professional status that they took these precautions in order to achieve that legitimacy which they struggled to obtain from the public.

Besides the short-term effects relating to income loss and popular perception, the proposed law also had long-term consequences for the trade. Ricardo warned that 'should this Bill become law, in a few years, there will be no great adult performers in Circuses, Theatres, Music Halls or other places of amusement'.[67] This was exactly the effect that advocates of the bill wished the law to have. 'If children were not allowed to perform in public', argued the Earl of Malmesbury, 'their parents would not think it worth while to train them.'[68] Not everyone in Parliament believed, as Malmesbury did, that the law could act as a deterrent to parents training their children. In a speech during the second debates on the bill in 1873, Shaftesbury argued that 'the bill [which only related to performance restrictions] would not touch the tortures [concerning acrobatic training since they] were perpetuated at home and under the secretary of privacy'.[69] Many believed, as he did, that parent/managers would, notwithstanding the bill, find ways of continuing their trade even if it meant forcing it underground.

George Sanger, a circus manager, injected such a view into the debates. He warned that the bill

> will not ... stop the practice. [It] will merely drive it into another channel. We shall then depend on the Continental artists or men [who] will take children from here, teach them across the Channel and bring them back efficient artists after the time of restriction has passed.[70]

In arguing this, Sanger hit an important and fragile chord: the itinerant lifestyle of many of these performers made them unlikely candidates for legal control, regardless of state intervention. For this reason, Shaftesbury sought the help of existing agencies in order to make these acrobat children answerable to an authority other than their parents. In particular, he enlisted the help of School Boards in order to 'put in force the compulsory powers of the [Education] Act [of 1870] in compelling [acrobat children] to attend the schools'.[71] In doing so, he hoped that they, like other child workers, such as flowergirls, matchbox makers, errand-runners, and 'little mothers', might be brought within the grasp of civil society, educated and reformed.[72] However, in assuming, as he did, that the statute would bring acrobat children under the authority of the school system, Shaftesbury made another erroneous assumption: children who performed with troupes were usually not permanent residents in any community long enough to warrant their registration in a local school district. Even if they and/or their parents-*cum*-trainers performed with a circus which was resident in a town (as many of them were), their engagements were typically no longer than several weeks, or possibly a season lasting several months. The problem was discussed in Parliament decades later when some observers, conflating 'gypsies' and circus performers into the category of 'moveable dwellers', asked what good it would do the school children or the 'infectious' itinerant children to be brought together. '[Such an act] would injure schools, retard school work, and disturb and dishearten the school management without [any] compensating benefit to [those children of moveable dwellings].'[73]

Ultimately, the Act of 1879 did not prohibit training practices *per se* since the peers could not agree on the idea of regulating all levels of labour in the trade. There was such a thing as 'overregulation', it was argued.[74] In addition, there remained the practical difficulty, if such a provision were adopted in the statute, of how to police private households where the alleged cruel training took place. The surveillance of homes, if put into law, would intrude on the rights of freeborn Englishmen to the privacy of their homes, a theme taken up in later debates, notably by Henry Stephens of the Liberty and Property Defence League. And, as some hostile contemporaries pondered, where would it stop? In its final form, the law represented a compromise between the pro- and anti-regulationists. It prevented children under fourteen from performing feats 'that were dangerous to the life and limb of a child, in the opinion of a court of summary jurisdiction', and further stated that any 'parent or guardian or any person having the custody of such a child, who shall aid or abet the same, shall severally be guilty of an offence against this Act, and shall be ... liable for each offence to a penalty not exceeding £10'.[75]

Of course, the debates over the Dangerous Performances Bill did not end with the passing of the statute. The child acrobat continued to occupy the attention of the public and legislators alike especially since, in the words of Shaftesbury in 1883, the provisions of the Act were being 'altogether ignored ... [and the evils of dangerous performances] prevailed to a greater extent [now] than [they] ever did before'.[76] Although inadequate from Shaftesbury's point of view, the statute did have the effect of opening the door to further reform; the provisions relating to acrobats in the Acts for the Prevention of Cruelty to Children in 1889 and 1894 were testament to this fact, as was the passage of a revised Dangerous Performances Act in 1897.[77] By the late 1880s, when the trade was inextricably tied in the minds of many to cruelty, the anti-cruelty laws threatened the parent and/or guardian of the performing child with more punitive measures.[78] In the meantime, during the 1860s and early 1870s, the public debates within Parliament and outside it provided the conditions for this change to take place.

Imbalance

Whether in the ring, in the contemporary novel or in Parliament, the child acrobat engaged the interests of the mid-Victorian public and in the process drew attention to tensions underpinning the social order. For patrons, the tensions were between morbid curiosity and a desire to admire and stare awestruck at the 'amazing' prodigy. For reformers the stress-line was between the moral cause and the dominance of the consumer demand for this spectacle. The contentious issues surrounding the acrobatic trade that were brought into focus by these two camps emerged in Parliament, where the conflicts between state interference and individual privacy, and between market intervention and *laissez-faire* politics, were played out. Yet the prospect of legal interference in the affairs of child performers exposed public anxiety, not the peaceful equilibrium that Burn saw in mid-Victorian England.

These 'wretched' acrobats, powerless and threatened by the Dangerous Performances Bill, provoked a paradoxical reaction amongst contemporaries: on the one hand, they became objects of revulsion; on the other, objects of pity who might be saved. While they were similar to other labouring children in so far as the conditions of their work were now, in the 1870s, brought before politicians for reform, they were unlike their peers in one essential way: their world was viewed as foreign, suspect and gypsy-like, despite the fact that the troupes with which they laboured belonged to the commercial entertainment market. Regardless, those stereotypes supported by sensationalized stories provided the seeds of discontent in the public mind and in Parliament. The parents and managers of these acrobats, unwilling to observe passively the dismantling of their trade by the legal system, challenged the arguments supporting the Dangerous Performances Bill and drew attention to larger issues about the relationship between the state and the individual. Their protests were, however, insufficient where matters of life and death were concerned, and for this reason the Dangerous Performances Act of 1879 was passed. Inadvertently, the mid-Victorian public's desire to see acrobatic spectacles involving children created the conditions for moral panic to reach its sensational pitch. Such anxiety encouraged public debate and was ultimately responsible for creating legal change. It was a historical paradox that the little acrobat, whose balancing performance relied on maintaining equilibrium, exposed deep cultural and political tensions, not equipoise, in mid-Victorian Britain.

Notes

1. W.L. Burn, *The Age of Equipoise: A Study of the Mid-Victorian Generation* (London: George Allen and Unwin, 1964), pp. 22, 61, 194–222, 267–8, 265.
2. Ibid., p. 8; On the mid-Victorian mind and the plurality of ideas, see G. Kitson Clark, *The Making of Victorian England* (London: Methuen and Co., repr. 1963); Walter E. Houghton, *The Victorian Frame of Mind, 1830–1870* (New Haven: Yale University Press, 1957), ch. 7; Jerome Hamilton Buckley, *The Victorian Temper: A Study in Literary Culture* (London: George Allen and Unwin, 1952); Gertrude Himmelfarb, *Victorian Minds* (London: Weidenfeld and Nicolson, repr. 1968).
3. Geoffrey Best, *Mid-Victorian Britain, 1851–70* (London: Weidenfeld and Nicolson, 1971), p. 136; C. Nardinelli, *Child Labor and the Industrial Revolution* (Bloomington: Indiana University Press, 1990), pp. 103–22;

Ivy Pinchbeck and Margaret Hewitt, *Children in English Society* (London: Routledge and Kegan Paul, 1969–73), vol. 2, pp. 387–413.

4. See Tracy Davis, 'The Employment of Children in the Victorian Theatre', *New Theatre Quarterly*, 2 (6) (May 1986), pp. 117–35.

5. Burn, *Age of Equipoise*, p. 8. My idea of 'instability', as compared with Burn's notion of 'equipoise', is connected to discussions of 'moral panics' which appear in Stanley Cohen, *Folk Devils and Moral Panics: The Creation of Mods and Rockers* (London: MacGibbon and Kee, 1972); and Judith Walkowitz, *City of Dreadful Delight: Narratives of Sexual Danger in Late-Victorian London* (Chicago: University of Chicago Press, 1992).

6. The 1960s was a fruitful and important period in which childhood received scholarly attention. In particular, see the seminal study by Philippe Ariès, *Centuries of Childhood*, trans. Robert Baldick (Harmondsworth: Penguin, 1973); on child labour, see E.P. Thompson, *The Making of the English Working Class* (London: Victor Gollancz, 1963), pp. 331–49. Over the next decade, other key works followed: see Pinchbeck and Hewitt, *Childhood in English Society*; Lloyd deMause, ed., *The History of Childhood* (London: Psychohistory Press, 1974). Later work on childhood and the industrial revolution includes Nardinelli, *Child Labor*; John Somerville, *The Rise and Fall of Childhood* (London: Sage, 1982). Along the same lines of 'decline', see L. Rose, *The Erosion of Childhood: Child Oppression in Britain, 1860–1918* (London: Routledge and Kegan Paul, 1991).

7. Margaret Nancy Cutt, *Ministering Angels: A Study of Nineteenth-century Evangelical Writing for Children* (Dorset: Five Owls Press, 1979); Gillian Avery, *Childhood's Pattern: A Study of the Heroes and Heroines of Children's Fiction, 1770–1950* (London: Hodder & Stoughton, 1975); J.S. Bratton, *The Impact of Victorian Children's Fiction* (London: Croom Helm, 1981), see ch. 3; cf. Anna Davin, *Growing Up Poor: Home, School and Street in London 1870–1914* (London: Rivers Oram, 1996), pp. 91, 162; cf. *idem*, unpublished article on waif novels.

8. Davin, unpublished article, *passim*; Bratton, *Victorian Children's Fiction*, *passim*, p. 84. In the mid-nineteenth century, literary output was also effected by a wider movement in children's cultural production, particularly books. This shift was especially noticeable after the repeal of the stamp tax in 1855 and the duty on paper in 1861; see Marjorie Lang, 'Children's Champions: Mid-Victorian Children's Periodicals and the Critics', *Victorian Periodicals Review*, 13 (1–2) (1980), pp. 17–31. There are, however, earlier examples of performing children who are waifs in children's fiction; see for example, Charlotte Adams, *The Stolen Child; or Laura's Adventures with the Travelling Showman and His Family* (London: J.W. Parker, 1838).

9. Davin, unpublished article, *passim*. Discussions of adult cruelty towards children assume greater importance in the waif novel of the 1880s when the campaign to save children from neglect and abuse earned legal and institutional legitimacy; see Brenda Assael, 'The Circus and Respectable Society', (PhD diss., University of Toronto, 1998), ch. 5; Bratton, *Victorian Children's Fiction*, *passim*, pp. 94–5.

10. Lord Shaftesbury had a previous rapport with waif fiction writers and their publishers; see Bratton, *Victorian Children's Fiction, passim*, p. 85.

11. *Public General Statutes*, An Act to Regulate the Employment of Children in Places of Public Amusement in Certain Cases, 1879, 42/43 Vic., ch. 34, s. 3.

12. 'In the Ring', *All the Year Round*, 28 January 1865, p. 20.

13. Ibid., p. 21.

14. 'Alarming Trapeze Accident', *Era*, 21 March 1869, p. 5.

15. *Royal Leamington Spa Courier*, 3 July 1869, p. 6.

16. *Hansard*, 3rd series, 199 (1870), c.1961; cf. 'The Exhibition at the Holborn Amphitheatre', *Era*, 20 March 1870, p. 13.

17. On the subject of female acrobats, see ch. 4 in the author's PhD thesis and Tracy C. Davis, 'Sex in Public Places: the Zaeo Aquarium Scandal and the Victorian Moral Majority', *Theatre History Studies* (1990), pp. 1–14; see also Davis, *Actresses as Working Women: Their Social Identity in Victorian Culture* (London: Routledge and Kegan Paul, 1991) for a perspective taken from the stage.

18. PP, vol. xvi, 1866, *Select Committee on Theatrical Licenses and Regulations*. Testimony given by Spencer Ponsonby Fane.

19. For a more general discussion of the commercialized leisure market, see Peter Bailey, 'Custom, Capital and Culture in the Victorian Music Hall', in *Popular Culture and Custom in Nineteenth Century England*, ed. R.D. Storch (London: Croom Helm, 1982).

20. 'Juvenile Acrobat Bill', *Era*, 21 July 1872, p. 12.

21. *Era Almanac* (1867), p. 69; (1877), p. 83; (1878), p. 84.

22. 'Mr Editor', *Era*, 21 July 1872, p. 12.

23. Based on the author's thesis, ch. 4.

24. Derek Hudson, *Munby: Man of Two Worlds* (London: J. Murray, 1972), p. 254. Diary entry for 7 September 1868.

25. Ibid., pp. 254–5.

26. 'Music Hall Celebrities: Madame Bertoldi', *Encore*, 9 June 1898, p. 9.

27. Davin, unpublished article, *passim*; Bratton, *Victorian Children's Fiction, passim*; Lang, 'Children's Champions', *passim*.

28. On the subject of mid-Victorian narrative fantasy, see Morton N. Cohen, *Lewis Carroll: A Biography* (London: Macmillan, 1995); see also U.C. Knoepflmacher, 'The Balancing of Child and Adult: An Approach to Victorian Fantasies for Children', *Nineteenth Century Fiction* 37(4) (1983), p. 501; On melodrama, see Peter Brooks, *The Melodramatic Imagination: Balzac, Henry James, Melodrama and the Mode of Excess* (New Haven: Yale University Press, 1976); M.R. Booth, *English Melodrama* (London: Jenkins, 1965); 'Sensational Novels', *Quarterly Review*, 226 (1863), pp. 482–514; Rohan McWilliam, 'Melodrama and the Historians', *Radical History Review* (forthcoming).

29. Davin, unpublished article, *passim*.

30. Margaret Simpson, '*Hard Times* and Circus Times', *Dickens Quarterly*, 10:3 (1993), 131; Philip Collins, 'Dickens and Popular Amusements', *Dickensian*, 61 (1965), pp. 7–19; Paul Schlicke, 'Dickens and the Circus', *Theatre Notebook*, xlvii (1) (1993), pp. 2–19; *idem, Dickens and Popular Entertainment* (London: Allen and Unwin, 1985); *idem*, ed., 'Circus',

Oxford Reader's Companion to Dickens (Oxford: Oxford University Press, 1999), p. 102.

31. Dickens and Collins deal with the subject of saving the circus girl in a different way from waif novelists. Dickens sees Jupe's exit from Sleary's troupe and into Gradgrind's schoolroom as a descent into a cold, utilitarian Benthamite world; Collins treats Madonna's release from Jubber's circus in slightly more critical terms. In both cases, however, the child performer does not engage with the sorts of issues regarding poverty, spiritual decay and irreligion found in waif novels.

32. Bratton, *Victorian Children's Fiction*, pp. 17–19.

33. Anon., *The Little Acrobat and His Mother: A True Story* (London: The Religious Tract Society, 1872), p. 3 (d).

34. Ibid., p. 20.

35. Ibid., pp. 6, 10.

36. Ibid., p. 22.

37. Ibid.

38. Anon., *The Mountebank's Children* (London: Society for the Promotion of Christian Knowledge, 1866), p. 6.

39. Ibid., pp. 7, 10.

40. Ibid., pp. 17–18.

41. Ibid., p. 18.

42. Peter Coveney, *The Image of Childhood: The Individual and Society: A Study of the Theme in English Literature* (Harmondsworth: Penguin, 1967); cf. Robert Pattison, *The Child Figure in Literature* (Athens: University of Georgia Press, 1978).

43. *Hansard*, 3rd series, 212 (1872), c. 619.

44. Anon., *The Mountebank's Children*, p. 18.

45. Hesba Stretton (pseud.) [Sarah Smith], *An Acrobat's Girlhood* (London: Society for the Promotion of Christian Knowledge, 1889), p. 52; cf. Patricia Demers, 'Mrs Sherwood and Hesba Stretton: The Letter and Spirit of Evanglical Writing of and for Children', in James Holt McGavran Jr, ed., *Romanticism and Children's Literature in Nineteenth Century England* (Athens: University of Georgia Press, 1991), pp.129–49.

46. Stretton, *An Acrobat's Girlhood*, p. 52.

47. Lang, 'Children's Champions', p. 20.

48. *The Little Acrobat and His Mother*, p. 8; cf. for a discussion of 'interiority' in connection with this story, Carolyn Steedman, *Strange Dislocations: Childhood and the Idea of Human Interiority, 1780–1930* (London: Virago Press, 1995), ch. 6, esp. pp.103–4.

49. *Hansard*, 3rd series, 312 (1872), c. 622.

50. Ibid.

51. Ibid.

52. In a different way, O.G. Rejlander depicted children belonging to the urban poor through photography in this period, see Jadviga M. Da Costa Nunes, 'O.G. Rejlander's Photographs of Ragged Children: Reflections on the Idea of Urban Poverty in Mid-Victorian Society', *Nineteenth Century Studies*, 4 (1990), pp. 105–36.

53. Cf. mid-Victorian *laissez-faire* principles in Burn, pp. 161–231.

54. *Hansard*, 3rd series, 212 (1872), c. 620.

55. Ibid., c. 618.

56. Jose Harris, *Private Lives, Public Spirit: A Social History of Britain: 1870–1914* (Oxford: Oxford University Press, 1993), p. 196; cf. K.T. Hoppen, *The Mid-Victorian Generation, 1846–1886* (Oxford: Clarendon Press, 1998), p. 96.

57. 'Acrobat Bill', *Daily Telegraph*, 22 July 1872, p. 2.

58. 'A Plea for Acrobats', *Era*, 14 July 1872, p. 4.

59. 'Acrobat Bill', *Daily Telegraph*, 22 July 1872, p. 2.

60. *Public General Statutes*, Children's Dangerous Performances Act, 1879, 42/43 Vic., ch. 34, s. 3; cf. *Bills, Public, etc.*, 'Acrobat's Bill', 1872, Bill 173.

61. Cited in Hugh Cunningham, *Children and Childhood in Western Society since 1500* (London: Longman, 1995), p. 140.

62. On the distinction between childhood and adolescence, see John Gillis, *Youth and History: Tradition and Change in European Age Relations* (New York: Academic Press, repr. 1981).

63. 'Infant Acrobats', *Era*, 14 July 1872, p. 4.

64. 'Mr Editor', *Era*, 21 July 1872, p. 12.

65. 'Mr. Editor', *Era*, 27 November 1870, p. 12.

66. 'Infant Acrobats', *Era*, 7 July 1872, p. 12.

67. 'Infant Acrobats', *Era*, 14 July 1872, p. 4.

68. *Hansard*, 3rd series, 216 (1873), c. 1244.

69. Ibid.

70. 'A Plea for Acrobats', *Era*, 14 July 1872, p. 4.

71. *Hansard*, 3rd series, 216 (1873), c. 1244.

72. Best, *Mid-Victorian Britain*, p. 178; see also Davin, *Growing Up Poor*, esp. ch. 5.

73. 'Moveable Dwellings Bill', *Era*, 4 February 1893, p. 16.

74. *Hansard*, 3rd series, 212 (1872), c. 620.

75. *Public General Statutes*, Children's Dangerous Performances Act, 1879, 42/43 Vic., ch. 34, s.3.

76. *Hansard*, 3rd series, 282 (1883), c. 1462.

77. See *Public General Statues*, An Act for the Prevention of Cruelty to Children, 1889, 52/53 Vic., ch. 44, s. 3, clause c; cf. *Public General Statutes*, An Act for the Prevention for the Cruelty to Children, 1894, 57/58 Vic., ch. 27; and *Public General Statutes*, An Act to Extend the Age under which the Employment of Young Persons in Dangerous Performances is Permitted, 1897, 60/61 Vic., ch. 52.

78. For a discussion of the effect of these anti-cruelty laws on circus families and managers, see the author's forthcoming book *Gaudy Dream: The Circus and Victorian Society* (Charlottesville: University Press of Virginia).

CHAPTER TEN

Harbouring discontent: British imperialism through Brazilian eyes in the Christie Affair

Ross G. Forman

> The relish [of the English] is hoarding, their happiness is in profit, their God is cognac, their promises are lies, their friendships falsehoods, and their pardons censures ... For a trifle, they buy our cotton, our sugar, our wood, the hides of our cattle and an immensity of objects that constitute a veritable fount of riches, for a trifle, that is exchanged for a small portion of cloth, that any other nation would furnish us at a more reasonable rate. They force all our produce to be sent to London, and after passing it through their factories, return it here to sell under the title of English manufacture, by virtue of which we do nothing more than buy very dear that which we have sold them very cheaply ...
>
> J.F.K. da Costa Rubim, *The English in Brazil* (1863)[1]

In playing the game of 'selective Victorianism' that W.L. Burn described in *The Age of Equipoise*, scholars of nineteenth-century Britain have concentrated on Victorian self-images and self-conceptions, overlooking how they themselves were viewed in other cultures and contexts. Burn himself, in a move surprising for one who was also the author of *Emancipation and Apprenticeship in the British West Indies* (1937), downplayed the importance of imperialism to the mid-Victorian period and focused, as many Victorians did, on domestic images and discourses about Britain's sense of itself. In the light of such selectiveness, this essay aims at a re-evaluation of certain elements of mid-Victorian imperialism through a consideration of the Portuguese-language literature surrounding the Christie Affair, a diplomatic imbroglio in the early 1860s that nearly provoked a war between Britain and Brazil.[2] As one of a series of diplomatic and commercial incidents of the period involving Britain and her trading partners in Latin America, the Christie Affair holds particular relevance because the publicity surrounding the débâcle played a key role in Brazil in exposing that country's perceptions of dependency on Britain, and in Britain in making British interests in the South American country more familiar to the public. Brazil, choosing to position itself in a proto-colonial relationship with Britain – rather than as an independent monarchy involved in a post-colonial relationship with Portugal – exposes the extent of Britain's overseas expansion during the nineteenth century and more particularly the ideological resistance that this expansion engendered abroad.[3] It also suggests an awareness that the publicity generated by ideological forms of resistance, such as political plays, could attract the attention of the public within Britain and potentially alter commercial and military relationships. Burn contended that the 'age of equipoise' saw a shift from a public largely uninterested in Britain's overseas activities to one actively invested in the process of empire, a shift he believes was induced by the exposure surrounding the Crimean War.[4] The Christie Affair, occurring as it did less than a decade later, offers yet another indication that such public awareness existed in Britain (whether or not it was the conflict in the Crimea that brought it into being) through its role in attracting public attention to Brazil. As *Macmillan's Magazine* noted in its October 1863 article 'Our Relations With Brazil':

> Of late years there has been considerable material progress, and a great development of the means of communication both with other countries and in Brazil itself, by railroads and steam navigation, chiefly effected by British capital, enterprise, and skill ... This sketch of anterior relations and of other questions of the English government with that of Brazil, is the prelude to the story of those proceedings which have lately excited so much attention and discussion, and which may almost be said to have made Brazil known within the last few months to a very large portion of the English public.[5]

By the 1860s, Britain's interventions in foreign affairs overseas mattered to the British people, and the writers of Brazilian plays intended to 'expose' British wrongdoing in that nation understood that echoes of their dissent might reach metropolitan shores. In addition, Brazilian observers speculated that in the long term the Christie Affair might actually be good for drumming up business. 'I think that at the end of the day Brazil owes to Mr. Christie a great debt', wrote a contemporary Brazilian publication.

> [H]e obtained for Brazil the most perfect recognition of its political existence, the esteem and admiration of the civilized world, awoke the nation from its placid slumber, stirred its spirits, made visible its opulence and resources, showed the advantages not only of the system that happily governs it, but also of the amalgamation of its extensive and numerous provinces in one big united state, growing in force, richness, illustriousness, and power.[6]

The Affair itself started as a reaction to two separate incidents: the shipwreck and subsequent looting of a British merchant ship off Brazil's southern coast and the arrest of three British naval officers and a chaplain several months later in Rio for purportedly attacking a police sentry in a drunken brawl. The stubbornness of Her Majesty's plenipotentiary minister in Rio, William Dougal Christie – his questionable assertion that the crew of the shipwrecked *Prince of Wales* had been murdered, his insistence that Rio's chief of police be censured for the department's treatment of the officers of the *Forte*, and his demands for large-scale indemnification for both incidents – provoked a call to arms on the part of the Brazilians, a harbour blockade and series of ship seizures on the part of the British, and a two-year-long rupture in diplomatic ties (1863–65). The Affair also provoked a series of comic sketches by Brazilian playwrights that reveal not only the Victorians' aspirations for economic and political control over Latin America's largest and wealthiest nation, but also how the Victorians were perceived in a country that they apparently dominated in commercial terms.

Despite the Christie Affair's role in putting Brazil on Britain's conceptual map, the Affair received little direct literary treatment in Britain, perhaps because it was overshadowed by the wealth of production inspired by the Indian Mutiny and events in other parts of the formal empire. No dramas or comedies about the incident appear to have been staged in Britain, although it found its way into prose in the decades following the incident. David Ker's 1876 *The Wild Horseman of the Pampas* considers the Affair in a comic light similar to that of the Brazilian plays, and with similar overtones of patriotism. His boy-hero Harry Falkland sneaks past a garrison guarding the strategic and symbolic Sugar Loaf Mountain in Rio, literally proving who is king of the mountain in Brazil. When discovered, the Brazilians mistake him for a criminal and send him to the English consulate. Ostensibly an autobiographical incident from the author's visit to Rio, this fictional portrayal clearly echoes the *Forte* incident, while transforming its outcome into a humorous, rhetorical victory for Britain. In a different vein, Emma E. Hornibrook's *Transito: A Story of Brazil* (1887) recasts the incident in patriotic Protestant terms. The aftermath of the Christie Affair allows a zealous English officer to smuggle in several Spanish New Testaments and escape punishment. Two of these Bibles form the basis for a series of incredible conversions surrounding the community that Hornibrook's title character and her family establish on the prairies of southern Brazil and offer the hope for a regeneration of Brazil through British influence. Hornibrook's representation of the Affair reiterates her government's concern to promote morality (especially anti-slavery)

through commerce and even settlement, but skirts the actual political
questions involved.

On the Brazilian side, however, the outbreak of the Christie Affair
fostered a series of extraordinary plays (all comedies) designed to rouse
a sense of nationalism among the urban middle classes and organized
around rhetorical, if not actual, opposition to Britain as Portugal's
replacement in colonial-style commercial relations. These comedies, written and produced during the incident itself, on one level depict the
British in familiarly stereotypical ways – as usurers, drunks, plunderers
and thieves – and on another level articulate a theory of Brazilian
culture and nationalism created in defiance of an informal and inexpert
brand of British imperialism. Considered collectively, the plays penned
about the Christie Affair go beyond a rabble-rousing rejection of the
colonizer by the colonized. Instead, they offer comic solutions to the
problems of interdependence within a global economy that encourage
patriotic indignation without really inciting a call to arms that would
have threatened potentially disastrous financial and military consequences. Drama censorship reports from the period – notably those of
plays on the Affair that were denied permission to be performed –
confirm the official mind's worries about inciting rioting and about
giving Christie potential grounds for further claims of indemnification
with broad-brush character assassinations. In this essay, I will focus on
three short plays produced in 1863 and 1864 in reaction to the Christie
Affair. The plays give an indication of the degree to which Brazil
believed itself tied to Britain in proto-colonial and economic terms, as
well as the way in which Brazil invoked notions of indebtedness in
order to resolve internal struggles over cultural self-definition and national redefinition. The three to be discussed here are culled from the
dozen or so plays about the Affair because of their authorship by some
of nineteenth-century Brazil's best-known dramatists and the involvement of two of its most prominent actors, Francisco Corrêa Vasques
and João Caetano dos Santos.

The first play, J.F.K. da Costa Rubim's 1863 *Os inglezes no Brasil*
(*The English in Brazil*), is a hilarious retelling of the *Forte* incident,
satirizing the English as an avaricious, drink-addicted set of plunderers.
With its characters of the young Lord Flask (exiled to Brazil by his
father to wean him from his London life of libertinism) and the diplomat
Lord Paunch (whose goal is to wring money, trade, and territorial
concessions out of the Brazilian government for its supposed infractions
on British sovereignty), *Os inglezes no Brasil* asserts a vision of Brazilian
nationality formulated almost exclusively around a rejection of Britain's
economic stranglehold. The play recycles a series of stereotypes about

British imperialism that work to suggest that if Burn's Britain was 'disciplined', this discipline maintained itself through the expulsion of the disruptive and the decadent: that debauched young nobleman served the empire to escape the embarrassment of their misconduct at home, that greed was intrinsic to the British character and alone explained his presence overseas, and that British imperialism, even at mid-century, was expansionist, and not reactive.

The second work, Joaquim José da França Júnior's 1864 *Inglezes na costa* (a title implying the double meanings of 'the English on our backs' and 'the English on our coasts'), sets up a connection between the English and usury that eighty years later resurfaced as Gustavo Barroso's and Tenorio d'Albuquerque's pro-Nazistic theory of the English as a Jewish civilization.[7] The plot of the farce features three poor students who decide to substitute the name 'English' for 'usurer' because '[a]fter the Anglo-Brazilian affair, I do not think there is a more appropriate epithet to call a creditor' ('Depois da questão anglo-brasileira, creio que não póde haver um epitheto mais appropriado para designar um credor', p. 6).

In the third play, *A questão anglo brasileira, commentado por Snr. Joaquim da Costa Brasil* (*The Anglo-Brazilian Question, As Told by Mr Joaquim da Costa Brazil*, 1863) by Francisco Corrêa Vasques, Britain is pictured as an old maid living on the best floor of Mr Brazil's house. Mr Brazil recounts that she is arrested after being mistaken for an intruder by his servant because she is dressed in men's clothes. This moment forms a direct allusion to Brazil's insistence that the sentinel who purportedly attacked the *Forte* officers was not to blame because he could not have recognized them without their uniforms, since their behaviour clearly did not match their rank. With Miss English's consistent misuse of genders in her broken Portuguese, her unrequited desire to marry her landlord, and her insistence on retribution for the servant's behaviour, the comedy asserts an embattled Brazilian independence assailed by an 'unmanly' British imperial policy based on force, disguise and extortion.

These pieces were all written and performed in 1863 and 1864 in Rio de Janeiro, the Brazilian capital. Production information for these specific plays remains scarce, but it is probable that, though penned earlier, many of these plays may not have reached the stage until after the initial hullabaloo about war had subsided but before diplomatic ties were restored.[8] They differ from earlier works about the British, such as Luíz Carlos Martins Pena's 1845 classics *Os dous, ou O inglês machinista* (*The Duo, or The Machinating Englishman*) and *As casadas solteiras* (*The Single Wives*) in engaging in political, and not social, questions – though the 1850 *Os inglezes no Brasil* (*The English in Brazil*) was

Lopes de la Vega's response to Parliament's 1845 Aberdeen Act to police slave trading in the South Atlantic. At the time the dramas were performed, Rio had an active theatre scene, catering to an ostensibly Europeanized élite and to a sizeable foreign population. Most plays were presented in Portuguese, although many were performed in French. Foreign theatre troupes gave the bulk of performances in the capital. Amateur theatricals – even by British naval officers of the South Atlantic fleet – were attended by the élite, including the Brazilian imperial family. Regional theatre was not widespread.[9]

Although the plays sparked by the Christie Affair provide perhaps the best literal representations of the dynamic between the British and Brazilian Empires at mid-century, the significant body of poetry published in newspapers, or in periodicals such as the Santos-based *O Caboclo*, or produced independently, also sought to frame the debate within a comic or carnivalesque tradition. Unlike the plays, these poems often directly invoked Christie by name or by mockery (the similarity in names between Christie and Christ forming the butt of many jokes). One of the most interesting of these poems is *O estandarte auri-verde: Contos sobre a questão anglo-brasiliera* ('The Gold-Green Flag: Cantos on the Anglo-Brazilian Question'), by one of Brazil's most famous and most popular nineteenth-century poets, L.N. Fagundes Varela. Fagundes Varela published these 'cantos', which take their name from the colours of the Brazilian flag (and thus make reference to the slogan it carries, 'Ordem e Progresso', or 'Order and Progress'), in 1863. With sections dedicated to Brazil, to the people, to Emperor Dom Pedro II, and an acid diatribe directed at William Christie himself, Varela reiterates the plays' concerns with the defence of national honour, but without the comic elements. Although the plays also harp on Britain's supposed aspirations for territorial control in Brazil, Fagundes Varela's poems share with earlier and contemporaneous political pamphlets about Britain an obsession with Ireland as a metaphor for Britain's overall conduct and as mark of its intentions in South America. This image stems from freely reorganized translations of such works as Élias Regnault's *Histoire criminelle du Gouvernement Anglais* (translated in 1843 in Brazil as the *História criminal do governo inglez desde as primeiras matanças na Irlanda até o envenenamento dos Chinas*, or *The Criminal History of the English Government from its First Murders in Ireland to its Poisoning of China*). The poems also set up an oppositional relationship between Britain and Brazil that radically alters standard British tropes of exploration and conquest. In the poem 'To William Christie', for instance, Varela conflates Britain's minister with the nation itself, contrasting images of the darkness and gloom of Albion with the light of the Brazils in a reversal of typical British images of the dark and mysterious Amazon that serve as a metonym for the subcontinent.[10]

To contextualize the role of this literary output in terms of the evolution of the imperial encounter between Britain and Brazil requires a short outline of their historical relationship. Throughout the century, Britain was the most important economic and commercial power in Brazil. Victorian investment in Brazil, though perhaps small in absolute terms, was surpassed in Latin America only by interests in Argentina and ran the gamut from trade in sugar, cotton, cocoa and manufactured goods to major infrastructural projects.[11] The mid-nineteenth century marked a key transition in Britain's relations with Brazil, both in terms of the kind of economic activities fostered and in terms of the increasing ambivalence on the part of Brazilian society towards the British presence. At the beginning of the century, with the British-engineered removal of the Portuguese court from Lisbon to Rio de Janeiro in 1808 and the signing of preferential trade treaties that continued after Brazil's independence from Portugal in the 1820s, British economic influence had been predominant and largely concerned with commerce. By mid-century, however, relations between the countries had grown more tense, with the expiration of the trade treaty, coercive attempts to control the slave trade – extending as far as the right to seize ships suspected of carrying, or of having carried, slaves even into Brazilian harbours – and the takeover of the New World's only independent monarchy by the pro-industrialist Dom Pedro II.[12] Britain continued to dominate trade, but Brazilian ports had now opened to competition. The Brazilian emperor's enthusiasm for industrialization also changed Anglo-Brazilian relations in two important ways: first, it brought British engineers and entrepreneurs to the country to build its railroads, trams, harbours, sewers, lighting systems and the like, and, second, it encouraged Brazil to seek large loans to finance industrialization through the London Stock Exchange.

To a certain extent, therefore, the Christie Affair represents an anomaly in the relations between the countries; it stands out as the only moment during the nineteenth century in which diplomatic relations were suspended. Yet Christie's reactions to the two incidents comprising the affair – his immediate call for reprisals and his willingness to order an offensive blockade of Rio – evince a trend towards increased vehemence in his country's relations with Brazil; his reaction bears out Burn's observation that the 'age of equipoise' witnessed a transferral abroad of violence formerly centred at home and around threats of revolution.[13] Burn asserted that this notion of violence was intrinsic to the affirmation and maintenance of the British civilizing mission, but implied that

the prevalence of violence stemmed not from a dominant cultural attitude, but from the specific sort of person involved in empire and in the
feelings of national and racial pride that emerged among Britons abroad
and at war. Rebellions in India and Jamaica aroused this pride at mid-
century and directed it overseas, given the limited tensions between
European powers at the time. As with the interpretation of the events of
the Indian Mutiny in 1857, the history leading to the 1862 Anglo-
Brazilian Question dealt similarly with native violence against British
subjects – the putative murder of the crew of the *Prince of Wales* and
the manhandling and imprisonment of the *Forte* officers. Despite lacking sufficient evidence to back these claims, Britain's consul acted in
kind, officially exerting his country's military might in a move intended
to secure immediate capitulation. Retribution replaced negotiation as
the means of procuring 'justice'. However, Christie's initiatives spurred
angry demonstrations and biting satire. Vasques's *A questão anglo
brasileira* typifies the Brazilian attitude through its portrayal of the
domestic shouting match between Mr Brazil and Miss English. Their
argument consists of exchanges of 'Pay – I won't pay' and 'Give in – I
won't give in', followed by Mr Brazil's statement that 'when she saw the
firmness of my words, she wanted to revenge herself, hitting me reck-
lessly and biting my right arm'('como vio a firmeza das minhas palavras
quiz vingar-se, apanha-me descuidado e da-me uma dentada no braço
direito', p. 7).

From the British government's point of view, the circumstances surrounding the *Prince of Wales* shipwreck and the 'ill-treatment' of the
Forte officers justified the level of intervention undertaken by Christie,
and officials countered opposition arguments aimed at rebuking Christie
for his actions by insisting that Christie had acted only according to
orders. In a document on the *Forte* claims later submitted to the King of
the Belgians during his arbitration of the incident, the government
claimed, 'it is submitted that, in the case of the officers of the "Forte,"
Brazilian law has been so administered as to cause serious offence to the
British navy, for which satisfaction ought to be made to Her Majesty's
Government by that of Brazil'.[14] The brief also included a letter of 8
October 1862 by Earl Russell to Christie enumerating the actions he
should take in response to the Brazilian position.[15] Arguably, as in the
case of the *Arrow* War in China less than a decade earlier, Britain had
been looking for excuses for an incident – especially in asking Christie
to produce an inflammatory report on the slave trade when he arrived
in Rio – and Christie received full backing from the government for his
actions during parliamentary debates. (In a speech in the Lords on 17
February 1863, Earl Russell stated, 'No proposal for arbitration was

made [by the Brazilians], and then he [Christie] had recourse to those measures of reprisals which have been complained of. I certainly cannot see anything to be objected to in this course, for it cannot be contended that when British ships are plundered and British officers insulted that we are not to make demands for reparation.'[16]) British officials at home and in Brazil had for a long time been upset by their failure to end slave trading and promote abolitionism, and some scholars have seen the incident as Christie's reaction to this stalemate over slavery. Yet the Brazilians and even other diplomats complained that Christie's bad temper, and not official policy, was the problem. The MP J. Bramley-Moore wrote to Christie in a letter published in *Correspondence between His Excellency W.D. Christie and J. Bramley-Moore, Esq., M.P.*,

> I could not help arriving at the conviction that the tone throughout was offensive and insulting, and manifested a disposition to quarrel. Nothing said by the Brazilians would satisfy you, and any facts or statements submitted by the Marquis of Abrantes [Brazil's Foreign Minister] were rejected with suspicion or not credited.[17]

Bramley-Moore himself had been in direct dialogue with the Brazilians over the issue, a dialogue conducted publicly when the newspaper *O Correio Mercantil* published a letter to him by Francisco Ignacio Marcondes Homem de Mello and Theophilo Benedicto Ottoni on 28 July 1863, and later printed his response.[18] In 1863, the US envoy and plenipotentiary minister, J. Watson Webb, published in Rio for private circulation an explanation directed at Bramley-Moore of the mistreatment he had received at Christie's hands, whom he accused of a 'reckless disregard for truth'. In the pamphlet, Webb went so far as to claim the following:

> I have said, officially to my Government, and I now repeat it to you, my deliberate opinion and the opinion of the soundest heads in Rio, that if there had been no quarrel between Mr. Christie and myself, there would not have been any reprisals upon Brazilian commerce, nor would your navy have been forced, much against its inclinations, to perpetrate an outrage upon the sovereignty of Brazil.[19]

MPs, including Bramley-Moore, raised the question of Christie's conduct in the Commons on 7 May 1863, after it became known that Webb also had written to Earl Russell impugning Christie's character.

In Brazil this opposition version of events was taken up wholeheartedly, both by politicians and diplomats conscious of the real need to avert Anglo-Brazilian hostilities and by the playwrights, who found it expedient to demonize a particular stereotyped version of a British type as a political statement that would satisfy their nationalist impulses for

autonomy without threatening the healthy economic relationship between the two countries.[20] One periodical, *O Conservador Vermelho*,
published a letter from a tradesman on 16 January 1863, alleging that
Christie owed his master money, which the plenipotentiary had refused
to pay, claiming that the work was unsatisfactory. Calumnies published
in Britain about Christie often appeared in translation in Brazil, allowing politicians and the culture industry there to exploit internal British
debates about the Affair for their own ends. According to the opposition view of the Affair, Christie was a maverick politician acting without
official sanction or with the sanction of a government that did not
accurately represent British opinion on the whole. (Russell had publicly
made disparaging remarks about Brazil, labelling it a miserable country,
without religious principles and without proper justice.)

Christie was a pawn used to air larger cultural and political griev-
ances against Britain, but in a mediated fashion. British violence was
personified, both in the popular press and in dramatic representations
of Britons, in the form of William Christie as an irascible and implac-
able individual who brooked no opposition. *O Caboclo,* a short-lived
weekly devoted to the Christie Affair, published a poem by Fagundes
Varela in its issue of 16 February 1863 calling Christie an 'insolent
diplomat' alongside an anonymous poem threatening 'John Bull' in
South America with imminent death. In Rubim's play, Lord Paunch
functions as a thinly veiled image of Christie. The play includes a scene
in which Paunch meets the British Admiral of the South Atlantic fleet to
instruct the Admiral to blockade Rio's harbour. Far from being a normal blockade, however, this one is to be a version of piracy, with the
British demanding the traditional 'your money or your life' of the crew
and letting through only those who pay. Such representations of robbery reiterate popular Brazilian sentiment that Britain's zealous efforts
to control slaving since the Aberdeen Act constituted piracy, while
making this sentiment topical by reformulating the piracy as part of the
perceived outrageousness of Christie's claims for indemnification. The
representations also make transparent Britain's own recognition that, as
Burn put it, 'such words as "justice", "morality", "Christianity", "peace"
and "free trade" had more than one meaning' (p. 71). Although a
character later claims of Paunch, 'This British agent, instrument for the
crimes of the British cabinet, minister of a government that oppresses
weak nations, will see how the Brazilian people defend their honour'
(p. 23), ultimately this defence is directed at the *agent provacteur*, and
not at Britain itself.[21]

As the play acknowledges, Brazil needs Britain for economic reasons;
the assertion of nationalism must be tempered by the recognition that

trade must go on. This assertion therefore is achieved by seeking the moral high ground in an interesting subversion of Britain's self-conception of imperialism as a civilizing mission. The representations of Christie's avarice and immoderate desires in the form of Lord Paunch and of Lord Flask's debauchery form a direct contrast to Brazil's ostensible morality and fairness. Taking up both the specific allegations of the *Forte* incident and Britain's national and international reputation for intemperance, *Os inglezes no Brasil* reacts to the temperance movement domestic to Britain by suggesting that the 'national vice' cut across class barriers, ran rampant among Britons overseas and reflected a generalized social indiscipline.[22] (Denials uttered by Christie and by the officers involved in the *Forte* débâcle that the officers were drunk carried little weight in the light of the well-known British propensity to overindulge.) Crucially, Brazilian morality in this play is seated in its middle-class status, while British immorality stems from its aristocratic leanings. Lord Flask's manservant Roger, whose subaltern position exempts him from the scapegoating of the Lords, clarifies this distinction by commenting on the 'decency of Brazilian pastimes' whose moderateness will lead his undisciplined master free to seek out 'English orgies' ('a decencia dos divertimentos brasileiros'; 'as orgias inglezas', p. 9).

In França Júnior's *Os inglezes na costa*, once again a single character, that of the usurer, is used to generalize about the economic relationship between Britain and Brazil without specifically repudiating the need for trade relations between them. The complaint is about the disastrous loans Brazil has contracted with Britain (or at least through British brokers). The debt-ridden student Felix allegorizes the young Brazilian government – itself a student of British law and politics – as a youthful rake sowing wild oats as he learns to grow into a mature nation. França Júnior suggests that perhaps young Brazil need not pay off the debts to Albion at all, although recognizing through the paternal intervention of Felix's uncle that in the end repayment cannot be avoided, and that resistance should come through not acquiring debts in the first place. (That such resistance was possible is corroborated by claims by Christie's successor that the Emperor was on the point of ending commerce with Britain and securing a loan from the French to liquidate all money owed to Britain when Christie left in March 1863. Instead, British bankers negotiated a loan of £3.3 million to the Brazilian government during the suspension of diplomatic relations, prompting one contemporary writer to comment derisively, 'there is no example in the history of the London market, nor that of any other European nation, of having contracted a loan with a foreign government in the anomalous circumstances in which we still find ourselves today'.[23])

In keeping with the desire to vilify Britain's activities and to promote Brazilian selfhood without encouraging the warmongering and militia formation proposed at the time by street demonstrations in Brazil's two largest cities (Rio and Salvador), the Christie Affair plays rely on comedy and, often, on the absence of British characters from the stage to circumvent tension.[24] The plays all have happy endings, in which Brazilians revel in their national identity in dances or monologues inspired by the British actions over the *Forte* and *Prince of Wales*, but in which the physical absence of Britons provides no ultimate object for violence. In França Júnior's play, for instance, the English never actually make an appearance; the author merely applies Balzac's epithet of them as usurers and metaphorically expands it in this tale of the plight of starving students in São Paulo plagued by a crotchety moneylender. In Rubim's *Os inglezes no Brasil*, the English literally exit the scene when patriotism enters, as the Brazilian minister of commerce comes on stage to announce that the British have backed down, for no apparent reason. The play ends with the characters dancing around Brazilian flags and singing the song of independence. The physical removal from the scene of Lord Flask and his pal Lord Paunch thus mirrors their country's supposed abandonment of claims oppressive to the Brazilian state, as if political resolution of the diplomatic conflict described by the play necessarily results in an isolationist-style independence for the younger nation. The visible presence of the flags on-stage in a circus-like atmosphere emphasizes the absence of the English ministers from the glorious spectacle of nationalism being presented. And even the patriotic hymn and battle-cry that ends the comic monologue *A questão anglo brasileira* practically overlooks the British in its efforts to promote 'the old Lie' (as Wilfred Owen has called it) *dulce et decorum est pro patria mori*.

In fact, middle- and upper-class Brazilian society's fears about British influence – in so far as they are represented in these plays and in the poetry, magazines and cartoons the Christie Affair also inspired – seem more concerned with safeguarding the integrity of Brazilian property than with altering structures of economic dependence, essentially discussing a conflict between land-based and currency-based economies. Scholars of nineteenth-century British fiction are accustomed to seeing this issue debated within the United Kingdom in novels discussing industrialization and the enclosure movement. These Brazilian plays replicate this debate in revealing ways. British interests in Brazil were overwhelmingly capital investments; few British subjects actually settled in Brazil, and most of those who did, did so later in the century with the coffee boom. Moreover, the British community's desire to maintain a separate identity safeguarded property and capital, as well as bloodlines, as firmly British and thus capable of removal at any time. British traders who married Brazilians, meanwhile, took care not to adopt allegiances to their wives' country, as Rubim states in his play: 'Very well you know, that rare is the Englishman who marries in Brazil, and when that happens, he quickly take cares to register his children at the English consulate as subjects of Her Majesty of Britain. For what son of an Englishman wants to be Brazilian?'[25] But for Brazil – with its agricultural, land-based economy and indigenous aristocracy – the anxieties about the British centred overwhelmingly on the conversion of these capital interests into land-based ones. These anxieties endured from the start of the nineteenth century to the Edwardian period, emerging particularly with relation to the Amazon, the southern area of Rio Grande do Sul and Santa Catharina (where the British had hoped to build a military base) and, in 1895, with the sovereignty dispute over the South Atlantic island of Trindade, where a British company wanted to land a submarine telegraphic cable that would have stretched from Europe to Argentina. Increased pressure on the part of the British to end the slave trade and limit the slave-based *fazenda,* or plantation, system heightened Brazilian concerns as well. With British money and expertise backing nearly all the wide-scale improvements in infrastructure begun under Pedro II's sponsorship during the mid-Victorian period (so much so that trams in Brazil became known as *bonds,* supposedly after the bonds on the London Stock Exchange used to finance their construction), Brazil's reaction to the Christie Affair could hardly have been other than a panic about British seizure of its territory. It must be remembered that part of Dutch Guyana had passed into British hands about half a century earlier, that the borders between British and Brazilian Amazon territories had yet to be resolved and that the Christie Affair itself involved a direct harbour blockade by British warships in Rio's Guanabara Bay.[26] Britain's intervention in the River Plate region, resulting in the separation of Montevideo from Argentina and the establishment of the Republic of Uruguay, also remained on Brazilian minds.

Rubim's play enacts these anxieties most starkly. Lord Paunch, Her Majesty's plenipotentiary minister in Rio, after earlier stating that 'money dominates the world' ('o dinheiro é quem domina o mundo', p. 6), explains that the real motives in asking for indemnities over the *Forte* affair are as follows: 'If we were fortunate enough to intimidate the government to the point that they ceded to us all we desire? That would be a pretty thing. Now 600 talents [contos], soon a trade treaty, and then the province of Pará or Santa Catharina ... This is the bounty that my diplomatic science must achieve ... '.[27] The ultimate aspirations of the British government, in other words, are for a successive weakening of Brazilian sovereignty that would eventually result in the relinquishing of two of its most important states, Pará (at the mouth of the Amazon) and Santa Catharina (a southern state adjacent to Rio Grande do Sul). The Brazilian ministers, of course, prove later in the play – and in the actual historical developments – to resist the ambassador's bravado and to force him to capitulate his demands. They envisage the British blockade of the harbour not as a legitimate attempt to settle the issue, but as harking back to an earlier form of plundering the British have practised on Brazil – piracy. These 'roast beefs', they claim, will soon find themselves *'assados'*, or 'grilled'. In the end, the spectator is left with an image not of the power of the British Empire, able to play and win a dirty game, but of an ineffective and boasting European power, represented by an unscrupulous and degenerate nobility and ultimately more afraid of those it pretends to dominate than they are of it.

A questão anglo brasileira treats the same issue of land control, but from the angle of the marriage plot. A revision of the 'comic scene' *O Sr. Joaquim da Costa Brasil* (1860), the monologue has noted actor Vasques relate the arrest and other misadventures of a cross-dressing and aged Miss English who seeks to subjugate the young and truly virile Mr Brazil to a perverted feminine will. Here, Mr Brazil is owner of a house and grounds that God has given him in his cradle and landlord to two tenants who have made his house their home 'but who decidedly do not live here' ('que decidadamente, não morão aqui', p.5). His property is of an incredible bounty and is coveted by the frustrated and 'demonic' English tenant who pesters him with her marriage proposals. This wanton, old, ugly, selfish woman wants to find her way to his pockets, where, Mr Brazil proclaims to the audience, 'you will always find *rivers of money* and *mines of gold*. I own *bays of diamonds*, farms filled with *lakes of silver*, surrounded by a *great jungle* of tobacco and coffee' ('VV.SS. encontrarão sempre *rios de dinheiro* e, *minas de ouro*. Possuo *bahias de brilhantes*, fazendas onde ha *lagôas de prata*, rodeadas por um – *matto grosso* de fumo e café', p. 5). But Mr Brazil ignores her proposals of marriage and her demands for retribution alike when, first, in a comic repositioning of the *Forte* incident she is surprised in her boudoir dressed as a man and arrested by the servant as a robber and, later, in a recasting of the *Prince of Wales* shipwreck in which some of the pack of hounds that she sends another of Mr Brazil's servants to wash drown in a 'Rio Grande'. 'Well, tell me, kind sirs', exclaims Mr Brazil of Miss English's demand for damages for the loss of her dogs, 'frankly, is it Brazil's fault that the animals were shipwrecked?' ('ora digão meus senhores, francamente, o Brasil tem culpa que os animaes naufragassem?', p. 7). Eventually, the unfeminine 'lioness of Albion' tries to make her landlord give in by biting him in the arm, but instead loses a tooth in the strong fabric of his coat. By comically reducing the Christie Affair to a battle of the sexes (as several published caricatures of William Dougal Christie do in depicting him as a squabbling woman), Vasques reverses traditional paradigms of passivity and femininity used by the British in their representations of Latin America, Asia and Africa, and asserts an independence based on the presumption that his country's riches lie in its land. At the same time, Miss English's persistent dogging of Mr Brazil tells the audience of the actor–playwright's belief that Britain needs an alliance with Brazil more than Brazil needs Britain. The play suggests how difficult it was for the Victorians, with their extensive formal and informal empire, to represent themselves as victims abroad without undermining the very authority they hoped their demands would cement and without opening themselves up to characterizations of weakness, peevishness and decadence. A *questão anglo brasileira* concludes with Vasques uttering a patriotic song and saluting the national flag. Although the song states, 'What does it matter if we lose our lives on the battlefield? If we die for Brazil, here is our shroud', the fact that Vasques's vehicle is a monologue – and that his vision of Miss English is told second-hand – again makes this call to action a symbolic one.[28]

Importantly, then, these plays, as well as much of the other literature produced in the self-styled 'land of Santa Cruz' about the Christie imbroglio, make the assumption that Britain's threats are more blustering than real, that to the Victorians resistance is so unthinkable that, when it happens, they are ill-prepared to meet it and give in. In contrast to internal British rhetoric and external British propaganda about the invincible position of the empire, of its moral leadership in the fight against slavery and the promotion of self-determination in Latin America and elsewhere, the literature of the Christie Affair offers an alternative vision of Victorian foreign relations that suggests that Britain's move during the 'age of equipoise' away from humanitarianism towards a view of ennobling commerce had its consequences. The Christie Affair shows that not only did Britain continue to use coercive means to press for emancipation in the world's largest slave economy during the 1860s – means that belied the popularity of 'a dogma that commerce was the "great emancipator"' (Burn, p. 70) – but also that British foreign policy engendered a counter-discourse in Latin America that saw commerce itself as a form of slavery. 'The best way in which to encourage social happiness and to spread Christianity and advance morality', Burn quoted Lord Russell as saying, 'was to let commerce take its own course'

(p. 70). That course in Brazil, as it flowed towards recriminations and harbour blockades and comic send-ups of Britain's 'civilizing mission', remained fraught with the perils of embarrassment and hypocrisy.

Notes

1. The original Portuguese runs as follows: 'O seu gosto é mesquinho, sua alegria está no interesse, o seu Deus é o cognhac, seus cumprimentos são mentiras, suas amizades falsidades e suas venias carantonhas ... Elles compram o nosso algodão, o nosso assucar, as nossas madeiras, os coiros do nosso gado, e uma immensidade de objectos que comstituem uma verdadeira fonte de riqueza, por uma ridicularia, que é paga em retalhos de fazendas, que qualquer outra nação nos forneceria por mais razoaveis preços. Elles fazem sahir para Londres todas as nossas producções e depois de as fazem passar pelas suas fabricas, mandam vendel-as aqui com o titulo de manufacturas inglezas, de sorte, que nada mais fazemos, do que comprar muito caro aquilo, que lhes haviam vendido baratissimo' (p. 7). See J.F.K. da Costa Rubim, *Os inglezes no Brasil: Comedia em um prologo e um acto* (Rio de Janeiro: J.P. da Silva Rocha, 1863). My translation. All translations from Portuguese are my own.

2. A good summary of the events involved in the Christie Affair can be found in Volume 3 of Leslie Bethell's 1985 edition of the *Cambridge History of Latin America* (Cambridge: Cambridge University Press) and Richard Graham's article 'Os fundamentos da ruptura de relações diplomáticas entre o Brasil e a Grã-Bretanha em 1863: "A Questão Christie"', trans. Maria Lúcia Galvão Carneiro, *Revista de historia*, 24 (49), January–March 1962, pp. 117–38 and 24 (50), April–June 1962, pp. 379–402. Christie's own book on Brazil, *Notes on Brazilian Questions* (London: Macmillan and Co., 1865) offers a brief and biased but informative account of the way in which the British government interpreted the events, while Bellarmino Barreto gives a characteristic Brazilian version of the events in *O Sr. Christie no Brasil, ou A descrição do conflicto anglo-brasileiro, dado á luz* (Bahia: Typographia de Camillo de Lellis Masson & Cia, 1863).

3. Note on terminology: because neither Brazilian nor British authors of this period were particularly careful of the distinction between England and Britain, the terms 'English' and *inglês* here can be taken to mean 'British' in the context in which Victorianists use the word today.

4. See W.L. Burn, *The Age of Equipoise: A Study of the Mid-Victorian Generation* (London: George Allen and Unwin, 1964), p. 56: 'It was natural that a country which lived by its foreign trade and its foreign investments should protect and extend them, in the last resort by force; it was remarkable that so many of its inhabitants did not realize that this had been done for years and treated the Crimean War as something different, not merely in scale, but in kind, from anything that had happened since Waterloo.'

5. 'Our Relations With Brazil', *Macmillan's Magazine*, 8 (48), October 1863, pp. 494–5.

6. See *Folinha de novas anecdotas e comedias para o ano bissexto de 1864* (Rio de Janeiro: Eduardo & Henrique Laemmart, 1864), pp. 76–7: 'Eu creio que o Brasil deve a Mr. Christie, no fim de contas, grande reconhecimento, alcançando elle para si as reprovações do mundo civilisado inteiro, que o considera como um tresloucado, titulo que lhe assenta bem, enquanto obteve para o Brasil o mais perfeito conhecimento da sua existencia politica, a estima e a admiração do mundo civilisado, acordou a nação da sua placida modorra, estimou-lhe os brios, fez-lhe apparecer a opulencia e os recursos, mostrou as vantagens não só do sistema que felizmente o rege, como as da agglomeração de suas extensas e numerosas provincias em um grande todo reunido, crescendo em forças, riqueza, illustração e poder.'

7. See, for instance, Gustavo Barroso's *História secreta do Brasil* (Rio de Janeiro: Civilização Brasileira 1934), and Tenorio d'Albuquerque's, *Atentados contra o Brasil*, Rio de Janeiro, n.d.), n.p.

8. However, according to the published edition, Vasques's play was premiered at the Theatro Gymnasio on 28 January 1863, at the start of the incident.

9. There is little scholarship on nineteenth-century Brazilian theatre to date, but Lafayette Silva's *História do teatro brasileiro* (Rio de Janeiro: Serviço Gráfico do Ministério da Educação e Saude, 1938), provides basic information on production and audience. See also Severino João Albuquerque, 'The Brazilian Theatre up to 1900', *Cambridge History of Latin American Literature* (Cambridge: Cambridge University Press, 1996), and Edwaldo Cafezeiro and Carmem Gadelha, *História do teatro brasileiro: Um percurso de Anchieta a Nelson Rodrigues* (Rio de Janeiro: Editora UERJ/EDUERJ/FUNARTE, 1996).

10. See L.N. Fagundes Varela, *O estandarte auri-verde: Cantos sobre a questão anglo-brasileira* (São Paulo: Typografia Imparcial, 1863).

11. For contemporary statistics, see William Scully, *Brazil; Its Provinces and Chief Cities; The Manners and Customs of the People; Agricultural, Commercial, and Other Statistics, Taken from the Latest Official Documents; With a Variety of Useful and Entertaining Knowledge, Both for the Merchant and the Emigrant* (London: Murray & Co., 1866). For more recent trade and investment statistics, if outdated analysis, see Richard Graham, *Britain and the Onset of Modernization in Brazil, 1850–1914* (Cambridge: Cambridge University Press, 1968) and D.C.M. Platt, *Latin America and the British Trade 1806–1914* (London: Adam & Charles Black, 1972). Beatriz Ricardina de Magalhães's study (1979) of the London and Brazilian Bank argues for that organ's control over exchange rates and economic life in general, despite the limited nature of capital investment. See 'Investimentos ingleses no Brasil e o Banco Londrino e Brasileiro', *Revista brasileira de estudos políticos* 49 (1979), July, pp. 233–52.

12. The well-known Aberdeen Act, which gave British naval authorities rights of search and seizure over any Brazilian ship suspected of carrying slaves and which was later extended to allow enforcement of the Act within Brazilian waters, was a continual sticking point. Even after the slave trade from Africa had ceased, the British government refused to repeal the Act. See Rory Miller, *Britain and Latin America in the Nineteenth and Twentieth*

Centuries (London: Longman, 1993), p. 54. See also Leslie Bethell, *The Abolition of the Brazilian Slave Trade: Britain, Brazil, and the Slave Trade Question, 1807–1869* (Cambridge: Cambridge University Press, 1970).

13. Burn, *Equipoise*, pp. 82–3.
14. *Ill-Treatment of Officers of Her Majesty's Ship "Forte," by the Brazilian Authorities: Case on Behalf of Her Majesty's Government* (London: George E. Eyre and William Spottiswoode, 1863), p. 11.
15. Ibid., p. 44. The memorandum included a call for the dismissal of members of the Brazilian military involved in the Affair, an apology from the Brazilian government and public censure for the chief of police.
16. *Hansard*, 169 (1863), 17 February, p. 369.
17. *Correspondence between His Excellency W.D. Christie and J. Bramley-Moore, Esq., M.P.* (London: Harrild, 1863?), p. 7.
18. The letter and response were reprinted in *Escriptos historicos e litterarios* (Rio: Typ. de Quirino & Irmão, 1868).
19. See J. Watson Webb, *A Letter from His Excellency J. Watson Webb, United States Envoy Extraordinary and Minister Plenipotentiary in Brazil, to J. Bramley Moore, Esq., M.P., in Reply to a Statement in the 'Times' Newspaper by His Excellency W.D. Christie* (1863), p. 15.
20. This view outlived the Affair. A historical article on 'Os ingleses no Brasil' published in 1915 in the *Revista do IHGB*'s special volume from the First National History Conference compares Christie and the Brazilian Foreign Minister, 'one, the British diplomat, was impulsive, violent, intractable, conceited, and rude; the other, the Brazilian diplomat, was a balanced man, serious but conciliatory, modest and simple, yet energetic and strong ... the Brazilian was a distinguished man of honour, [whilst] the Englishman was a vulgar instrument'. See *Revista do IHGB* 130 (77), (1915), p. 348: 'um, o diplomata britannico, era um impulsivo, violento, intractavel, orgulhoso, e rude; o outro, o diplomata brasileiro, era um homem equilibrado, severo mas conciliador, modesto e simples, embora energetico e forte ... o Brasileiro era uma consciencia illustre; o Inglez era um instrumento vulgar'.
21. The original reads as follows: 'Esse subalterno bretão, instrumento dos crimes do gabinete inglez, ministro de um governo oppressor das naçoes fracas, ha de vêr como o povo brasileiro defende a sua honra.'
22. Cf. Burn's discussion of temperance, *Equipoise*, pp. 280–84. In particular, Burn notes, 'Freedom to drink was a freedom that the Englishman cherished, not merely as a matter of academic theory but as an enthusiasm' (p. 283). This 'enthusiasm' provided an easy target for Brazilian satire. In its issue of 25 January 1863, for instance, *O Caboclo* printed a poem about the Affair implicitly accusing Christie of drunkenness.
23. See Lillian de Amorim Fritsch, 'O *Affair* Christie: Diplomacia da força', *Reflexões sobre a escravidão: Tráfico e sociedade escravocrata*, Papéis Avulsos 7, December 1988, p. 9; *Emprestimo brasileiro contrahido em Londres em 1863* (Paris: J.P. Aillaud, Guillard, & Ca., 1864), p. 10.
24. A contemporary description of popular sentiment and demonstrations can be found in Barreto, *O Sr. Christie no Brasil* p. 39. Further discussion can be found in Mello Barreto Filho and Hermeto Lima, *História da*

polícia do Rio de Janeiro: Aspectos da cidade e da vida carioca, vol. 2, (Rio: Empresa A Noite, 1944), pp. 268–71.

25. See p. 12: 'Mui bem sabeis, que raro é o inglez, que se casa no Brasil, e quando isto acontece, elles tem logo o cuidado de matricularem os seus filhos no consulado inglez, como subditos de sua Magestade Britannica. Pois qual é o filho de inglez, que deseja ser Brasileiro?'

26. Negotiations over British Guyana's border with Brazil began in 1838, following an expedition by the Royal Geographic Society under German explorer Robert Schomburgk, but were suspended from 1843 until 1888. See Jorge A.G. de Araujo, *Ensaios de história diplomática do Brasil no regimen repulicano* (Rio de Janeiro: Imprensa Nacional, 1912), p. 152.

27. 'Se nós formos tão felizes para intimidar o governo a ponto delle nos ceder quanto desejamos? Seria uma coisa encatadora! Agora sessenta contos; logo, um tratado de commercio, e depois, a provincia do Pará ou a de Santa Catharina! ... Eis o prodigio que a minha sciencia diplomatica deve operar' (p.11).

28. See p. 9: 'Que importa deixar a vida/Lá no campo da batalha?/Se pelo Brasil morreremos/Aqui está nossa mortalha!'

Index

INDEX

253